BACKBONE

MT Adams

The x-ray on the cover is from my 1990 surgeries. For
additional pictures, commentary, and information visit:
www.facebook.com/BB2020MT

Memories are fragile restorations of actual events. When
possible, specific details were researched. As a memoir, to protect
privacy, character names and descriptions were fictionalized.

DEDICATION

My son, Sam

Dr. Michael MacMillan

CES patients around the world

Unsubdued

S.E. KISER

I have hoped, I have planned, I have striven,
To the will I have added the deed;
The best that was in me I've given,
I have prayed, but the gods would not heed.

I have dared and reached only disaster,
I have battled and broken my lance;
I am bruised by a pitiless master
That the weak and the timid call chance.

I am old, I am bent, I am cheated
Of all that Youth urged me to win;
But name me not with the defeated,
Tomorrow again, I begin.[i]

Introduction:

BACKBONE is a medical memoir about my life's journey. A fortune cookie wisely sums it up, "The axe soon forgets, but the tree always remembers."

In 1987, I compiled notes—a lost catheter inside my heart—on a manual typewriter. I slammed out twenty-four single-spaced pages, no margins, at 3:00 a.m. on a steamy August night. Glaring typos, along with alternating case letters in the middle of words reflected the panic of the survivor. At the time I didn't know a second error, from the same surgery, was progressing.

My spinal cord was being severed. In 1990, six doctors, including a neurosurgeon who abandoned due to the catheter implication, missed the diagnosis. Emergency surgery averted impending paralysis.

Complications, chronic pain, and invisible limitations became my normal. After my spine was rebuilt, and rebuilt again, I too, became a different person. At first in barely visible ways, I learned to stand up for myself.

A whole new backbone enabled me to defy my past, alter my present and reroute the future. In 2015, at age 57, I transformed the ending of one chapter of my life. Decades after dropping out, I finally graduated—from the same university—with my Bachelor of Science degree. *"Tomorrow again, I begin."*

TABLE OF CONTENTS

Scoli Girl Speaks

Thirty years had passed since I was last on campus. The young people I walked by were the time-warp reflections of my younger face. Rather than graduation, my life's trajectory ricocheted elsewhere.

In April 2007, almost 50 years old, I was the guest speaker at my former university. The winding route through their medical center complex brought me to my destination at the opened double doors of an auditorium. I smiled. The overwhelming aroma of freshly baked chocolate chip cookies filled the air.

Marlene, future doctor, said, "We found an overhead projector, they're almost obsolete. May I set up your x-rays?"

"No. I prefer to do it myself. How many people does this lecture hall hold?" I eyed the steady stream of health-care students, lugging backpacks, lunch, and laptops. I heard hurried cell phone conversations, and metal chair legs dragging across the worn floor as they took their seats.

"Seventy-five, in addition to pupils, several health-center professors, as well as physicians, are in attendance. Your flyer generated quite a bit of interest." She adjusted the battery pack at my waist, then my lapel microphone.

The physical therapy student on Marlene's team rushed by, paused. "Hey guys. I've been keeping count. It's standing room only. We've got ninety people in attendance." He faked a full-mouth scream, "No pressure, Mary."

I laughed, "You guys said twelve people, twenty at the most. They're here for your cookies."

Marlene said, "Imagine it's only the three of us."

"I've only given talks to garden clubs. I've never spoken about my medical history before."

"You'll be fine." She walked towards the stage.

My thoughts were on full-tilt spin cycle. *With my medical events, when I fell through the cracks, I tumbled all the way, zoomed through the core of planet earth, flew out the other side, and was lost in outer space. How do I put a light-hearted slant on my story for these young students?*

Soda cans popped and sandwich wrappers rustled. Marlene bounded up the steps, "Welcome. I'm in my first year in the College of Medicine. Ms. Adams, our speaker, has quite the exceptional medical history. We hope. Today, she will share her most memorable events as an orthopedic patient." Marlene flipped the light switch for the overhead.

There was brief polite applause. I walked up the three steps, with a death grip on the handrail. At the lectern I exhaled nervously. *Why in the world had I agreed to do this?*

Marlene took her seat. She and two classmates had organized everything, including baking chocolate chip cookies until the wee hours of the morning. "Our professor said home-made cookies would pull in the audience, to leave plates nearest the stage, to fill the auditorium from the front."

At barely five feet tall I was almost completely hidden behind the enormous oak podium with the large orange and blue university logo. A trio of classmates I'd talked to over the course of a school year sat in the front row. Ascending seats behind them revealed row after row of young, chattering, college-age people. I felt like a weathered combat veteran looking at the faces of fresh recruits. *That used to be me.* Then I noticed their mature counterparts: doctors and professors, who sat along both edges of the auditorium, their heads bent down, distracted by whatever was in front of them.

"Hello, before I start, I want to say that I'm in awe of every student in this auditorium. I applaud you. School is difficult. I was enrolled here decades ago, accepted into the College of Pharmacy at age 19. I met my first orthopedic surgeon not long after that, and partially because of his diagnosis, I foolishly dropped out after my junior year.

"Please don't let anything or anyone trip you up. I scored in the 92nd percentile on the PCATs, but without a diploma that doesn't mean anything. It's what you finish in life that counts." Aware of the brightly lit screen behind me, I placed my postured fingers in front of the light bulb of the prematurely lit overhead, "Look, a bunny." A ripple of laughter rolled through the audience. I turned off the switch and walked out onto center stage. "Let's begin." With a royal wave, partial bow, I announced, "I am your patient. Let's talk." The sound of cell phone covers slapped shut. One student in the front row loudly declared, "This'll be good."

"I'm not sure how to condense thirty years into fifty minutes. There are a lot of backstories you won't hear. Pun intended.

"We all use the word, 'backbone,' as if our spines are solid bone. As upcoming health care professionals, you know the typical spine is made up of 26 vertebrae, with spongy discs in between to absorb the jarring of all our movements. In some patients there is a medical condition that causes vertebrae to fuse together, like the long bone of the femur, thigh. My spine is in the same category due to fusion overgrowth from an experimental device. We are the people with true backbones.

"My case started with a birth defect at the base of my spine, a malformed extra lumbar vertebra, which likely caused my scoliosis. At age 10, when first diagnosed, my family doctor told my parents, 'Don't worry about it.'

"When I was a sophomore in college, an organic chemistry classmate walked up, and said, 'I've been watching you.' I was so flattered. I thought he was asking about a date. Instead, he said, 'You. Have. Scoliosis.'"

From the audience a few moans.

"I was mortified. He might as well have said, 'You have a big zit on your nose.'" A cackle of laughter arose. "He insisted a brace would fix my problem. I pursued medical treatment. A surgeon said my twisting rib cage would crush my heart and lungs, resulting in a premature death. He also said my spinal deformity was as severe as the Elephant Man. Not true, by the way. And that patients like me were classified as 'freaks' by the medical community."

The audience gasped.

"I accepted his diagnoses as the word of God. Since I was going to die young, I dropped out of the University of Florida."

I walked over to the podium, placed my first spine x-ray onto the overhead and hit the switch. "Then six years later, in 1983, at age 26, with a different surgeon, I had my first scoliosis surgery. Here's a reference point. The leaning Tower of Pisa is tilted by 8 degrees. My lumbar spine was a 70-degree curvature. Plus, I had rotation of the entire spinal column. Think spiral staircase."

A physical therapy student raised her hand, "Your sagittal plane is distorted, plus the S-shaped curves?"

Oh, right, UF, these are sharp students. "Yes. Not all scoli patients have that. Unfortunately, seven months post-op, as soon as I was out of my brace, a new type of lower-back pain developed. My surgeon insisted nothing was wrong. Eventually, he said, 'You're so used to being in pain you don't know what it feels like not to be in pain anymore.'"

The audience howled with laughter. A professor with a salt and pepper beard, near the front row, stopped doodling in his Blackberry. He turned, scanned the room. As he rotated his neck, his eyes returned to the stage, and met mine. *Scoli girl wants to be heard.* He deposited his device, clicked his briefcase closed, folded his arms across his chest, leaned back, and listened to the rest.

"I had no way of knowing my surgeon had fused my spine to the wrong level. He'd failed to include the birth defect, as we'd planned. That deformed, unstable vertebra had to bear all the weight of my movement. It was especially stressed as the weak link sandwiched between the surgical scoli fusion and the biological fusion of the birth defect.

"I learned to live with the pain. An improbable seven years later, in 1990, seemingly unrelated symptoms evolved. Stop. Let's role-play that you all work in the ER. There's been a serious car accident. A patient arrives with numbness in a leg and unable to urinate. Think anatomy. What would affect both of those body parts?"

The audience in unison thundered: "Spinal cord."

I ordered myself not to cry. Bit my bottom lip. *Why did I have to fight so hard to receive that correct diagnosis in 1990? Did my case alter future generations of doctors? It must have been Dr. BrownEyes. He was always a team player. He must have told the ER.*

"In defense of the emergency room staff, without a recent physical injury, no one thought that was possible."

A murmur went through the audience. A poised woman in a nursing uniform raised her hand. "Symptoms are symptoms regardless of the cause."

Others shouted out: "Yes," "Of course," "Definitely." A medical student from the last row jumped up. "It must have been *Cauda equina* syndrome, CES. That's a medical emergency. Paralysis is imminent."

Without intent, I stood up on tippy toe. "Yes, that's correct." Game-show style, I yelled out, "Give that man a cookie." When the last chuckle dissipated, "I'm sorry to report that six doctors, including three visits to the ER, and a neurosurgeon missed that diagnosis in 1990."

The audience became eerily silent. A doctor wearing a stethoscope put down the book he was reading. *They're all listening.* Sandwiches mid-bite returned to desktops uneaten. A hesitant hand went up, from the third to the last row, and a male voice asked, "Were you paralyzed?"

A bushy, red-haired, doctor in a white lab coat, turned and snapped, "She walked in here, didn't she? She's standing there isn't she? Use your skills of observation."

I appreciated his solidarity, and chimed in. "Yes, scrutiny is critical for a correct diagnosis. Don't forget you have two eyes, two ears, and only one mouth. Look and listen twice as much as you speak, or rather diagnose. I was fortunate. If not for meeting an astute orthopedic surgeon, I would have been paralyzed in 1990. During that CES operation, it was discovered that my prior scoliosis surgery had failed. The fusion never bridged. So, in addition to the spinal cord decompression surgery, they had to re-do my scoliosis operation, too. And then, as fate would have it, a week later that newly installed hardware broke. The manufacturer had inadvertently shipped a defective batch. That resulted in my third spine surgery."

A part of my brain registered the composed, confident tone of my voice: clinical, mechanical, robotic mode. Zero emotion. My coping mechanism had kicked in. *Stay tough. Swallow those sniffles. Wait until I'm alone.* I slid another x-ray onto the machine. There was an audible gasp from the audience. One student toward the rear of the auditorium did my crying for me, loudly. The professionals craned their necks in her direction, scowled. I continued. "As you can see, the upgraded construct included five metal rods, two spine-length verticals, and three horizontal cross-bars, in addition to six two-inch screws."

A bald physician near the front row, slid his glasses down the tip of his nose, scowled over the top rim. He covered his mouth with a bent index finger, while he noisily drummed his pen on the desktop with his other hand.

The students and I volleyed in a question-answer session. A physical therapy student informed his classmates, "She has permanent damage for biomechanical function."

I interjected, "Yes, that's accurate. I've not heard it explained that way. Thank you."

The medical students argued their point-of-view with their nursing and physical therapy counterparts. "Her surgeries were a success. How is that possible?"

While they debated, I returned to the podium, to prop myself up, some relief from the pain of standing. *Does this generation know about FDR and his polio? He was a four-term president who used a wheelchair. Official photographs only revealed him sitting in cars or standing for speeches. His leg braces were hidden by his pants. He leaned on podiums, too, for support. He was able to walk a few steps with punishing effort. I, too, had learned to keep my challenges hidden and appear healthy to the outside world.*

My thoughts were interrupted when one of my students from the front row pointed to her wristwatch. The wall clock confirmed. "Thank you all so much for listening. Don't be late for class."

I was pleasantly surprised to hear thunderous applause. Some students collectively gathered their belongings, tossed half-eaten sandwiches into the garbage can at the door as they exited. An elderly, thin, grey-haired physician stood up. He flashed a congratulatory smile, mouthed, "Good job," then gestured a double thumbs-up with two straight arms over his head.

Other students, professors and another physician joined me on the stage. The young learners lined up behind the professionals. All of them shook my hand. My student contacts waved from the front row as they cleaned up the cookie crumbs.

When the professionals left, the students in line broke formation and circled, all talking over each other. "My cousin has scoliosis…" "My roommate was misdiagnosed by ER staff…." "Can you speak to the Holistic Physicians of America club?"

They dashed off to their next class. Within minutes, I was alone. Relieved and exhilarated I exhaled, self-satisfied. I gathered my x-rays and left, still buzzing with the success of the talk. Distracted, I exited the wrong door. Typically, I would have retraced my steps. It was a monstrously huge medical complex to get lost in. My curiosity won out. I didn't know what was ahead. I did know what I was leaving behind: memories of major surgeries, countless procedures, injections, failed experimental devices. So, I thought.

As I walked down the unfamiliar breezeway, to my left was a highly varnished, oak, double door. I recognized it immediately. It was the entrance to their medical library. I touched the brass handle to confirm. In 1987 I had spent hours dredging through their research journals, desperate for information about the catheters. *How had I even known this library existed on campus?*

I kept walking as if hypnotized. The area seemed vaguely familiar from some ancient dream. I opened one of a pair of glass doors onto an open-air internal oasis surrounded by the towering buildings of the facility. Lunch vendors and patio tables with decades old, faded red-and-white metal umbrellas filled the area. Looking straight up I saw a patch of blue sky, the only light in the enclosure of man-made, steep, cement cliffs. I turned to leave, stopped dead short. I recognized my former medical terminology classroom, my flyer taped to their glass door.

In 1978, that was that course where I learned about their medical library around the corner. That decade I researched the word "scoliosis." I wasn't lost. I knew exactly where I was in the medical complex. With that realization I shuddered. My eyes moistened. With my fingernails I pried off the tape, pulled down my lecture announcement.

Stiffly, I turned around, gazed upwards to the top floor. I could still hear them laughing at us. *That's when it all went wrong. What if I had not been so naïve? So, trusting? What if I had not been a stupid 19-year-old who dropped out of college?* I collapsed onto a cement park bench and opened the floodgate of my memories.

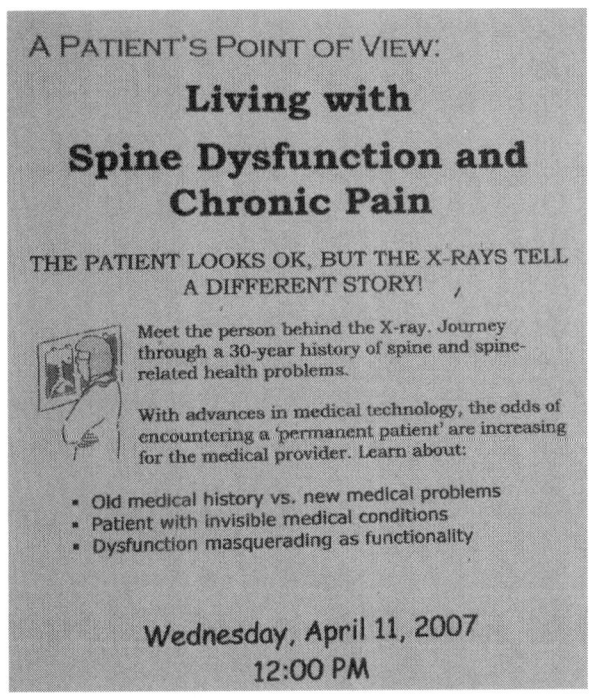

A PATIENT'S POINT OF VIEW:

Living with
Spine Dysfunction and
Chronic Pain

THE PATIENT LOOKS OK, BUT THE X-RAYS TELL A DIFFERENT STORY!

Meet the person behind the X-ray. Journey through a 30-year history of spine and spine-related health problems.

With advances in medical technology, the odds of encountering a 'permanent patient' are increasing for the medical provider. Learn about:

- Old medical history vs. new medical problems
- Patient with invisible medical conditions
- Dysfunction masquerading as functionality

Wednesday, April 11, 2007
12:00 PM

Cookies to Crumbs

It must have been the smell of those freshly baked cookies. My thoughts wandered to childhood, my family, my sister's home-made bakery, my mother and I making doll furniture for a local orphanage, and the day I was first diagnosed with scoliosis.

I was a child, in Ohio, during the 1960s. Our backyard neighbor was an ancient widow, with nooks and crannies of a deeply wrinkled face. She grew tall stalks of corn along our fence line. My mother plucked a few ears for us. Concerned for her after-life, I repeated what I had learned in parochial school about venial, versus the "mortal, burn-in-hell-for-all-eternity," sins. Nuns would draw a large circle on blackboards to represent our souls. Tiny flecks of pecked-out chalk were the partial untruths of venial sins, white lies. Violently drawn, edge-of-chalk, solidly filled circles represented the more serious ones. Stealing was a mortal sin. I was sure of it.

Mother blew off my concerns about hell-fire damnation. She educated me on the topic of property law rights. Each time she flicked an ear of corn in our direction, she said, "Our side of the fence, our corn."

We did share our harvest with that neighbor, whether out of guilt or reciprocation. We brought the old woman bowls of fresh raspberries from our bushes, peaches, and apples from our trees, along with tomatoes and cucumbers from our garden. As a child I was expected to be silent, sit still, while the two women chatted for hours. I played a game: I observed every detail of my surroundings, closed my eyes tight, tried to remember everything I'd seen, and then cracked one eye partially open to see what I missed.

While the women chatted, my mother often quoted our priest, with her own interpretations. "Sure, it's better to give than receive. Better to be rich enough to do the giving, rather than so poor that you need the receiving."

My sister Judy, eight years my senior, had always been the baker in our family, from complicated cakes—a replica of Daddy's B-24 Liberator bomber—to crème puffs, and lots of home-made chocolate-chip cookies.

As my parents were older than the norm, in their early 40s when I was born, Judy was my touchstone for all things contemporary: movie theatre, Halloween, and listening to rock-n-roll music on her record player. She alternated between her dual roles as modern mom and big sister—both protective guardian angel and tormentor. As the latter she teased nonstop. When young I couldn't verbalize the "h" sound. She would gather her friends, point to Daddy's ashtray, "What do you call this?" Gales of laughter erupted when I said, "Daddy's ass-tray."

Aside from my angst, I admired her bravery and wanted to be like her. At a neighborhood kids' baseball game, too young to play, I sat on the sidelines to watch. My sister was the catcher when a wild swing caused the bat to hit her square in the eye. She didn't cry. With her hand cupped around her injury, we rushed home to find Daddy. I sprinted to keep up.

Our mother banned neighborhood baseball games for us after that, even as spectators, due to my sister's black eye. "Too dangerous."

When either of us needed stitches for deep cuts, Dad would sterilize a sewing needle in the flame of a candle, and sew it closed using standard thread. I must have been pre-kindergarten age when I tripped and fell against the brick casement of a basement window. Blood ran down my face from a deep gash at the tapered edge of my eyebrow. Dad opted out. "Too close to the eye." At the hospital, on the exam table, an angled white cloth over my eyes left a revealing gap on the right side. Looking upwards I watched the doctor sew the gash closed. I wasn't afraid. He wasn't doing anything Daddy didn't do.

My mom avoided doctors after her own mother died abruptly, age 56, after being taken to a hospital with a "cold." My mother never knew the cause of death until decades later when I wrote the Ohio Historical Society for the death certificate, and we learned my grandmother had died of pneumonia. What my mom did remember was being chased down the hallways of the hospital by a dozen doctors, medical students, begging her to sign consent for an autopsy. "You're not cutting her up! She's suffered enough in her lifetime."

My father took me to all my medical appointments. Afterwards, at the drugstore, he bought me comic books— but only from the Classic series: *A Tale of Two Cities, Don Quixote, Oliver Twist,* and *Gulliver's Travels.*

One time, Daddy and I stopped at the neighborhood tavern, The Grey Wolf, for a beer on the way home. I revealed my delight at swirling on a barstool to my mother. That feature might have passed for the ice cream parlor, if I had not mentioned the huge jar of pickled pig's knuckles on the counter. Poor Daddy never heard the end of it. My mother took me to appointments after that, no more comics.

In 1967, the summer of my 10th birthday, my life transitioned. After her senior year in high school Judy moved out to live in a nursing-school dorm, only coming home on the weekends. My parents moved from Cleveland to the suburbs. I was diagnosed with scoliosis.

At my parochial school, our uniforms were a skirt, blouse, and vest. The hem of our skirts met the top of our knee-length socks. At any given time, girls were ordered to kneel. If the hem of their skirt didn't touch the floor, they were sent home for the indecency of revealing the skin of their knees.

The nuns were confused by my dress code glitch. The hem of my skirt was perpetually crooked. One side touched the floor, the other side didn't. My mom, a former factory seamstress, noticed the garment was horizontal when hung.

Our family doctor said, "Mary has scoliosis. Her spine is crooked. That makes her hips lopsided, causing the uneven uniform." Neither of us had ever heard the strange word. He continued, "Don't worry about it. Everyone has something wrong with them. Some people have flat feet."

Mother was relieved. Daddy had flat feet. No big deal. I wasn't so sure. It must have been a Friday. Judy was home for the weekend. I ran from room to room searching for her, and then rushed down the basement stairs. Those cool, underground caverns were the alternate living rooms during the hot summer months in Ohio. No air-conditioning.

My sister, all of 19, was lying on our faded, navy-blue, throw-covered couch. Winded, I arrived in front of her. Reading as usual, knees bent, a book propped up on her lap, she took a bite from a half-eaten apple with her left hand, while slowly turning a page with her right. I yelled out, "Judy, I have scoliosis. What does that mean?"

Without looking up, she said, "That means you'll be a cripple and, in a wheelchair, when you grow up." She took another bite of her apple and turned a page.

Dazed, I waited. *Was she joking?* She kept reading. I ran up the worn, green, linoleum steps. When at the landing I turned and stuck my tongue out at her. *I know who to trust: the doctor. He said it's nothing to worry about.*

Our move to the suburbs that summer had been like landing on another planet. No more vegetable gardens, clotheslines, or stores within walking distance. Sodded lawns were off-limits for children, "too expensive" to ruin. Block after block of brand new, brick, cookie-cutter houses, all looked the same. Daddy hated them. "They look like army barracks." We were fortunate there was an open field behind our home. Countless fluttering wildflowers of Queen Anne Lace created an image of an ocean's cresting waves as a breeze blew through them.

Alone, I walked our dog around the field of pungent wildflowers. One day, I braced myself as a strong gust of wind kicked up. The lacey blooms bent, all except for one solitary flower. Upon closer examination the stem was deformed. The flower was the same, only smaller than its counterparts. The stem was as flat and wide as a piece of ribbon. All that summer I would wait for a gust of the wind to reveal the rigid flower's location. I fully expected it to wither and die long before the others due to its deformity. Powerless to bend, its blossom was tattered by the wind, but survived. In memory that battered wildflower became a metaphor for my spine.

My mom was always weeding our backyard in the summer. After school one day I found her sitting on the couch in the living room petting four baby rabbits squished together next to her. "They were in a nest in my flower bed behind the house."

"Mom, you can't bring them inside. Their mother will be looking for them."

"Are you sure? I had pet mice as a little girl."

• "Yes."

My father used to tease her by calling her Saint Francis, for Saint Francis of Assisi, patron saint of animals. We had a platform bird feeder outside our kitchen window for the wild birds. Inside we always had a dog, cat, and parakeet. She loved animals.

Another day, my mom was weeding. I walked behind her towards the open field behind the house to walk the dog. Over her shoulder, "Mary, make sure you close the gate."

"Yes, Mother."

"And don't climb on that pile of bricks."

"Yes, Mother."

Twenty minutes later, of course, I climbed onto the jagged three-foot pile of construction crews' discards. At the summit I slipped and fell. The cut to my knee was sharp and deep. In the split-second before the blood flowed, I saw two white cord-looking things cut in half. In the few minutes to walk home blood covered the entire front of my leg, filled my white tennis shoe, and gushed with each step.

As quietly as possible, I opened the gate of our chain-link fence, as I unhooked the dog's leash. My mom was still kneeling, head bent over. I tried to walk past without making a noise. Without looking up, she called out. "Lock the gate."

"Yes, Mother."

"And put the leash where it belongs."

"Yes, Mother."

I walked through Daddy's rose garden, across the patio, through the attached garage, to our avocado-green kitchen. As usual, Daddy sat at the kitchen table reading the newspaper, a long ash of spent cigarette dangling precariously. When I spotted him, my fearless resolve erupted in waterworks and a long-drawn-out wail. "Daaddy!"

He jumped up, snuffed his cigarette, and was kneeling beside me in a moment. "This is too deep for me to stitch, Mary." From the kitchen drawer, he grabbed a clean towel, ripped it in half, and tied a tourniquet. It was soaked crimson in minutes.

My bottom lip quivered, "Daddy, I saw two white cord looking things inside cut in half…."

"We have to go to the hospital." He stood up. "Ask the doctor when we get there. I don't want you to be afraid of doctors like your mother." He paused, "Always ask questions. That's how you learn. All knowledge is of value."

"But Daddy, what could that be?"

"Sounds like tendons." He shoved a pack of cigarettes into his pocket.

In the attached garage he flung open the screen door, yelled out. "Mother, come on. What's taking you? We've got to get Mary to the hospital for stitches."

"I'm busy weeding."

Neither of my parents questioned why I walked past my mother that day. She couldn't handle anyone being hurt. The emergency room doctor confirmed the cut tendons.

During my freshman year in a public high school, the second time in my life I heard the word, "scoliosis" was when I questioned a classmate wearing a brace that showed at her neckline. I felt sorry for her; she didn't know my trick of hemming my pant legs, an inch different in length, so they would look even when wearing them. In my ignorance I thought that fixed my scoliosis. Little did I know.

The third time I heard the word "scoliosis" I was a college sophomore. An organic chemistry classmate stopped me in the open-air breezeway of my Florida community college. "I've been watching you," he grinned. I had noticed him for weeks staring at me and had rehearsed my reply, *yes, pizza and a movie sounds great.*

He loudly announced, "You. Have. Scoliosis." His tone of voice made it clear this was a bad thing.

"How do you know that?"

"It's obvious."

I was embarrassed. Then remembered the diagnosis from the prior decade. "My family doctor said it's nothing."

"All you need is a brace to correct the problem." I was 19, he was easily 25. I believed him.

Later, I remembered the girl from my high school. *A brace won't interfere with my classes for the upcoming fall quarter at UF.* I had already been accepted into the College of Pharmacy and decided to take his advice.

My spine was x-rayed for the first time in my life in the spring of 1977 at age 19. Multiple referrals and months later I found myself at a local hospital with my mom. They, too, filmed my spine. We returned to the top floor of the hospital. I handed my film to a young doctor wearing a stiffly starched white jacket. He and a dozen other young doctors, with their backs to us, gathered around an illuminated screen.

My mom and I were instructed to sit on the opposite side of the large, carpeted office. We waited patiently with our ankles crossed. Mother held her purse tightly on her lap. The doctors neither introduced themselves, nor said anything to us. I was clueless about the ramifications of a "teaching hospital," or what it meant that I was scheduled to see a surgeon.

I stood up, walked over to the window. Directly below was a courtyard of brand-new red-and-white metal umbrellas. I felt uneasy at the doctors' overheard conversations.

"Can you imagine this level of deformity?"

Another doctor responded, "All we need is signed consent. That's why we're meeting in his private office, no need for clinic visits on this case." He excitedly said to me, "You have a double curvature. Your thoracic spine is 37 degrees, lumbar 52."

The first doctor interjected, "Plus, rotation!"

I had no idea what they were talking about. As I started to inquire, my mom called out, "Mary, come here, sit down. Don't bother them." I joined her, annoyed. I had questions. *Consent? What is the normal curvature of the spine supposed to be?*

No one showed us the x-ray. Their statistics meant nothing. I didn't know anything about scoliosis. The only image I'd seen of a spine, at that point in my life, had been Halloween cardboard cut-outs.

An elderly man with bushy, grey hair, also wearing a white jacket, entered the office. He didn't introduce himself or the other doctors. He, too, peered intently at my film.

"I'm only here for a back brace," I advised.

He turned, "It's too late. You should have had a brace as a child when your bones were still growing. You have a fully mature spine."

He faced the other doctors. "Surgery is the only option. We'll need to make a large incision, likely from the base of her neck down to the tailbone, the sacrum." He pointed at the film. A wave of excited chatter, rippled through the white coats. He continued, "We'll break each and every vertebra of her spine—."

Sacrum? Vertebrae? My fears escalated, but I didn't question them. The older doctor continued, "...make two additional eight-inch incisions over both hips, to remove marrow. We'll re-set the whole spine into alignment, fuse with the hip bone material, and finish by drilling in metal rods and screws for stability."

My stomach churned. I felt like I was going to throw up. I didn't know putting screws and rods into a person was ever done surgically for any reason.

With that, the older doctor turned towards us. "You'll need to be hospitalized, bedridden, for one year in a full body cast, then another year in a rehab facility to learn to walk again."

To the younger doctors, he said, "This is groundbreaking surgery. You're fortunate to be on my team. The severity of her deformity is rare in the United States, due to screening in our elementary schools." He turned to us. "How long have you lived in this country? You speak English beautifully."

"I was born and raised in Ohio."

"I take it you refused to wear your brace when a child." He shook a scolding index finger.

"I wasn't offered a brace as a child. Our family doctor said not to worry about it. I'm here today for a brace. I'm a junior at the University of Florida. It's my first quarter. I've already been accepted into the College of Pharmacy. They can only take 30 students a year. I'm in the number one position for next fall. They told me to take electives until then." *Didn't he know? I was one of them.*

"You'll have to drop out of school for a few years."

It was the worst possible thing he could say. Before I could form my own opinion, my mother spit her words through clenched teeth, "Don't you dare touch my daughter." She stood up. "Mary, come on, we're leaving." I hesitated. She hissed, "Now, Mary."

The older doctor was clearly surprised. He said, "I'm not harming her. Mrs. ...." He looked down at my chart. "Besides, she's old enough to make her own decisions. My students..." he waved in their direction "... are only a few years older. They'll soon be practicing physicians."

They're only students? Like me?

The surgeon handed me his clipboard, "Sign here. Let's schedule surgery. Your mother doesn't understand."

My mother shouted, "I said no. Your boys can go practice on someone else. I'm...her...mother. I make her decisions."

The students all laughed. I wanted to crawl in a hole.

The older doctor paused, as if to think, then to me, said, "Patients with a spine abnormality as severe as yours are classified as freaks by the medical community. You'll never have children. Without surgery, you'll be in pain the rest of your life. A cripple confined to a wheelchair. The twisting deformity of your rib cage will eventually crush your heart and lungs, resulting in premature death."

Horrified, I tried to take it all in. I looked at my mother's stony expression as she stared out the window.

To the doctor, my mother said, "We're leaving. How much do I owe you?" She fumbled to open her purse and pulled out my father's green checkbook, and a pen. Holding her purse tightly between her hip and her elbow, she opened the cover, ready to write.

The older doctor said, "You pay the receptionist." He then handed me his business card.

Before I could look at the card, my mother yanked it out of my hand. At arm's length she held it out to him. "I understand plenty. You want to cut her up. To experiment." She opened her fingertips. His card fluttered to the floor.

We left without talking. I knew medical care was unaffordable in my mother's childhood home. The rich thrived while the poor died. *She's old-fashioned.*

It was a long walk through the winding corridors of the enormous hospital. Once outside she sprinted ahead of me.

"Mom, wait up!"

She turned, shouted, "Once they cut you, you'll never be the same," and kept walking. I stood there bewildered.

My thoughts swirled. *I don't want to be the same. I want to be able to have children.* I broke out of my stupor and scrambled to catch up.

In my mind, doctors, priests, and God were all on the same level. Not to be questioned or doubted. It was a death sentence as far as I was concerned.

Soon, I questioned my major. I'd always wanted to take botany. Ultimately, I dropped every single class except one, throughout all three quarters of my junior year. When the College of Pharmacy mailed their paperwork for the upcoming fall quarter, I threw it out.

An invaluable resource did come from that faltering year at the University of Florida. A medical terminology class, adjacent to courtyard patio tables with red-and-white metal umbrellas, had introduced me to their massive medical library around the corner. After meeting that first surgeon, dubbed Dr. Unknown since I never knew his name, I spent hours studying their research journals to learn everything known about scoliosis.

Dr. Fixit

Six years passed. In 1983 I was 26 years old. After playing tennis I experienced my first major episode of lower back pain. It was so severe I couldn't stand, rolled off the edge of my bed, gently lowered myself to the floor, and crawled on my stomach to the bathroom. I so believed Dr. Unknown's earlier dire predictions about my future that I blamed my untreated scoliosis. It never occurred to me that it could be a temporary muscle, ligament, or tendon pull.

That year I met a second orthopedic surgeon, an aged man with a few strands of comb-over on his balding skull. Again, my mom joined me on the hours-long drive to the out-of-town facility. There I was delighted to discover the new surgeon had a completely different personality. He greeted us warmly and introduced himself with the all-important words: "I can fix your spine." *Dr. Fixit, my savior!*

There were only the three of us in the examination room, no students. "You'll be more comfortable in the waiting area Mrs. … how do you pronounce your last name?" Through blaring white teeth, he flashed a caged smile in my direction. When he escorted my mother out, she flinched when he touched her arm. He turned to me and said, "My nurse will bring you a gown for your exam." He winked.

His nurse arrived, handed me a gown. "You need to completely undress. That includes your bra and panties, too. I don't know why. I've worked for lots of other doctors. They usually let their patients keep their panties on. Opening in back, so he can examine your spine."

When the doctor returned, he measured my height, and then the distance between my outstretched arms. "I'm afraid your scoliosis is quite severe. Your height is three inches less than your arm span."

"Doctor, what does that mean?"

"Did you do cartwheels, when a child?"

"No, I always fell. How did you know that?"

"Scoliosis compresses the spine." As he motioned for me to turn, I held my gown closed on my hips. "Let go. I'll hold it. I need you to bend completely forward from the hips." He slowly slid his open palm from side-to-side, along the length of my back. I felt uneasy. He seemed to linger too long, especially at my hips.

"As I thought, you have a significant rib cage hump."

"What?" I bolted upright, turned to face him.

"Due to your scoliosis the ribs are pulled apart on one side of your spine like a fan, the other side crowded together. When bending forward, one side of your rib cage raises up. The other side descends. Hasn't anyone done an exam like this on you before?"

"No."

"You're 26. I wish I'd met you when you were younger. Your spine is surprisingly flexible for someone your age. A brace would have corrected the curvature, even as late as age 20. How unfortunate, you wasted your time at that teaching hospital six years ago. You could have benefited from my expertise. We'll reconvene after x-rays."

"Can I have children?" I was still haunted by Dr. Unknown's dire diagnosis.

"We'll discuss that when you return."

Afterwards, his nurse ushered us into his large, private, carpeted office. Opulent, burgundy, leather chairs faced his desk, in front of a wall of glass. The view of enormous skyscrapers in the major metropolis looked like daggers pointed at a cloudless sky. There were no trees anywhere. Along the side wall was an enormous oil painting. I exclaimed, "Wow, that's a big boat."

The nurse chuckled. "That's no boat, Sweetie. That's his private yacht." She instructed us to take a seat and wait.

The surgeon entered. As he walked past the artwork, he appeared to fall off the bow as he rounded his desk. He carried my film. "You have a 69-degree curve along with a second birth defect. You have an extra lumbar vertebra, six rather than five." He didn't say anything about the upper back curve or rotation, like Dr. Unknown, so I assumed my debut surgeon was mistaken.

"That extra vertebra is deformed and caused your scoliosis." He looked directly at my mother as he said, "I see from my questionnaire, you were 40 when Mary was born. Birth defects increase with age."

Wide-eyed I tried to telepathically message her. *Oh! Please. Don't tell that story.*

"My doctor said I had leukemia, was going to die. I couldn't leave my daughter, Judy, so, I prayed. God was good to me. He spared my life but gave me a different cross to bear." She tilted her head in my direction. "It turned out I was pregnant with Mary. Can you imagine at my age? I don't know how that happened, my husband and I worked different shifts. The Rhythm Method failed twice in my life." As I glared at her, imagined crawling under the carpeting.

The doctor chuckled, cleared his throat. "Let's stick to the present day. Due to this sixth lumbar vertebra not separating from your spine, we must include it in our fusion. Otherwise, the weight of all your movement would rest on one partially deformed level. That would be a potentially dangerous situation."

My mother interrupted. "She looks okay to me."

"Yes. Only an experienced surgeon would be able to discern the severity of her scoliosis, visually."

My chemistry classmate noticed.

"We'll list it as idiopathic, unknown source, to keep the insurance companies satisfied. They don't like to pay for congenital scoliosis surgery. Not for patients her age."

I had no idea what he was talking about. "Doctor, are you sure about the degree of curve? Three months ago, it was 62 degrees when x-rayed in my hometown. How could it advance seven degrees in three months? My original film in 1977 was 52 degrees. I've been reading up—" He noisily drummed his fingers on his desk. "The journals say it takes twenty years for a scoliosis curve to advance twenty degrees."

"Where did you read this?"

"At the medical library, my former university, I plan to finish my degree there someday."

"Well, someone has done her homework. Well, apparently your scoliosis is advancing at an alarming rate. After my surgery you'll be able to have children. You'll never experience back pain, again. I'll be able to reduce your curve by at least fifty percent. Probably down to a 30-degree curve."

My mom interjected, "But, she'll always be weak."

"No. Actually, her spine will be strong enough to play tackle football. This is 1983. There have been many advances in orthopedics. Only one incision is required. There's no need to break vertebrae these days. We use a ratcheting device to straighten the scoliosis. Stainless-steel Harrington rods are hooked onto the spine, no need for screws. Two months recovery, you'll return to work by the third month. The brace is worn for six months, only as a precaution.

"You don't have to decide today. Make an appointment to return in three weeks with any questions."

My mother stood up, held her purse tightly. "She's not having an operation."

"Madame, other than surgery, there simply is no other option." He looked in my direction, "Not if you ever want to have children, Mary."

At the follow-up appointment, I signed consent. Dr. Fixit said, "Here's a prescription for iron. Donate three units of blood. We'll be using your own because there's a new disease called AIDS that some donors carry. Also, cut down to two cigarettes a day while donating."

That weekend I went out with a girlfriend. A good-looking guy with a nice tan asked me to dance, then for my phone number. Aaron and I dated over the next couple of months.

In the interim my mom did her best to talk me out of the scoliosis surgery. "Mom, I want to marry, to have children, a family of my own someday."

"You think that new boyfriend of yours is going to marry you? I've got news for you, Missy. He's going to dump you like a hot potato. No man wants to be stuck with a cripple for the rest of his life."

I was admitted the day before surgery. My sister's husband, Ed, drove the three of us. As soon as we arrived, at noon, an aide instructed my family to leave. "Her pre-op tests will last all day. She won't be in her room." I handed my mother my clothing, shoes, and purse after pulling out a lighter and two cigarettes. The aide said, "Keep the whole pack. You've already donated your blood for surgery. Smoke as much as you want. It doesn't matter now."

Except for a plaster cast at 4:00 p.m., to manufacture my hard-plastic back brace, there were no other tests. When I questioned a nurse, she said, "Much later. You can walk around. Stay on this floor. Smoking is allowed in the visitor's lounge." She gestured towards my pack on the nightstand.

Wearing the pink bathrobe my mother had bought, I walked the deserted hallway, then to their waiting room. The only other occupants were a middle-aged couple. The woman softly wept, leaning against the man's shoulder. He held her with both arms. Within minutes they left.

Dust particles, illuminated by the setting sun, were suspended, like my future life. With the shifting light the previously clean-looking windows revealed hidden streaks of dirt. I lit a cigarette and watched my reflection through the haze of smoke in the ceiling-to-floor gold-speckled wall mirror on the opposite wall. I wished the couple had stayed.

In my hospital room, the phone rang around 7 p.m. A friend called. I didn't know long-distance calls were allowed.

At 9 p.m., I tossed my bathrobe onto the foot of my bed and turned on the TV. My door flung open. A flock of white uniforms, like sea birds, swooped in. One person took my blood pressure, another vitals, a third vials of my blood, while a fourth person attached sticky patches to my chest. They chatted with each other.

After they left, a female barely out of high school entered. She carried a brown, pint-sized glass bottle, along with a large, rectangular-shaped, hospital-blue, plastic-coated dressing. I turned onto my stomach as instructed and she poured the liquid over my back. The dark red betadine dripped off the side of my body. The white sheets were soaked. When she applied the large pad and sticky latex tape to my wet skin, the plastic dressing fell off. She did this three times. Each time, she left to obtain more supplies, then re-washed my back with soap and re-applied copious amounts of the liquid.

After her third attempt, I rolled over and bolted upright. "Tape doesn't stick to a wet surface." I didn't know the opened bottle was on my bed. The entire contents dumped. The crimson stain soaked through the bathrobe in seconds. In exasperation I said, "You don't know what you're doing. Please, stop."

"You can't have surgery without this, it kills germs."

Will the surgical team be this incompetent? Out loud I said, "That's a good idea. No surgery." She left. With one hand holding my gown closed, I sprinted down the hallway to the nurses' station. "I'm cancelling my surgery. I want to go home."

"No, you can't do that. All your pre-op tests are done. Dr. Fixit will be angry if we let you leave. Have a cigarette, relax. Someone will drop by to talk to you." She motioned down the hall.

In the lounge I chain-smoked the rest of my pack of cigarettes. Every frightened fiber in my body screamed at my brain: *Cancel surgery. Get out of here.* I debated. *How would I get home? There's no one I can call. I have no money, no purse, no clothing, not even shoes. Could I sneak off the floor? Use the stairwell? Where would I go?*

In my hospital room, I threw the ruined bathrobe in the garbage can, lay down on the wet, stained sheets. A nurse came in, "Oh, this is quite a mess. Today was her first day, no training available. A more experienced aide will be in shortly to take care of everything. It's too late to call your surgeon to request a prescription to take the edge off. Plus, your anesthesiologist still needs your signature for consent. You can't sign when under the influence. It's against the law." She looked at her watch. "It's midnight. He should have been here hours ago. I'm certain he'll be here any minute, I'll have him write for a drug when he arrives."

The anesthesiologist failed to show up that night or the following morning. Neither did the aide. In the wee hours I dozed off into a restless sleep.

At 7 a.m. I was taken to the pre-op staging area, where another nurse repeated, "We can't give you any meds until consent is signed." When the tardy doctor arrived, he read off the disclaimer, and shoved a generic brown clipboard into my hands. The nurse said to him, "You'd better hurry. You're late." I barely scribbled my signature, handed the clipboard over my head to the nurse, as the anesthesiologist shoved my gurney out of the holding area.

Once inside the operating room, the anesthesiologist dashed out. The temperature was freezing. Blinding bright lights from the ceiling bore into my eyes. Everything was white, except for five or six latex-gloved unisex creatures dressed in surgical-green gowns, with matching caps and face masks. Portals of eyes and noses looked like the nuns from grade school. No one said a word. The reflection from a pair of eyeglasses revealed a frightened, deathly-white, familiar looking, young woman—me.

The mute people transferred my body to the operating table. They continued their prep, hushed murmurs between them. I looked to my left, a long buffet-style table held dozens of objects: saws, drills, scalpels, long meat-hook rods. With a sickening feeling, I realized those tools were all for my body.

The anesthesiologist rushed in, out of breath. "I need to start your central line." Through the corner of my right eye, I watched, and felt, the clear plastic tubing being stabbed into my neck. Later, I learned they were used in long surgeries—mine eight hours—to monitor blood pressure internally, the tip barely placed inside the heart, rather than an external blood-pressure cuff.

I was an eyewitness to the initiation of the first of two major surgical errors in 1983.

A rubber mask was placed over my face. I counted in reverse from 100, finally drifted into blackness at 88 as I recognized Dr. Fixit's voice, "What's taking so long? Why isn't she under yet?"

I woke in a dimly lit hallway, freezing cold like a meat locker. My whole body felt like a glacier. I couldn't swallow, my throat felt scraped raw. Heavy eyelids barely opened; my eyes followed the staff. At first, I didn't recognize the fringed vertical black lines as my own eyelashes.

Employees bustled around a zig-zag pattern of gurneys with moaning patients. One uniform walked up, "Well, you shouldn't be awake." She injected a vial into my IV. In the dim sound of distant voices, staff joked with each other, one laughing loudly. The black curtains of my eyelashes closed the show.

When I woke up, I was alone in a small square room of white nothingness: walls, ceiling, sheets. In the direction of my feet, I could see a closed door. Firmly shut ivory blinds blocked the window view.

There were tubes and wires everywhere. Hemovacs drained blood from both sides of my flank. A Foley catheter drained urine. IVs in both arms replenished lost fluids. Heart monitor pads were stuck to my chest. The eighteen-inch incision was thoroughly bandaged.

Tethered like Gulliver, my mind was free to roam through the fog of endless, static, whiteness. I moved my toes. I'd overcome the terror from last night. *Scared, that's all. Nothing horrible happened.*

Required to lie flat for the next ten days, I remained motionless. A white uniformed pair of nurses entered, deep in conversation. Using a sheet, they rolled my re-built spine from side to side to prevent bed sores.

One of them asked, "How ya' feeling?"

"Wonderful!"

She laughed, "That's the morphine we gave you when you arrived." They left.

Within minutes, I felt blissful, light as a butterfly hovering on a gentle breeze. I was warm and cozy inside, safe, secure, and comfortable. I felt a profound sense of peace.

Then everything vaporized. First, the window blinds vanished. The door disappeared. My stomach had an unusual, pleasant fluttering feeling. My bed evaporated, the IV poles dissolved... then I was gone, too. In a vibration of transparent glistening white light, gentle warmth like sunshine on my skin on a cool spring day, my body dissolved into particles, soared into infinity. I was free.

Loud buzzers returned me to the reality of my physical body. I jolted awake. The sound of a heavy metal door flung open, hitting the wall, repeatedly. There was confusion and movement nearby. I could sense their presence. People rushed into my room. The sound of multiple voices yelled, at first, indiscernible words. I couldn't see them. With my fingertips I felt my eyes, they were open. *Why can't I see?* Someone ripped a blood pressure cuff off my arm. A dozen uniforms came into focus. A voice rang out. "We're losing her. BP bottomed out, 50/20."

A third voice said, "This is an overdose, people. Recovery already gave her morphine. Pull that morphine drip." The nurse closest ripped the tape off the inside of my elbow and yanked the needle out. Morphine sprayed my face, the sheets.

Without a word, they filed out. The last person said, "You can't have anything for pain, until the drugs clear your system." The sound of the door latched shut. I was alone.

Within hours, waves of nonstop, unbearable torture took over my body. I gave into the sensation and screamed, over and over. I felt as if every instrument I had seen in the operating room was still being used on my body.

The same nurse to whom I'd reported my earlier euphoria returned, her hair pulled into a bun. As she bent over my body, wisps of thin grey hair escaped and floated around her face. She grinned, "Feeling some pain now?"

She left. I was alone with my horror.

The hours on the clock trudged at a camel's pace. Minutes lasted an eternity. As the night progressed, the intensity escalated. I screamed and begged them to help.

At 4:00 a.m. a young nurse arrived. "We can't give you anything for pain. You had a negative reaction earlier." She kept her eyes on the floor. The word, "overdose," was never used again.

"Where's my surgeon?"

The nurse said, "He's out of town, a trip."

Weakly, I asked, "Isn't there anyone else?"

The on-call doctor arrived, rested his hand on my shiny bed rail. With trembling fingertips, I barely touched his skin, seeking some warmth and humanity. He yanked his hand away.

Around 7:00 a.m., an IV line with morphine was started again. Soon after, my mother arrived. She gently held my hand in hers. I felt loved.

Twenty years later, in 2003, my mother was 86 years old, and I was 46. Her memory was like a shattered mirror, tiny unconnected reflections of the past. She often said, "I'm at the end of my life, if you have any questions about anything, ask now."

"Mom, do you remember anything about the day of my surgery in 1983?"

Without hesitation, she answered. "That morning, Ed drove me, as I walked around the corner, the nurses were all laughing at you. They pointed to your room and mimicked you screaming."

"Did you file a complaint? Speak to my surgeon? Do anything?"

I already knew her answer.

"You can't complain. No matter what anyone does to you. That's life. You'd better get used to it, Mary."

Souvenirs

The next ten days passed. My new boyfriend, Aaron, drove the long distance to visit. His sandy blond hair complimented the remnants of his summer tan. On his first visit he brought a dozen red roses. The second time, he arrived with a friend, and carried a bouquet of pink carnations.

Aaron's friend lounged in the empty bed next to mine, eyes glued to the TV, while he rotated through the channels. Aaron pulled up a chair. He bragged about our first date to his buddy. "You should have seen Mary, I took her to a really expensive steak house, and she orders chicken, the cheapest thing on the menu." He laughed, "You Catholic girls."

   •   "Maybe she likes chicken."

"No, I saw her, she ran her finger down the list of prices, then slid over to the entrees, 'I'll have the chicken.'"

So, I tell her, "Don't you like steak? Are you a vegetarian? We could go somewhere else if you prefer."

She says, "Oh, no, I love steak."

"Great, would you like an appetizer?" And get this, she says, "Oh no, that's too expensive. The steak is already a lot of money." They both laughed.

"Outside the restaurant, I told her, 'Hey, you might not want to go out with me again. You might as well get a steak dinner out of it.' Then get this, she says, 'If I order an expensive meal, you might not ask me out again.'"

The guys roared with laughter.

I said, "Yeah, it was a real *Gift of the Magi moment*."

A few days later a nurse came in on rounds. She said, "There's blood on your sheets. Your incision ripped open. I'll page your surgeon." I was scared.

When Dr. Fixit arrived, he said, "Let's take a look," and gently rolled me onto my side. I felt a twinge of embarrassment as my hospital gown opened. I reminded myself he was a doctor and a professional.

Without warning, Dr. Fixit shoved his ungloved fingers into my vagina. I quickly rolled over to face him. Furious that I'd lost all rights to my body. He held up two bloody fingers, "Yes. Looks like chewing tobacco. You're on your period."

Dazed, somehow, I managed to ask, "How is that possible? My period was only two weeks ago."

"Stress can bring on an extra period. Didn't you have some situation in SICU, a drug allergy"? He winked.

In that instant I remembered my scoliosis exam in his office two months prior. *Had I blocked this out?* As I'd stood, wearing only the examination gown, he had asked me to bend forward from my hips. At first, he held my gown closed at my hips, as promised. When it opened, he mockingly commented, "Oops," then wolf-whistled, "Nice view." I'd bolted upright, humiliated. *I should have walked out.*

But who would fix my scoliosis? I decided a straight spine, and being able to have children, was more important.

As my release date approached, Dr. Fixit came into my room. "You need to get out of bed young lady." I had been horizontal, with my head barely elevated for meals, for almost ten days. When I tried to stand the dizziness was overwhelming. My body sagged like a sack of potatoes.

My surgeon grabbed my waist, held me too close. The odor of his after-shave was intense. I turned my face away from his. I wished that anyone else was available to help with my first steps.

Later that day, I shared my surgeon's instructions with my mother and sister. "He ordered an ambulance. No sitting. No jostling in a car."

Judy said, "There's no need for that. You can lie flat on the back seat of my car."

My mother questioned her, "Are you sure? She can't be bounced around. You'll have to drive slowly."

On the day I was to be released, Dr. Fixit examined my incision. He said, "You've developed an abscess. I'll drain it. However, it will need to be drained again tomorrow.

You're welcome to spend another night in the hospital. He winked. I cringed remembering his prior assault.

I brought my mother and sister up to speed when they arrived. My mother refused for the three of us to stay in a hotel for the night or stay with a local relative. "I have to sleep in my own bed."

"And I can't spend another night in the hospital, Mom." I was afraid to tell her about my uneasy feelings about my surgeon. I didn't think about the logistics, or inconvenience for them to make the trip twice in two days. Judy was livid. She banged cabinets shut, and then with one shove, the wheeled cart with my food tray went flying across the room.

The three of us drove home in silence, with me lying flat on the back seat, no seatbelt. About half-way home my sister hit railroad tracks hard, at 60 mph. I screamed in gut-wrenching pain from the abrupt bouncing. My mother scolded her.

I wondered, *Were these last ten days for nothing.*

I moved in with my parents for my post-op care. In my former bedroom my mom gently washed my back, replaced the dressing daily. She insisted I wear my father's bleached, white T-shirts. "We don't want dye from the fabric near where they cut you."

My mother didn't allow any visitors, not even Aaron or my sister. Two weeks after I was released from the hospital, while lying in bed, I suddenly started coughing. Within minutes it escalated to choking, even though I hadn't eaten anything for hours. I jumped up to grab a glass of water from the bathroom. The water ran down the sides of my mouth. I couldn't swallow. Each attempt for air became a shrill, harsh squeaking sound. I struggled to breathe. Against my surgeon's orders, I took my brace off to expand my lungs.

In the living room, I found my mother blankly staring out the window, barely whispered, "Where's Daddy?"

She glanced in my direction.

"Take me...hospital."

"What for? So, one of your fancy doctors can tell me I wasn't a good mother? Besides, I don't know where to park there." She continued to stare out the window.

Did they have an argument? In the kitchen I reached for the wall phone.

"What are you doing? Don't you dare call anyone."

Replaced the receiver. *It's too late anyway.*

Back in my bedroom, with outstretched arms I steadied myself against the molding of the doorway and tried to cough. Nothing. I crouched to the floor, tried again. *I'm choking to death.*

In the bathroom, with one last ounce of adrenalin strength I threw my body against the counter of the sink. The suffocation cleared. Nothing came out of my mouth. I inhaled a burst of air, as if I had been under water too long. With my sweaty face and palms pressed against the cabinet I had sunk to the floor, then realized I had urinated all over myself. Eventually, I pulled myself up, caught the countertop, and stood, as sweat dripped off my chin. The bathroom mirror reflected a lobster red face, including my scalp. My eyes were wide with fear, the whites filled with broken blood vessels. *What just happened?*

When I reported the bizarre incident to my surgeon, he wasn't concerned. "Nothing to worry about." He recorded the issue as, "a chronic cough."

Soon the episode was forgotten, but over the years, I often wondered. *Was that choking episode the catheter? Even if unrelated, if we had gone to the hospital, maybe it would have shown up on an x-ray?*

Within two months, right on schedule, I returned to work. The rest of my recovery was uneventful. However, my back pain returned, much worse than prior to surgery. There were several trips to Dr. Fixit, who responded with increasing hostility. "There is no reason for you to be in pain." Except for standard x-rays there were no other tests.

Meanwhile, Aaron introduced me to both sides of his family. One day he mentioned, "When we have kids someday." My happiness was complete. We were married a year after my scoliosis surgery. I bought myself a pearl-hued dress. On top of my curly permed hair, I wore a wreath of tiny flowers. We said our vows under the arms of an enormous Live Oak tree at a relative's home.

Life with Aaron was adventurous. On our honeymoon he wanted to drive a go-cart on the abandoned beach of winter despite the bitterly cold whipping winds. It was fun, though we hit all the ruts. Later, in the Bahamas, he wanted the experience of driving a scooter on the left side of the road. We wiped out, going around a corner, as he swerved to avoid hitting a truck with long metal poles sticking out at eye level, no red flags. Fortunately, each of us only suffered road burns from skidding across the pavement. Then he signed us up for golf lessons. I took one swing with the golf club, and literally saw stars. I didn't dare twist my spine after that. As my pain worsened, a coworker said, "Your muscles must be really weak from being in the brace so long." She suggested physical therapy, which I had never heard of.

Dr. Fixit refused to write the orders, when first requested. When I asked, again, saying I wanted to join my husband to play golf, he begrudgingly consented. "This is totally unnecessary. However, as you're a wife now, you'll only need two sessions."

It seemed a peculiar comment. I didn't question him. My first appointment lasted fifteen minutes. I was shown the correct body mechanics when pushing a broom. At the second appointment, another quarter-hour meeting, I was taught to oscillate, like a rocking-horse when vacuuming.

Neither helped my pain levels. Dr. Fixit decreed, "You've been in pain for so long you don't know what it feels like not to be in pain." Speechless, I stared at him.

By 1986 I was having unexplained, recurrent, episodes of coughing. My family doctor diagnosed "bronchitis." Dr. Mayberry was a crusty, country gentleman, middle-aged, with a lean wiry build and curly hair. The sparkle in his eyes made him seem younger than his years.

His booming voice easily came through thin office walls. Patients always came first. Staff had better be on their toes. Once I overheard him as he grumbled to his nurse.

"What do you mean she can't pee? Well then, give her a can of cola to drink."

Dr. Mayberry blended wisdom with medical knowledge. In my early twenties I had often felt overly tired. On the very first visit he questioned, "Before we order blood work, when did you last eat a fruit or a vegetable?" He was right. I had lived off pizza and hamburgers for months since moving out of my parent's home. My health improved. I didn't need the blood test. I had the utmost respect for Dr. Mayberry after that.

In spring 1986, several courses of antibiotics had failed to cure my symptoms. After three months of the gagging cough, with many follow-up visits, the good doctor ordered a chest x-ray. At our follow-up appointment, he stared at the floor. "The test results were normal."

When I became ineligible for a major promotion at work because of "too many absences" I returned to my family doctor the following week. While there I fell apart and started to cry. "Why am I always sick? Why aren't any of these antibiotics working? Not only did I miss a raise, but my job is also in jeopardy. The company I work for has a strict policy: Three absences in three months are grounds for dismissal."

Dr. Mayberry casually answered, "You'll always be susceptible to bronchial trouble, due to the metal and plastic in your body. Bacteria tend to attach to foreign objects. Didn't your scoliosis surgeon tell you to take prophylactic antibiotics when you have your teeth cleaned?"

"No." I dried my eyes. "What? What does dental work have to do with my scoliosis surgery?"

"During dental cleanings the gums are loosened, and all the bacteria in your mouth transfer directly into your bloodstream. Once there, they attach to anything inorganic in your body, making it extremely difficult to rid them from your system. Was there a dental cleaning a while back?"

I thought for a moment. "Yes."

Dr. Mayberry continued. I didn't hear another word. *Plastic?* I interrupted, "Wait a minute. Did you say plastic? What plastic? I only have stainless-steel Harrington rods."

He cleared his throat and then looked directly into my eyes. "The plastic in your chest, the catheter, I assumed you knew about it. It showed up on your film last week."

I thought of the prior week's office visit, an overheard conversation through the partially opened door of the exam room. His nurse touched the back of his hand as he reached for the knob. She said, "Wait. You'd better take this call first. It's the radiologist. An unusual finding has shown up on this patient's report." Apparently, "this patient" had meant me.

Dr. Mayberry continued, "You'll need to call your surgeon. The radiologist and I looked at the film together last week. I wanted to see it for myself. We're both confident it's part of the central line catheter. It should have been removed after surgery."

"It's been three years since my scoliosis surgery. What's a catheter? They've taken several x-rays at their facility. No one said anything. How did it get there?"

"They're used to monitor blood pressure internally."

"Where is it, how big of a piece?"

"It's near your collarbone. I would say, several inches long. You'll need to take antibiotics for teeth cleanings, or any procedure involving germs going directly into your bloodstream."

"For how long?"

"The rest of your life," he pulled my chest x-ray out from a large manila folder off his desk and held it up to the overhead lights, while he pointed out my collarbone with his index-finger. The film was a blurry side view of my angled ribs, with one, distinctive, vertical, white line.

Driving home I began to sob, and shake, uncontrollably. In Payne's Prairie I pulled onto the edge of the road. As I took a step out of the car, I collapsed onto my hands and knees. *Is this really happening?*

As cars whizzed past, I rolled onto my heels and sat upright. Along the freshly mowed strip of grass, there was movement. I dried my eyes, stood up, and looked all around. The movement was a solitary wildflower, blowing in the breeze. The lone survivor after the state's massive riding lawn mowers had cleared the highway edge. *You're still alive, too?* Once home, I left a message for my surgeon with his nurse, as I had done in the past.

When the phone rang, it was the operator asking if I'd accept a collect long-distance call from my surgeon's office. That was a first, in the three years I'd been his patient. They had never called me collect in the past. I was surprised to hear the voice of Dr. Fixit, himself. The conversation with him was brief, terse, and antagonistic from inception. Not even a hello, my surgeon was enraged, shouted, "I performed a perfect surgery. What's this about a catheter?"

Stunned, I paused a moment, then stuck to the facts. "My family doctor and the radiologist are both saying there is a plastic, central line catheter, in my chest, from surgery. I saw the x-ray myself."

He snarled, "Why were you seeing a doctor?"

"Bronchitis, I'm coughing constantly."

He barked, "Clearly, you must have a fever and are hallucinating from your illness."

"Dr. Fixit, I'm not a doctor. I don't know how to read x-rays. I'm repeating what two doctors have said. My family doctor said to call you."

"All the doctors in your town are incompetent idiots. None of them know how to read an x-ray." With those words he slammed his receiver down.

I held my handset mid-air, as the dial tone buzzed.

Bewildered by my surgeon's hostility, I returned to Dr. Mayberry. He said, "I've been looking into this. Rarely, when being pulled out a small piece breaks off. Typically, the patient is taken in for emergency surgery to have it removed. In your case, since a few years have gone by I'm afraid it's too late. It's already grown into tissue by now. I promise you. It won't move any further. Besides, a lot of veterans have retained shrapnel. Don't worry about it."

No tests were ordered, not even a confirmation x-ray. There was no mention of seeing a specialist.

Father's Day 1987

I had complete faith in Dr. Mayberry's prognosis. Why wouldn't I? A doctor's words in those days implied an eleventh commandment had chipped off when Moses came down the mount. "Thou shalt not question your doctor."

Nevertheless, I was defiant and indignant about the surgical error. I went to my father. Dad bit hard into the filter of his dangling cigarette, blew out a cloud of smoke. "It might be best to leave it alone." He looked away.

Silently, I stared at him, *Why aren't you angry?*

As the days went by, I remembered my father had a small piece of shrapnel embedded in his leg from an explosion while he was in the army. Daddy had said, "One minute I was talking to my best friend, the next minute he was blown to pieces."

My grandfather, a coal miner, had been buried in a mine collapse. Every Christmas when he'd visited, he would point to the chunk of coal embedded under the skin of his forearm and explain what it was like to be buried alive.

Shrapnel? Coal? How could I complain about a little piece of plastic? I had relayed to my father what my doctor said: "Plastic tubing inserted into the neck, near the collarbone, inside your chest."

> "The heart is normal … There is a tubular structure in the area of the superior vena cava measuring approximately 14 cms in length and this extends from the upper portion of the superior vena cava to the lower portion and may project into the right atrium a short distance. The lungs are free of active infiltrates.
>
> IMPRESSION … THE APPEARANCE OF A RETAINED VENOUS CATHETER"

In 1986, age 28, I didn't know to ask for the report. A year passed before I read it. I wouldn't have understood but would have visited the medical library to look up the definitions, as I had done when researching the word, "scoliosis" the prior decade.

The "14 cms" would have caught my attention. From my college physics and chemistry classes, I knew that was around five inches.

Six months after the discovery of the catheter, 11 p.m. on November 30th, I received a call from my sister. "Dad is at the VA hospital. They're taking him in for exploratory. No, don't come."

The phone rang again at 3 a.m. "He's out of surgery, and he's full of cancer. He's going to die. There's nothing they can do. They're sewing him up, sending him home."

It was unsettling when I walked into work at 7:30 a.m. and heard Christmas music. *Was the call in the middle of the night a bad dream?* Coworkers were putting up holiday decorations. I sank into my padded office chair. On my cleared desktop was a small spiral-bound calendar, updated the prior day: December 1, 1986. *November was yesterday? It's Christmas and my father is dying….*

The VA surgeon informed us Daddy's liver cancer had metastasized from somewhere else—we all assumed lungs—he'd been a chain-smoker after his combat years. The doctor gave my father six months to live. Through the month of December, I mechanically reported to work. After work, my sister and I took turns visiting our parents.

Daddy deteriorated daily. In his darkened bedroom his green eyes were the only hint of color. Each visit I opened the blinds to let some light in.

Five weeks after his diagnosis my father quit speaking. He only stared at the ceiling from his bed. He had already lost quite a bit of weight. I sat on the edge, leaned in, scrunched my arm under his bony-thin shoulders and stroked his forehead. "Daddy, it'll be okay. Don't be afraid. I'm here. I love you." There was a flicker of skin near his temple.

A week later, in January, my husband bought tickets for us to join another couple for a concert. When I tried to beg off, he rationalized, "You've got five more months of this. Take a break, I never see you anymore." I arranged for my mother's friend to stay with her, and sub for me.

At the 10,000-seat venue the house lights darkened. Within minutes, on again. The loudspeaker announced my name. "You have an emergency phone call at the office."

My mother shrieked. "He's dying. Come home now!"

I sat with my father until 2:00 a.m. In the blackness of night my mother took over. As she settled in, I brought Daddy a wrung-out washcloth and placed it on his forehead, kissed his cheek gently. He was barely breathing, eyes closed. Then I joined Aaron to sleep in our clothes on the living room floor.

When Daddy died at 3:00 a.m., mother woke us. She insisted the three of us kneel together in front of his dead body, while we prayed aloud. "Holy Mary, Mother of God, pray for us sinners now and at the hour of our death, amen." When they left, I was alone with my father's body. I tried to close his eyelids like I'd seen on TV shows. They wouldn't budge, so I held his cold hand. *Daddy, it's only been six weeks, I thought we had more time.* I couldn't even cry.

The next day, I went to the funeral home by myself. My mother didn't want to go, and my sister couldn't take time off from work. In a room full of caskets, overwhelmed with grief, indecisively I circled repeatedly. When I saw the small coffins for children, I burst into tears for all the families who had been there. The funeral director suggested I call my sister.

"I'm at work! Don't bother me. You can put him in a shoebox for all I care." She hung up.

In the weeks following my father's funeral, my thoughts swirled with memories of prior conversations. Often, when I had visited after work and asked, "How are you?" he had always answered, "My belly hurts."

I was young. I didn't think anything of it. Or did I subconsciously know? Luckily, years earlier, I had decided to tell him words never verbalized in my childhood home. I had my opportunity one day, when I stopped by for a visit. We were alone, which was rare. We sat across from each other at the kitchen table. I had practiced for days, in a mirror, at my place. *How could words so genuine feel so awkward to say aloud?*

I gushed out the words: "Daddy, I love you." I'd not anticipated a response.

"Mary, I love you, too."

"Oh! Daddy!" I bounded around the table, hugged his shoulders, and kissed his cheek. It was the only time in my life we said those three words to each other.

Father's Day, that year, 1987, brought a double dose of grief as it coincided with what would have been my father's birthday. I asked my husband to skip his routine of watching a baseball game on TV, for the two of us to take a day trip, anywhere, to take my mind off the absence of my father. But even though his workplace was normally closed on Sundays, he had to go in for all-day inventory.

Alone with my sorrow, I wandered beneath the dark canopy of our deeply wooded acreage. A pair of mourning doves cooed to each other. I looked up. A halo of bright sunshine, where we had cut trees, shone on the corresponding bare patch of earth below.

The enormous oak trees were covered with long, two-inch-thick, Tarzan-like, swinging vines and tumbling sheets of Spanish moss. Crying and angry that my father was gone, I kicked my watering can into the air. The water sprayed down like a priest's blessing. I looked skyward and seized one of the monster vines. Briefly, I hesitated. *Is this okay for my fusion? No, the pain can't be any worse than it already is.*

I tugged repeatedly. Nothing happened. With one last hellacious adrenaline burst of energy I yanked for all I was worth, as if I were reaching up to Heaven to bring my father to me. The vine didn't budge. Pop! A loud noise from my upper back. I knew immediately it was a huge mistake.

At home after work, Aaron said, "There's a lump the size of a walnut, it's red and feels hot."

I couldn't raise my right arm above my shoulder. Dr. Mayberry diagnosed, "Pulled muscle. Give it a couple of days to settle down."

A week later, on the morning of my 30th birthday, I woke up at 3:00 a.m. from an intense dream, saturated with sweat despite the air conditioner running full blast. In my dream I was swimming in a small, isolated grotto encircled by rough-textured, deep coco-brown steep cliffs, so tall only a circle of blue sky was visible. I swam to the edge, hoping to climb out, noticed teal-colored vertical striations in the ragged bluff. They erupted from the water's edge. No handholds anywhere. I circled, in the cool turquoise waters, looking for escape. A speck of bright light coming from the opposite wall revealed a tunnel at the base. I swam through the narrow opening.

The bright sunshine was blinding in the open ocean. Waves gently bobbed as I floated in the indigo waters. Overhead, pink tinged cotton-candy clouds swirled against an azure sky. Behind, further out at sea, cresting white waves formed and released before rolling along. The water was warm, I felt safe. At that moment a rumbling sound, from my left side, commanded my attention. In moments, the tunnel of my escape solidified with rock. Then the grotto of my confinement slipped into the ocean. I pivoted again and saw a distant shoreline. Unafraid, I swam towards the unhabituated dunes of sea oats.

Reality intruded when I felt the rough texture of our blanket with my hands. I opened my eyes, bolted upright. Aaron slept soundly. Five minutes passed as I repeatedly swept my palm across our coarsely woven blanket, incredulous that the smoothness of the water was gone.

The dream was bizarre. I didn't know how to swim, no one in my family did. Plus, I had an intense fear of deep water from a near drowning episode in my early twenties. In the dream I was fearless despite being in the middle of the ocean. It was empowering. *Would I learn to swim someday?*

•

Pricks, Needles, and Pins

Within a week after the dream, the pain worsened. I struggled to finish my eight-hour shift. After work I went to a new, "no appointment needed" medical clinic. I explained about pulling the vine weeks earlier.

The clinic doctor, blonde hair piled on top of her head held in place with loose hair pins, pulled the stethoscope out of her ears, and said, "Your lungs don't sound right. You might have a cracked rib or pneumonia. We have equipment here. I need to see a chest film."

The look on her ashen-white face when she returned told me that undeniably something was wrong. "Have you ever had major surgery?"

"Yes, four years ago for scoliosis." Then I remembered. "Oh, I know what you're worried about. Last year, on x-ray, a plastic catheter showed up."

"Why wasn't it removed?"

"My family doctor said to leave it alone. That it had grown into tissue."

When I saw her confused look, I relayed additional information. "It's in my chest, near my collarbone."

The doctor fidgeted, turned her stethoscope over repeatedly. "Yes, an intravenous catheter did show up. Not in your chest though…. There are three pieces. They're all in your lungs."

When I found my voice, I said, "No. You're mistaken. There's only one piece. I saw the x-ray myself last year."

"There's nothing in your chest. It must have broken apart, transported."

I shouted, "That's impossible. Dr. Mayberry promised it would never move! He said it had grown into tissue."

"Come and see for yourself."

I ran down the hall after her, barefoot, barely holding my gown closed. There was my illuminated spine. She didn't have to point them out. There were twin one-inch pieces in one lung, a third, of similar length in my other lung. The catheter in the middle of my chest was missing.

The clinic doctor continued, "You'll need surgery. It's too late to call for a referral. Return first thing in the morning, we open at 8:00 a.m., a thoracic surgeon is the specialist required." She paused, "They'll likely have to remove your lung." In memory she became *Dr. Panic*.

As I drove home, a death-grip on the steering wheel, it was an effort to blink. My stomach was in knots.

The next morning when Aaron and I arrived, there was a different doctor. He introduced himself as the owner of the clinic. The woman who accompanied him was not introduced to us. She was well-dressed, wearing a black pin-striped business suit, and carried a leather briefcase. Her spiky high heels further indicated she wasn't in the medical profession. Aaron whispered, "She looks like a lawyer. Why would they have a lawyer here?"

The four of us looked at the lit monitor. The owner said, "I've already made calls to thoracic surgeons. They might be able to go down your throat and pull the pieces out, either way, these need removal immediately. They can't stay in your lungs."

I heard my voice as if in an echo chamber, "Your partner...said I might have to have a lung removed, since there are pieces in both lungs...how is that possible? I can't lose both lungs."

He hesitated, cleared his throat, then continued. "Well, yes, that's true. If they need to remove your lung, it will have to be the most severely damaged of the two. That would be a major operation. They'll have to crack your sternum, your chest, open."

Oh my God! Please help. We waited three hours. Nothing. The clinic doctor said, "Go home. I'll call you as soon as someone returns my call."

We stopped at my mother's house. I fell apart with hysterical sobbing and shared my news. She only frowned and commented. "I told you not to have that surgery. You didn't obey me. Don't come here and upset me for nothing."

I missed my father even more.

The phone was ringing the minute we walked into our home. It was the clinic doctor. "None of the surgeons I spoke with will take you as a patient. They all said the same thing, 'It's a clear-cut case of medical malpractice.'"

My voice escalated. "I've known about the catheter for over a year. There's no lawsuit. I trusted my family doctor. I trusted my surgeon. They were both wrong. Now I'm penalized for believing them? Wouldn't there be a specialist at the teaching hospital?"

"No one will take you as a patient. You should call the orthopedic surgeon who performed the surgery. He won't be able to do the surgery himself. It's not his specialty. You'll need a thoracic specialist. I'm certain your surgeon can refer you, though. He'll have a friend who owes him a favor."

"Favor? Your partner said this is an emergency. My surgeon knew about the catheter a year ago and he hung up on me. Would you please call him? He'll believe another doctor." Within 30 minutes the clinic doctor phoned. "Dr. Fixit said he doesn't know any thoracic surgeons. He wants you to bring our x-ray to him, so he can see it for himself."

I dialed Dr. Fixit's office, spoke to his nurse. "Could my husband and I please come in today? We've both already taken the day off from work. We're out of vacation leave."

"No. He's already left for the day. It's Wednesday afternoon. All the surgeons golf on Wednesdays. We can fit you in next month."

The next day I raged as I vacuumed the house, my thoughts percolating. *A golf game is more important than my life? Wouldn't one of the other players know a thoracic surgeon? If he hadn't abandoned me a year ago none of this would have happened. He's only curious. He can't help.* I cancelled the appointment.

I returned to Dr. Mayberry. "Mary, you're too young to have a lung removed, nothing can be done to remove them."

At work, coworkers demanded, "Call a lawyer."

"Why? They can't remove the catheter pieces from my lungs."

A mature woman advised. "Mary, an attorney can help you find the right specialist. They affiliate with doctors who provide expert testimony in trials. I'm sure those physicians provide medical treatment, too."

Aaron knew an attorney. His office was in a small, single story, cinder-block building within a strip shopping center. Inside were dozens of crucifixes on 1960s-style brown paneling, along with the quintessential cursive-inscribed plaques: "Jesus Loves You." I had never met a lawyer before. The familiar symbols from my childhood were reassuring. He was a genuine Christian, and I could trust him.

At his desk in the inner office, which contained an equal number of religious memorabilia, the attorney said, "You have a case. Yes, I have friends who are doctors. I'm confident one of them will be able to remove these catheter fragments."

"Thank you."

"Let's meet weekly, so I can gather all the facts."

"Okay."

Three weeks later, attorney Mr. Christian still had provided zero referrals. At work, I had whispered conversations with my friends. All their voices echoed the same idea: "Since when do lawyers work for free?" "You'd better get a contract signed."

I felt confused, but decided my coworkers were right. On my fourth visit, I sat down in front of his paint-chipped metal desk covered with dusty piles of jagged papers. He said, "Pardon me. I'm finishing my lunch." He slid away his plate of half-eaten fried chicken, leaving a trail of grease, across his blotter on his desk. He hastily wiped his hands on a paper napkin, and then meticulously picked off the fragmented pieces from his fingertips

"Mr. Christian, please, can we sign a contract today?"

"No rush. We'll sign later. I promise. First, let's have you see a specialist. Do you own a typewriter?"

"Yes."

"Oh! Praise, Jesus!" He clasped his palms together, looked upward. I followed his gaze. Droplets of water clung to the water-stained brown ceiling tiles. "Type up the events, list everyone you spoke with, your conversations, word-for-word. Let's contain, I mean collaborate. Make sure you include the names and phone numbers for all the doctors who know of your situation."

I felt uneasy but couldn't formulate the words to go with my gut feeling. When I stood to leave, he hastily wiped his hands again on another paper napkin and then stepped around his desk. He clasped his fried-chicken-greasy fingers around my hands, and ordered, "Pray with me!"

He closed his eyes. Mine were wide open.

"Praise the Lord!" he exclaimed, "Our Savior! He protects all the lambs of the flock."

He cracked one eyelid open, tightened his grip. "Dear Lord, we pray for the quick resolution of Maribel's—"

"My name is Mary...like...." I motioned to my namesake on his walls.

"—oh yes! Dear Jesus, we pray for the quick resolution of Marilyn's illness."

I scanned the pictures of the wall, sighed. *Which one of you is Marilyn?* When I saw him adjust his hearing-aid, rather than embarrass him, I said nothing. I didn't want to hurt his feelings.

When the situation didn't improve, my mother-in-law suggested I try acupuncture for relief. At first, I brushed off her idea. Later, I took her advice, desperate for relief. I was thankful for her suggestion, even more so as the years and decades rolled by.

So, not long after I met my first attorney, I met my first acupuncturist. Michael's office was impeccably clean. The air smelled fresh, like laundry in the breeze on a sunny day. Relaxing, mellow music played softly. He was an educated man, evidenced by his diplomas, including a PhD from Oxford, which hung on the wall. His voice was calming. He gently inserted one tiny, diameter-of-a-hair needle into the top of each foot. "Some people feel a pinprick, others don't feel anything."

"I don't feel the needle. I thought you would place it at the source of the pain."

"In Chinese medicine this is the pathway to that part of the spine."

Later that afternoon I had minor relief. However, by evening the sensation returned even more intense.

Michael had scribbled down his home number. "In case you need me."

I dialed him. "My pain is worse!"

He calmly explained, "Yes, I understand. That occurs with a minority of people. It's a rebound effect. It's rare. I truly feel acupuncture can help you. Please continue treatments."

He was correct. Each visit provided greater intervals of relief. After the fourth appointment, I enjoyed three glorious days before the gnawing sensation returned.

Once again, I returned to Dr. Mayberry's office. He leaned into his squeaky, forest green, Naugahyde office chair, as if deep in thought, and then slapped his knees and jumped up. He circled his desk, stood with his hands on his hips. Uncharacteristic of his syrupy-slow Southern drawl, he shot out his words like a rifle blast. "Mary, I'm going to be honest with you. The catheter shouldn't have broken up like that. It traveled through your heart to arrive inside your lungs. Quite frankly, you shouldn't be alive."

"You said it was inside my chest."

"Didn't I tell you last year?"

"No, you did not."

He held up his palm. "A year ago, it had been my experience that foreign objects grew into bodily tissue. Since that was my assumption, perhaps I thought there was no point in upsetting you about the exact location." He looked at the floor.

When he looked up, he said, "Mary, there are medical events that doctors can't explain. Despite our best efforts, we lose a patient we should have been able to save. Or, in your case, a patient survives. I have faith in a higher power. It's my opinion the good Lord wants you here, for a reason."

"Dr. Mayberry, no disrespect, but last year you promised it wouldn't move." I straightened my shoulders. "I would like to be seen by a specialist."

He sighed, paused for a moment, circled to his side of his desk, dropped into his noisy chair. His steely eyes locked on mine, while he loudly exhaled. "Okay, that's the least I can do for you. I'll find someone. It might take a while. A lot of these specialists have their appointments scheduled months in advance."

His tone softened. "Peace of mind is important. You're handling this better than my wife would have. He skimmed the photos facing him on his desk. With that he vaulted out of his chair, stepped around his paper-cluttered desk, and warmly shook my hand between both of his calloused palms. "Mary, you're going to be okay. Twenty years from now you'll still be alive. If the catheters haven't killed you by now, trust me, they never will."

At home Aaron thumbed through the yellow pages of the phone book and made an appointment for me with a vascular surgeon. He told the receptionist, "My wife had an unknown object show up on a chest x-ray."

When he hung up, I asked, "We need to lie to obtain a doctor's appointment? Dr. Mayberry's going to help."

"You're allowed to see two doctors. Besides, he might not be able to find anyone."

A couple of days later we saw the vascular surgeon. My hopes were high. I'd brought my film from the clinic. We were in his office less than ten minutes. He couldn't answer any of my questions. He didn't listen to my heart or order a new x-ray to confirm the findings. He barely glanced at my film. "Don't worry about it. Nothing can be done." As we were leaving, the doctor stopped us. "Wait a minute. Who was your surgeon?"

I told him, "Oh!" Then as an afterthought, "I thought he had a good reputation. It's very odd that the catheter moved and crumbled. That type of plastic is indestructible. It has a 100-year shelf life."

The vascular surgeon's written report was brief. I was surprised to see his secretary had mistakenly cc'd a copy to Dr. Fixit, rather than Dr. Mayberry, as I had requested.

I wasn't giving up. After work each day I sat with the phone book's yellow pages in my lap and made many calls over the ensuing weeks. Each doctor's office responded with the same answer: "No. We can't get involved."

Finally, a cardiac surgeon's secretary in another city answered my prayers. "Yes, he will see you. There is one provision. He asks that you arrive at 3:00 a.m. and enter the hospital through the loading dock entrance. There's to be no record of your visit." Desperate to have the catheters removed, I agreed.

The next day I hurled a full mug of hot coffee against the wall. It shattered. *Why should I have to sneak around like this? I haven't done anything wrong. What if the clandestine exam revealed I did require a lung removed? Would the surgeon perform the operation under a tarp with a flashlight in the parking lot? Would he throw sections of my lungs to the stray cats in the alley?* I cancelled the appointment.

Ultimately, twenty-two physicians in three cities, various counties, hundreds of miles apart, refused to provide medical care. Each said the same thing. "No. That's clearly medical malpractice." Others further advised, "No one will take you as a patient."

With each rejection, the original error multiplied and quadrupled as, one by one, those sworn to inflict no harm refused to provide medical care. I rallied, dialed, and spoke to one last secretary. She repeated the same words. "No...clear-cut...malpractice."

In that instant of lost faith, I realized my life was less important than an unblemished career. I felt like a condemned person facing a firing squad, but rather than a last meal I requested an answer. "Why?"

The secretary coolly replied. "Doctors don't testify against other doctors."

At work I had only told my closest friends. My boss, to my irritation, announced my medical crisis to a sixty-employee section meeting. After that, the news spread throughout our 800-employee two-story building. I was confronted at the water cooler, in the lunchroom, even the bathroom, by complete strangers from other departments, who verbalized and reinforced all my fears. "Don't you think you'll die from this?" My research at a local medical library indicated that was a real possibility. Each person then offered the same unsolicited recommendation. "Sue."

Dr. Mayberry's referral came through. The appointment was with a thoracic surgeon. When we arrived, I was sent for x-rays. The radiology technician asked, "Any chance you're pregnant?"

"Highly unlikely. We did decide to start a family after my 30th birthday. But, only a few days later, the catheters were discovered in my lungs, so we resumed birth control right away."

The technician said, "I'll call your doctor."

Dr. FalseHope messaged, "No x-ray."

Once in his office, without new films, the surgeon looked closely at the two I brought. The original from 1986 revealed a six-inch catheter. It was a side view, grainy, hard to make out. The clinic film from July 1987 showed a total of three pieces in both my lungs, none near the "collarbone." The doctor said, "Apparently, the tip always extended into your heart. It's unfortunate we can't take an x-ray today. Film is developed differently depending upon whether we're looking at soft tissue or bone. Neither of your prior studies had been x-rayed looking for catheters. "I've never seen one break into pieces."

"Can they be removed?

"No. The only way to remove them is to surgically excise those sections of your lungs. You're too young to survive a lifetime with partial lungs. Plus, your history of asthma since childhood precludes pulmonary surgery."

"Doctor, that's not accurate. I never had asthma as a child. I developed chronic bronchitis last year."

"No, you've had asthma since childhood. That's what your records say." He tapped papers on his desk.

Moot point. Not worth correcting their typo.

The three of us stood in front of the lit monitors. With both x-rays side-by-side, he continued. "The broken pieces in your lungs don't add up to the single piece from the 1986 film. There must be another, about an inch long, I suspect, hidden behind your metal rods and fusion mass on the film.

"At some point in the future that fragment will loosen, too. It'll feel like a heart attack. It's quite fascinating how the circulatory system works—."

I interrupted, "After my lungs, where does it move from there? Won't it continue…somewhere?"

"No, once inside the lungs, they'll wedge into tiny capillaries, where it's impossible for them to move any further. Those surrounding areas of your lungs died off from lack of oxygen. There are plenty of other capillaries to make up for the lost supply. Don't worry about it."

"Did their movement cause my upper back pain?"

"No, that's a coincidence. You'll have to see a musculoskeletal specialist, that's not my field of expertise."

The thoracic surgeon walked us out. At the receptionist's desk I rested my purse on the counter, pulled out the checkbook to pay.

"No charge," he said, and knocked his knuckle on the counter.

His receptionist objected as she waved papers in the air. "Doctor, I've already filled out the forms…. Her insurance will cover the visit."

The doctor paused, reached over the counter, snatched my paperwork from her hand, tore my bill in half, then into quarters, and eighths. "No problem." He flashed a self-satisfied grin. "Now, there's no bill." He flung the remnants in the air over a nearby wastebasket in the waiting room. A few pieces fell onto the carpeted floor. He winked in my direction, "I didn't really help. It's not fair to charge you."

My mouth said, "Thank you." I stared at the paper scraps. *Should I pick them up?*

His knuckled triple-knock on the counter signaled the end of our conversation.

The next day my period confirmed I wasn't pregnant. I called and requested the cancelled x-ray.

His secretary forwarded his answer, "No need. Nothing needs to be on file here." I thought it was an odd response but didn't question her.

Decades later, I had the opportunity to question the department head who had worked there for more than 30 years. He said, "It was always our policy, even in the 1980s, to send a patient for a pregnancy test, and then proceed with the x-ray."

A few days later, I was still thinking about the events of the past month. After work, I kicked off my heels, slipped into faded jeans and my favorite, well-worn, beige T-shirt with a teddy bear print.

Outside, the dogs ran into the thick underbrush, chasing squirrels. At the summit of a hill on our five-acre property I sat on my favorite boulder. I felt safe there among the oak and pine trees. A soft strand of Spanish moss fell against my arm. Up close it looked like a grey, cable-knit, zigzag of fallen sky.

From the trees, under the darkened canopy of the forest, a pair of owls hooted to each other. Mindlessly, I dug my heels into the soft dirt. The words that kept gnawing at my thoughts came from both specialists and my family doctor: *"I've never seen a catheter break up like that." No tests? Not even a stethoscope to listen to my heart.*

At age 30 I had met with eight physicians in my lifetime, including four surgeons. I ticked off on my fingers, *Fifty percent of their diagnoses were wrong. Was the thoracic surgeon wrong, too? What if the last missing fragment could be removed?*

In 1967, our family doctor, who made the initial scoliosis diagnosis, had said, "Don't worry about it." There was no x-ray, follow-up appointment, or a referral to a specialist.

In 1977 Dr. Unknown, "Without scoliosis surgery, your heart and lungs will be crushed by the deformity of your rib cage." Now those were the exact two organs in jeopardy.

In 1983 Dr. Fixit had promised, "You'll never have back pain again." By age 30 I already avoided trips to the mall at all costs. I kept a pair of flat shoes in the car, to make quick grocery store trips after work bearable.

Those three unrelated physicians, in different cities, states, over the decades, had all said the same thing: *"Don't worry about it."*

I cupped my hands around my mouth and screamed into the dense jungle overgrowth of vines around our home. "Well, I'm worried about it!" In frustration I picked up a dead branch, swung at the base of a grandfather pine tree, chunks of bark went flying. The dogs ran, retrieved the "let's play" stick. My anger dissipated with the game.

Nights were the worst. There was no distraction from my thoughts. My mind rattled with questions, as if some somatic information stored in my gut tried to bubble up to my brain. I was confident with every fiber of my being. *My life was in danger.*

Aaron suggested I go for counseling. Psychologist Greg was sympathetic. We met weekly. We discussed my mounting fears: the catheters, mystery upper back pain, and the odd lawyer. Greg encouraged the pursuit of my instincts.

The next time I met with my lawyer I once again asked, "When do I meet your doctor friend?"

"My friend needs to read your surgical reports first. Ask your family doctor to request them."

"Shouldn't we sign a contract?"

"Later."

Dr. Mayberry refused, as did the thoracic surgeon. It was a ping-pong game. Apparently, my role was to be the net: motionless and uninvolved.

My surgical records, is the answer there? Why did this happen?

Incidentally Noted

I missed my father. He was calm, logical, and decisive. He would have known what to do. One morning I cried uncontrollably on my way to work, passed the interstate exit, and instead drove all the way to his cemetery. Sitting on the grass by his headstone, I tried to remember his advice over the years. *Daddy, what should I do?*

When I was first married, my father had said, "You should both take out a life insurance policy, with each other as beneficiaries, while still young, before either of you has any medical problems."

That was easy. I worked for a large insurance company. Employees were often encouraged to buy all lines of insurance "in house." We could apply—while still on the clock—freshly licensed agents were anxious for new customers.

Aaron was approved. I was denied, "Due to medical reasons." I was upset. *Turned down for life insurance at age 27? Why?* My insurance agent had been equally puzzled, he said, "The Underwriter won't disclose the reason."

As an employee in the Underwriting Department for auto insurance I was confident the guidelines for my counterparts in life insurance had to be similar. The names of policyholders weren't hung on a dart board and flung at with reckless abandon. When we turned down an application there had to be documentation from a reliable source. When I cancelled policies for DUI, the form letter I signed stated, "Due to information obtained from your state Motor Vehicle Division." By law we were required to list the source.

The out-of-state life underwriter, and his assistant—my counterpart—both refused to take my call, even though they knew I was an employee as well as the applicant. When I insisted, the Underwriter sent a letter stating, "Contact your surgeon, Dr. Fixit. He'll provide you with the specific reason. We cannot disclose medical information directly to a patient."

Dr. Fixit's response: "Scoliosis surgery has nothing to do with life expectancy."

I ran my fingers across my father's name on his headstone. *Was it the catheter? Is that why they turned down the life insurance? Why else the specific instructions to ask my surgeon for a reason*? Out loud, "Thanks Daddy!"

Within days, I drove the long journey to the hospital where I'd had my surgery four years earlier. There, the Records Department clerk said, "Your surgeon has been notified of your request. He needs to review them for accuracy and then sign off before we can give you a copy. You might have to wait all day. Plus, we'll have to charge you a dollar a page. Do you still want them?"

"Yes. I'll wait." I picked up a stack of magazines and settled in.

Later that day, at home, I scanned over the pages of the thick file. There were EKG reports, dozens of pages of barely legible handwritten notes. It came as a surprise to me that there was a problem at the end of the surgery: the drains had pulled out and they had to re-open the incision.

Another item caught my attention. The recovery room form was an entire page of neatly typed instructions. At the bottom edge of the page, a cursive scrawled hand-written order, "DC CVP line," was written as if an afterthought. *Were there no orders to remove the line? Wouldn't someone have seen it sticking out of my neck*?

KCL/500 ml at
/ #2 For Hemovac repla
4. IPPB with 2 1/2 ml NS + (
5. H & H at 6PM - Call Dr. I
SHA$_G$ & ABG's in AM; H & I
6. NPO - ice chips & lemon :
7. TED hose
8. Foley catheter to BSD
AP Thoracolumbar sp
DC CVP line

When I called to tell Mr. Christian of the notation, he said, "Your surgeon has a lot of friends. Don't make any copies. Bring them to me, the sooner the better. I'll take care of everything. I'm sure the difference between typed and hand-written means nothing. I'm surprised you noticed a minor detail like that. I'm sure there were always orders to disconnect the line. Are you implying they were written the day you picked up your records?"

"Huh? What?" I didn't grasp his meaning.

At work I sought out the help of a mature coworker. She was furious when she heard Mr. Christian's request. "He shouldn't be requesting them from you. They're not admissible in court since you obtained them. Any lawyer would know that."

"What does he mean about them being altered the day I picked them up?"

She sighed. "You're too honest and trusting for your own good. Do not…are you listening? Do not give him these records! Who the hell is this jackass of an attorney? Didn't you sign a contract with him weeks ago? Hasn't he done anything?"

"No, he said we had to wait."

"Can't someone in your family help you?"

At Mr. Christian's office, without my records, he ordered. "Go home. Bring them in, immediately."

I mustered the bravery to repeat my coworker's words, "Aren't they inadmissible unless you order them? Are we signing a contract today so I can see your doctor friend?"

He fidgeted. "It turns out the statute of limitations runs out two months from now. I'm not going to be able to take your case after all. I don't have enough time to prepare."

"Didn't you know about the statute of limitations when I first met with you?" I lurched up from my seat. "You promised your friend would help."

Without answering he stood up. "Drop off your medical records first. I'll pray for your health. Don't worry about it." He waved me towards the door.

The next morning before I left for work, I called my husband's out-of-state aunt for advice. Her voice intensified. "Get another attorney! Immediately! Hang up and do it now! What are you waiting for?"

"Aaron will be angry. It's his lawyer."

She hissed a soft shout, "Let him! You don't need his permission. It's your body, not his."

I pulled the receiver a few inches away from my ear. Hand to my heart. I knew she cared.

She continued, "Make an appointment with an Internist, too. Pick one out of the phone book. Tell him you want a complete physical. He'll send you for a routine chest film. Maybe the film has an artifact, and there is no catheter."

"Okay, thanks, good idea."

"Why hasn't anyone ordered a second x-ray to confirm?"

"I don't know."

A week later the Internist said, "I'm sorry, there really are three catheter segments in your lungs."

> "A total of 3 fragments of catheter are seen apparently lodged in the pulmonary circulation. One is in the right midlung measuring 3.5cm. One is in the right lower lobe measuring 2.5cm in length. There is another in the left lower lobe measuring 3.5cm in length.
>
> IMPRESSION: ... NO ACUTE ABNORMALITY."

I nodded, unable to speak. *I'm living a nightmare.*

When I shared the report with a coworker, she provided me with the name of her attorney. That morning, while on my 10-minute coffee break, I called him from the pay phone in the vending machine area. His friendly receptionist said, "I'll leave a message. He's tied up today. He'll call you much later this afternoon."

Not three minutes after I returned to my desk, my desk phone rang, it was the new attorney. "I'm not allowed to make or receive personal calls on the job."

"Can you come by my office today, after work?"

"Yes."

I sat across from him at his shiny mahogany desk. The young lawyer said, "It's odd the other attorney didn't sign a contract. Yes, I'll take your case. Do you need a couple of days to think this through? Perhaps, discuss it with your spouse?"

"No, I want to sign the contract today, right now." I accepted as true Mr. Christian's claim about the statute of limitations. My office friend had said, "It's better to sign a contract. Drop it later if not needed and pay the attorney for his time rather than need it and find out it's too late to file."

Later I learned the law hinged on "date of discovery," not date of surgery.

The attorney buzzed his secretary. "Standard contract, please." While we waited, he said, "My name is Josh, we're a team." We shook hands.

Meanwhile, acupuncture helped for a while. Two months post injury, Dr. Mayberry found a specialist. The new doctor examined and felt both sides of my spine with his fingertips. He said, "It feels like a rib has pulled out of your vertebral column. That would explain the lump under your skin when it happened. I'll order an x-ray and send you for physical therapy."

Dr. Ribby wrote orders for PT but forgot the x-ray before he went on a "month-long vacation to Europe" per his secretary. Without the film the physical therapist instructed me to use an overhead weighted pulley. My upper back pain worsened dramatically,

When the doctor returned, I questioned his "pulled rib" diagnosis. He insisted, "No, you misunderstood, I said, 'os-te-o-arth-rit-is of the spine.'" He slowly enunciated each syllable.

"How would I have developed arthritis in my upper back? Besides, isn't that what old people get?"

"That's my diagnosis."

"Dr. Ribby, the words 'osteoarthritis' and 'pulled rib' don't even sound alike. 'Pulled rib' was a surprising diagnosis a month ago. You told me it was from tugging on the vine. You said, my rib popped out because of my scoliosis fusion surgery."

"Pulling a rib out of the vertebral column post scoliosis surgery would indicate a serious problem with your fusion. It's osteoarthritis of the spine." He quickly stood. With his hand on my back and walked me out. Over the years I came to realize a hand on the back was a dismissive gesture from someone trying to dominate, terminate, or control the situation.

Greg, my counselor, had encouraged journaling. I paged to the entry in my notebook and from the date I met Dr. Ribby, "diagnosed pulled rib."

The delayed x-ray was ordered. My physical therapist requested that I pick up the actual x-ray for her to review. At home when I yanked the black film out of the envelope, a sheet of paper floated to the floor. *No mention of the catheters. Great! Must be a mistake?* Then the all-cap last paragraph caught my eye:

> "CONCLUSION: NO CHANGE …
>
> INCIDENTALLY NOTED ARE RETAINED VENOUS CATHETER FRAGMENTS IN THE LUNG FIELDS."

Researchers Never Quit

Greg, my counselor, suggested I pursue the topic on my own. A local librarian mentioned the Lung Association, and they recommended an affiliate. No luck. Then I tried a physician referral service. No help. The information desk at my local library provided the number for the Scoliosis Association in New York. It was a non-working number. This mystery was solved when it was discovered they had moved to North Carolina. Their answering machine: "Sorry, we will be on vacation for three weeks."

The Institute of Health Statistics in Washington D.C. instructed, "That's not an illness. That's a medical error. We don't record those statistics. I don't know any agency that does."

Three weeks later I called the Scoliosis Association, again. An older man's voice answered. "My daughter had the same surgery fifteen years ago and she's always done great. She's not had any problems since then. Best decision she ever made. Your surgeon must have not fused enough of your back."

It was consoling to be talking to anyone's father, even if not my own. Three years later I learned the accuracy of that stranger's last sentence.

In 1987, as we chatted that day, the paternal voice on the phone continued, "I've not heard of a catheter being left after surgery. Nor have I ever heard of taking preventative antibiotics because of Harrington rods. My daughter wasn't told that. She still has her hardware."

My fears heightened. *Was Dr. Mayberry's antibiotics prescription only because of the catheters?* Before we hung up the man offered one last suggestion. "If I were you, I'd call the National Health Information Clearing House in Washington D.C. They have statistics on everything. They'll be able to help you. Good luck."

Nope. They didn't record medical errors either. Then I called the National Heart, Lung and Blood Institute in

Bethesda, Maryland, the State of Florida's American Medical Association, then the national AMA in Chicago, and the Florida Medical Society. Call after call, I was ultimately referred to the Lung Association, the same agency where I'd made my first call days earlier. Exasperated, I slammed the receiver down. I was at square one. I dreaded seeing our long-distance phone bill. I had made a total of fifteen calls over the course of ten days.

My longing for advice from my deceased father was constant. In 1969 he had helped me with my summer science project, prior to 7th grade. I chose the topic, "Nuclear Reactors and Atomic Fission." Our local library didn't have any information. "Too new a topic," per the librarian. Daddy said, "Mary, go to the source." He helped me locate the address for the out-of-state Atomic Energy Commission. I corresponded with them all summer, received a dozen booklets intended for the public. I studied them, looking up each word I didn't understand. Using scrap cardboard bent in a trifold, from a new refrigerator, I presented everything I learned.

That autumn, when school resumed and the projects were lined up and judged in the cafeteria, mine won first prize: a set of Audubon Encyclopedias. Now, multiple moves and decades later I still owned them. I wandered over to the bookcase, ran my fingertips across their binding. *Go to the source, thanks Daddy.*

From the yellow legal pad on the kitchen table, where I had been recording all my calls, date, time, phone number, and name of the person I spoke to, I paged to the coffee-stained information for the AMA in Chicago. It took me a couple days to get up enough nerve to call them again. A different employee answered the phone, said her requested coworker was off that day. I was in luck. The sub provided information that changed everything. "We don't have a physician referral for things like that, that's not an illness. Try calling the University of Maryland. Their library should have a computer access program called Medline and that will provide a list of articles in medical journals, if there are any, on the subject. The doctors who authored the articles should be able to help you."

Finally! A clue!

The librarian at the University of Maryland was extremely gracious. She answered my pleas for help with a solitary empowering word: "Yes." She apologized. "It will cost $30 to run the list for you and mail it out. By any chance do you live near a major university? If you do, they might have the Medline program and likely a reduced fee."

"Is the University of Florida a major university?"

A moment of silence passed, and then she gushed. "Oh, yes, most definitely. They're a research university. I didn't realize where you were calling from. If the UF people can't help you, we will. Call back if you need us. Then she provided information utterly unique to all the phone calls I had made so far. She spelled her last name, slowly, and said, "Here's my direct extension."

A stranger had become an ally.

Holding for The University of Florida's medical library's staff, I was startled when a familiar voice answered.

"Kate, is that you?" It was an old friend I hadn't seen in a few years. I didn't know she had switched jobs. I unclenched my jaw and brought her up to speed. Kate said. "We do have the program. It's a flat $5 charge plus $1 per minute the computer runs."

"Okay, do it." That was Friday afternoon. Monday, she called at 4:00 p.m. "We'll have to run it again. We didn't specify 'foreign object.' There were no results."

Tuesday, I went in to pick up the list of articles. I struggled to walk the few feet from the parking lot. My upper back pain was in excruciating pain.

My friend handed over the list. There were only sixteen articles from the top journals around the world. Scanning the titles, nothing seemed to apply to my situation. Most were about intentionally placed catheters in legs.

One title seemed relevant. With some help from Kate, we found the right medical journal. I didn't grasp the content. Lifting the weight of the thickly bound periodicals accelerated my anguish. At the copy machine, I held it upside down precariously trying to copy the article without truncating the edges.

At home, I found the information discouraging. It stressed the importance of removing a central line catheter before it perforated the heart, caused an embolism, or septicemia.

I dropped off a copy to my lawyer, Josh. He asked, "Did you look up the articles referenced?"

"No, but I will. Good idea."

Once again, at the medical library, one essay led to another. Twenty-year-old articles from 1967 were about catheters showing up in Vietnam Veterans during autopsy. They weren't coated with a radio-opaque material in the 1960s. Once lost inside the body they were impossible to locate. It was those autopsies that prompted the idea to manufacture the catheters with a radio-opaque coating.

My roller coaster of rising optimism descended into hopeless depression. The articles described diagnostics. *Why wasn't anyone running tests on me?*

At the kitchen table, I spent hours re-reading the information. With my medical dictionary, I translated each word, sometimes entire paragraphs, like I was taught in high school Spanish classes. Dr. Mayberry had not been exaggerating when he said, "You shouldn't be alive."

One day, my entire kitchen table was covered with those crooked, poorly made copies from the medical library. Some I had highlighted, others dog-eared. Overwhelmed with a sense of rage, I flung the papers with one sweeping motion off the table. *All I want is medical care, why is this so difficult?* I picked up the chair and slammed it on the floor. With that release of anger, I plopped down, folded my arms, and sobbed. When I opened my eyes, from my sideways vantage point, the top article caught my attention. I bolted upright. *This isn't from the 1960s. It had been published in 1984, only three years ago.* I dried my face. The doctor who authored the article was from Missouri. *Why not? One more call.*

Multiple attempts later, wrong area code, wrong hospital, a secretary at the VA hospital in Missouri put me on hold, after exclaiming, "I'm so sorry this happened to you. You need diagnostics run by an expert."

She returned, "Yes, you've reached the doctor who authored that article. He'll be happy to take you as a patient here in Missouri. Where in Florida did you say you're calling from?" "Hold, please."

When she returned, she said, "I have good news and bad news. Our doctor here in Missouri was at a medical conference a year ago in Israel. He met two doctors there, both from your hometown. He's confident either of them is qualified to help you. One is a cardiologist, the other a thoracic surgeon."

She paused, and then continued. "There's only one hitch. He can't remember either of their names."

Into My Heart

The Kansas City secretary continued, "He completely blanked on one doctor. The other, he thought, was some type of cracker."

I didn't know I had already met one of the two.

When I hung up, I whipped the phone book off the microwave cart and thumbed to the physicians' section, scanned every entry in the alphabetical listings, until I came to a Dr. Ritz. I crossed my fingers before checking his specialty: cardiac surgeon. It had to be him. His secretary confirmed. "Yes, he's familiar with retained catheters. Call his appointment secretary and tell her you need the first available."

As it turned out, that was a month away. It would be a long thirty days. Greg, my counselor, was pleased, yet cautious. "Mary, I'm proud of you. However, in case this Kansas City recommendation doesn't work out, perhaps the thoracic surgeon you've already seen has access to another expert. It's only one more phone call." My shoulders slumped. I knew he was right.

The doctor's secretary was friendly and caring. With a pleasant voice, she said, "He'll return from lunch in an hour. I'll either call you this afternoon or first thing tomorrow morning at the latest." I wrote down her name.

Three days later, I made the, *they must have been busy and forgot to call,* call. At first, I was relieved when I realized it was the same secretary. "He's on vacation. Out of the country. Europe. Several weeks. No, make that a month." A pause, and a terse, "I have no way of contacting him." After every couple of words, I could hear another voice in the background, whispering, as if prompting her.

"Umm, I didn't ask you to contact him. You know, three days ago, you said he was at lunch." *Europe? A month? Isn't that where Dr. Ribby disappeared to?* I shook off the odd coincidence, shifted to the reason for the call. "The journal articles I've read mention 'death is a possibility'.

This is kind of a big deal. Isn't there another doctor there you could ask?"

"No." A pause, whispering. Then she continued, "It was a courtesy visit." Pause. "Besides, all doctors will have the same opinion."

"I have insurance. I didn't ask him to tear up the bill. What are you talking about? Doctors don't all have the same opinion."

She enunciated both syllables, "It was a fa-vor. Besides, there's no record of your visit here."

"Of course, there's a record of the visit."

She raised her voice, "Lady, don't you get it? As far as we're concerned you don't exist. And you were never here." She hung up.

I sat there, numb, dumbfounded, *a favor to whom?* A shiver went through my body. *Whether it's my second opinion or my twentieth, it's my body.* Defiant, I dialed the number, again. On the offensive, I asked, "Was a written report sent to my family doctor, with his opinion? Isn't that customary for a specialist?" Greg had trained me well.

"No. He verbally discussed your case with your family doctor. There was no written report." Click.

I sat in my kitchen, stared at the receiver still suspended in mid-air. In slow-motion the mechanical claw of my former flesh and blood appendage returned the handset to its base. It was beginning to hit home. *No bill. No report. No x-ray.*

When I shared my news with Greg, he frowned, and uncharacteristically raised his voice, "This is definitely a cover-up."

The days passed, slowly, summer faded into the shadows of fall. Labor Day weekend I was glued to the Jerry Lewis Muscular Dystrophy Telethon, shamefully jealous. Those patients were allowed to receive medical care, not asked to sneak around hospital loading docks in the middle of the night or told they didn't exist.

When the month finally passed and I was ushered into the exam room, Dr. Ritz's nurse asked with a light, bouncy voice, "What brings you to clinic today?"

"I have three catheter fragments embedded in my lungs."

She stared wide-eyed. I was sent for an EKG and an x-ray. Shivering, three hours later, I was still in the same, overly air-conditioned cubicle of an exam room. I scrunched up my legs, tried to pull the threadbare hospital gown over my knees. I had read all their stale, obsolete, magazines cover to cover and was starting on the diabetes pamphlets when Dr. Ritz came in. He held my latest film.

After introducing himself, he was business-like. "You didn't have respiratory issues until last year?"

"That's correct, Doctor."

As had the family doctor, original radiologist, internist, vascular, and thoracic surgeons, Dr. Ritz said, "I can't fathom why the catheter would crumble like that."

"A thoracic surgeon said it broke due to the beating of my heart."

"I disagree. Catheters are virtually indestructible. More likely, it was accidentally cut when being removed from your jugular vein. That happens, rarely, when the line is being pulled out. One cut would be feasible. But, for the line to be cut three times would be utterly amazing.

"Another concern, comparing your current film to the one from a year ago I see that the pieces in your lungs don't correspond, in total length, to the solitary piece seen on the original 1986 film."

That opinion the thoracic surgeon and Dr. Ritz agreed upon. Even I could do the math: The original segment was six inches long. The three fragments in my lungs totaled slightly over five inches.

Dr. Ritz went on to say, "It's unfortunate I didn't see you last year, before it fragmented, I could have removed it." I swallowed my grief. *Haven't I heard this before?* Before my memories came up with an answer, Dr. Ritz turned to his nurse. "Take her upstairs to the fluoroscopy lab. I'll join them shortly."

All the medical journal articles I had read mentioned this test as imperative for diagnosis. It was like a live movie rather than the still shot of standard film.

The fluoroscopy technician was not surprised at the reason for my visit. "We don't see this every day, typically one or two a month. Referrals come in from all over the country. What type of surgery did you have this morning?" As I lay on the exam table, he bustled around, took his measurements with squares of light on my chest, and then palpated my hips for landmarks. He paused, waited for my answer.

"Four years ago. I had surgery four years ago."

He stopped dead. "That's wild. Typically, patients are brought in as soon as possible after a central line is cut and a fragment lost. You're in the right place though. As a teaching hospital we take the cases that other institutions don't have the expertise to handle."

"How did this happen?"

"The edge of the device that holds the CVP line is sharp, if angled the wrong way when being removed, it's possible for a tiny piece, like a fourth-of-an-inch, to be sheared off. Even with a piece that small you don't want it circulating inside your body."

A male nurse who introduced himself as Matt entered the room. He was friendly and professional. We ended up chatting about my vegetable garden while he did his prep work. I appreciated the distraction. Our conversation ceased when Dr. Ritz walked in. To the technician, he said, "Okay, let's see what we've got here." There was a large machine suspended from the ceiling directly over my chest and a black-and-white television above my feet.

I saw my ribcage move with each deep breath or requested cough as well as the three catheters within both lungs. The six-inch catheter "in my chest, near my collarbone," from the 1986 original diagnosis, was gone. The elusive remaining one-inch piece was a no show, too.

Dr. Ritz's eyes were glued to the monitor. He told the technician, "Tilt the table about ten degrees. This remnant must be here somewhere."

Two seatbelt-like straps cinched my body as I shifted sideways as if on an amusement park ride.

I screamed, "Oh! My God! What is that?"

Even the hum of the machinery, in the room, seemed to dim. Split seconds dangled like a slow-motion droplet of molasses. I held my breath, terrified to breathe. My brain couldn't assemble words to express what I saw. At my feet, on the TV monitor, was the exact same six-inch catheter from the 1986 x-ray.

There were two notable differences: it was no longer near my collar bone and was whipping back and forth with each heartbeat. My shell-shocked mind found the words, "Doctor, is that piece completely inside my heart?"

"Yes."

"How large would you say...?"

"I estimate, fifteen centimeters, about six inches."

"Is this the same piece from 1986?"

"Yes, I'm afraid so."

"Then where did the segments in my lungs come from? Those totals are around five inches."

"I was wondering the same thing. It's my conjecture that they're not breaking off from the bottom. They must be breaking off from the top, doubling over this portion as they circulate through the chambers of your heart, then into your lungs."

Dr. Mayberry's words echoed in my thoughts. *You shouldn't be alive.*

Somehow, I shut down my emotions, focused on the problem. "Doctor, I've had three x-rays since 1986 and this six-inch segment wasn't there. We all thought this one had fragmented and deposited into my lungs."

"Watch. Don't take your eyes off the catheter." To the technician, "Return the table to a full horizontal position." Like a magician making a rabbit disappear, the catheter inside my heart vanished behind my Harrington rods and fusion mass.

Dr. Ritz continued, "Clearly, it has not grown into tissue. It must have slipped completely into your heart sometime in the last year. I don't know why it's breaking up. I'm afraid many more pieces will end up in your lungs.

"I want you to schedule a cardiac catheterization. We'll attempt to retrieve it. However, the wound is no longer fresh; when we tug, it might tear a hole in your heart. We'll have to be prepared for emergency open-heart surgery."

Before I could collect a thought, or ask a question, he evaporated from the room like a fast-moving fog. Mechanically I dressed. My appointment was in three weeks. Cement legs found themselves in the parking lot. My ears only recorded the constant pounding of blood in my brain.

The numbers felt like awkward, spinning, data units. I tried to convert *centimeters to inches. Or is it inches to centimeters? Divide? Multiply? I can do this.*

Thunderstruck, I sat in my car in the parking lot for the longest time, took a fast-food napkin and a pen out of the armrest. Several times, I scrawled out the calculation, despite shaking hands. The numbers confirmed: the total length of the four catheters, including the one still inside my heart, was over ten inches, twenty-five centimeters. *These aren't sheared-off fragments. Is this the entire central line?*

In October 1987, 30 years old, I was admitted to the hospital early in the morning, as an outpatient. Aaron, my mother, sister, and her husband Ed chatted with each other. I stared at the tan carpeting. I wore my orange Cleveland Browns T-shirt. A young resident arrived. To my family he said, "This will take about an hour. Mostly for set-up, the actual procedure doesn't take more than ten minutes. Once we grab the piece it'll come right out. You'll be able to take her home by 10:30 a.m."

Things didn't quite go as planned. None of us knew, but my cardiac cath was to last five hours.

In the cardiac cath lab a young doctor offered a hospital gown and motioned. "You can get undressed in the employees' bathroom." He noticed my T-shirt, "Hey, are you from Cleveland? I did my residency at Case Western. Those are some wicked winters up there. Great pierogis, though." It felt reassuring to chat about a non-medical topic as if this was any average day and the outside world still existed.

The employees' cocoon of jackets, pants, and shirts on both walls was so thick, it was impossible not to knock their belongings onto the floor. Terrified I couldn't stop shaking. As I bent to pick up their clothing, more items fell. My mouth went dry. *Why did I pursue this?* After my fourth attempt, I gave up and left a pile heaped on the floor.

When I emerged, gowned and barefoot, the soles of my feet recoiled when they hit the floor's chilly surface. I squinted from the room's bright lights. Once on the exam table, other staff members, around twenty people, entered the lab and took their places. Each person acknowledged me by name, as if I were someone important.

Dr. Case Western gently inquired, "Are you ready, Mary?" Dr. Ritz asked, "Do you want a pain medication to take the edge off?"

"Yes, I'm ready. No, I want to be fully alert. I want to be the first to know, not the last, if any surprises...."

On my left, the visiting French doctor, an expert on the experimental angioscopy procedure, entered the glass booth. I was the third human in the United States, after animal testing, to have a camera inside my heart. It transmitted the image to a second, TV-like color monitor at my feet.

Meanwhile, six doctors tested microphones hanging from the ceiling over their heads. Above my feet was the fluoroscopic monitor, along with a VCR below it to record the procedure. I watched the six-inch central line wiggle back-and-forth with each beat of my heart, like a worm on the sidewalk after a heavy rain.

On my right was a stainless-steel table with medical instruments. Above my body, there hung two huge, beige machines of an irregular shape. My groin area was shaved on both sides. Though they kept me covered as much as possible, I was still embarrassed. More people entered the room. Matt, the nurse I had met three weeks prior, was joined by another nurse, Laura. They applied Betadine to the shaved area.

9:05 a.m. I was given two injections, both sides of the groin, to numb the area. The needle was paper-cut painful. Nothing. The drug didn't work. The area never numbed.

They re-injected, both sides, at least five times. Dr. Case Western exclaimed, "This is impossible. She has enough drugs on board to numb everyone in this room!"

Two long catheters were inserted into both sides of my groin. They felt like two pencils being stabbed into my body. My muscles tensed. The retrieval devices—claws and baskets—alternately were placed inside those catheters. From the journal articles I recognized the names of all the items.

Dr. Ritz said, "We don't know which tool will work best, until we attempt retrieval." The microscopic camera was advanced towards my heart. The doctors had been accurate in their predictions. "There will be a burning sensation inside your chest."

10:40 a.m. I watched both the fluoroscopic and angioscope monitors. The first retrieval basket looked like a skinny black snake on the screen. I pretended I was still a college student, privileged to watch an exciting procedure on a patient. It wasn't my body up there with the Harrington rods.

When I was a kid growing up, my father always said, "Everything you learn is of value. Always ask questions."

"Why aren't you using the jugular vein in my neck? It's a shorter distance to the heart. That's where they inserted the central line. I was still awake when they put it in."

Between face masks and corresponding surgical green caps, I noticed a few of the doctors' eyes darted, as they looked at each other. One voice thundered, "A patient who wants to self-educate. Good. That makes my job easier."

Another voice answered, "Yes, of course, you're correct. However, this route is a straight line. Not the curves we would encounter if accessed via the jugular vein. With a catheter of this size, we need to be able to pull it straight out."

I replied, "Okay, that makes sense." My fear dissipated. Until the next wave of panic took hold. Repeatedly, Dr. Ritz said, "Take a deep breath and hold it, don't move. Stay perfectly still." The nurses, Matt, and Laura stood on either side of my shoulders. Laura said, "Squeeze our hands as hard as you need to."

The anticipation of each advancement felt like I was perched on the edge of the galaxy, one step from falling into a black abyss. The multiple areas of physical sensations were intense. The worst feeling was inside my heart. It felt like it was being pounded with a hammer. Then it would skip a beat. Mercifully, the doctors had forewarned about both sensations.

My thoughts ran in a continuous loop: *I can't believe this is happening. How did this mistake occur?*

My hands and feet were blocks of ice. Through a gap in my line of view, I could see the bloody latex-gloved hands and soaked crimson pieces of gauze everywhere.

Matt and Laura were both remarkable. When they weren't helping the doctors, they held my hands, stroked my forehead, or squirted water into my mouth. During intense moments they engaged in questions requiring a complete answer, not a "yes" or "no" reply. The distraction helped.

Matt remembered our conversation from three weeks earlier. "What types of veggies are you growing in your garden?"

I watched the clock on the wall on my left side as another half hour slipped by. Lightning strikes shot diagonally, in a straight line, across my torso up to my right shoulder. I felt as if I was being sliced by a fast, burning, laser-beam sword from a Star Wars movie battle. I reported every sensation.

Dr. Ritz asked, "Do you want a narcotic for the pain?"

"No, I can tough it out."

One by one each attempt failed, for various reasons. Until one closed claw-like device, like an amusement park's candy grab, traveled the distance. However, once inside my heart, the width of my vein wasn't wide enough for it to open. They pulled it back out of my heart.

I stared at the translucent button on Laura's nurse's uniform. The rest of the room faded away. I felt dizzy, as if passing out. I turned the block of ice that used to be my head to stare at non-stop ashen ceiling tiles and started counting them. When those episodes occurred, like roll call, every few minutes a different doctor called out. "Mary, are you okay?" "How are you doing?" "How do you feel, Mary?"

I weakly whispered, "I'm okay." The warmth of my own breath rolled across my arctic lips. They were true professionals. Despite everything, I knew I was safe there. If any issues arose, they would handle the situation, not abandon their patient like Dr. Fixit.

As I looked up at Laura's face, I focused on her smoky-blue eye shadow; the color reminded me of the sky and ocean. Places far away from here.

Dr. Ritz said, "Let's take a minute, people." He stood in front of the monitor gazing intently. Those surrounding my body stepped away. *Light. Air.* I exhaled deeply, then kicked into student mode to cope. "Where is the third piece in my lungs, I only see two on the monitor."

Dr. Ritz, at my feet, index-finger pointed at the monitor, "Here it is. The severity of your scoliosis, the fusion mass, and the hardware, makes it difficult to visualize."

At precisely that exact moment, as we all watched, a piece broke off from the top-most portion of the six-inch central line. It doubled up against the remaining five-inch segment, and traveled, looping, and careening throughout the chambers of my heart to deposit itself exactly parallel to the solitary fragment in my lung, the one his suspended index finger was still pointing to. The monitor confirmed. There were now four pieces, two in each lung.

The entire room became deathly hushed. Faces and machinery turned to stone. Microphone conversations with the booth stopped. Dr. Ritz abruptly took a step away from the exam table. He maintained a sterile position: bent elbow, arms, and hands upright; fingers spread wide apart. His Mount Rushmore face flickered with fear deep inside the pupils of his eyes.

Everyone, including myself, was incredulous. None of the snaring devices were inside my body when the newest segment broke off spontaneously.

In a split second, a determined Dr. Ritz was again at my side. He reported to the booth, "It's extremely friable. We must quickly remove the remaining five-inch portion before it, too, crumbles and transports to her lungs."

I heard the child's version of my own voice, "What does friable mean?"

Dr. Ritz answered, "It means the catheter is crumbling."

A male voice, with a French accent, from the glass booth ordered. "We need a thoracic surgeon immediately."

He's back early from his European vacation?

Within minutes Dr. FalseHope appeared. I was furious yet resisted the overwhelming urge to ask him to leave. My urgent situation didn't seem like the place to be indignant. In that instant, I knew he must be the second unnamed specialist referred by the Kansas City doctor.

Clearly Dr. Ritz's superior, Dr. FalseHope shot down every one of my cardiologist's ideas. "Don't pull." "Leave it alone." "Don't do anything else." "End the procedure."

Dr. Ritz asked, "Mary, do you want me to continue?"

"Yes," I spit out with bitterness. "Please don't give up on me. It took me two months to find you."

He immediately advanced the device. He was able to hold onto a half-inch piece, as it too, broke off. He snaked the fragment out of my heart, down the length of my torso and removed it from my body.

I cried with relief. Each time the plier type device snatched the catheter, another half-inch piece would break off.

Inside my chest there was the sensation of movement. With each portion removed, the snaring device had to be introduced from the groin, then advanced to the heart, and then pulled out again. They went into my heart dozens of times as the hours passed.

"Can I see one of the pieces?" I asked.

From the table to my right someone held up the bloody piece of gauze cradling the tiny catheter fragment. I strained my neck to see what threatened my life. I felt dejected. In all the articles I had read and pictures I had seen the entire segment came out with one yank, not crumbling like this.

Dr. FalseHope eventually acknowledged our relationship. He chuckled, "I didn't expect to see you return to us with additional concerns." He winked.

Someone interjected, "Mary, you saw Dr. FalseHope over a year ago." *Not true. More like two months ago.*

I asked, "Doctor, how was your month-long vacation in Europe? I spoke with your secretary a few weeks ago. Guess you didn't receive my message. I received yours."

Dr. FalseHope's eyes flickered; his lips tightened into a narrow line. "Well, I, umm, well …." He walked away. Staff gave each other questioning looks.

Before Dr. FalseHope left the room I overheard him boast to another doctor, "Four years? That's nothing," He clicked his tongue. "Tomorrow I'm removing a catheter from a man who has had it retained internally for ten years."

It was apparent that he was quite an expert on the subject. If he had done a fluoroscopy test, he would have known the supposed one-inch remnant was a six-inch piece, whipping inside my heart with every heartbeat.

Tiny fragment, by tiny fragment Dr. Ritz was able to remove most, but not all, of the line. Several more hours passed. No luck. Two pieces remained embedded near the tricuspid valve of my heart. I was exhausted. The latest snaring device moved through the maze of veins in my lungs, to retrieve the newly deposited fourth piece. As I was about to tell Dr. Ritz to quit, he said, "Mary, I've tried everything I know."

"I agree. It's time to stop."

All the doctors left. The two nurses remained. At 2:00 p.m. they rolled my gurney towards the recovery room. Then the excessive bleeding caused my blood pressure to drop. The nurses ran pushing my gurney back into the lab, and paged Dr. Case Western. He came running, as they hooked me up to oxygen, and an IV drip.

Once stabilized and in the recovery unit, a different pair of nurses, aware I hadn't eaten, bought me lunch from the cafeteria with their own money. "No need to reimburse. We're all blown away about the reason for your procedure."

Dr. Ritz came in, he said, "The catheter pieces were sent to our lab for analysis. The other doctors and I are puzzled. A catheter should never crumble like this. We've contacted the manufacturer. They might be defective."

By 6:00 p.m. Dr. Case Western replaced my bloody bandages. "You're being released. Keep your right leg straight. Complete bed rest for the next three days, no work. There is a sizable puncture wound."

Later, when questioned under oath, Dr. Ritz reported, "She felt no pain during the procedure."

Cracks

My first day home from the cardiac cath, hunched over with pain and unable to stand upright, I lurched toward the bathroom, and truly saw myself in the mirror. The months of fear, uncertainty, and sleepless nights had left their mark. Fissures of facial lines appeared on a ghostly white face, with dark circles under sunken eyes. Gently I pulled up my floor-length, cotton nightgown with the small cornflower-blue flowers, looking for the entry point for all the devices used. I carefully removed the blood-soaked gauze, my eyes tearing with self-pity. The gaping red opening was the diameter of my index finger, not the needle mark I expected. *I'm still alive. That's all that matters.*

I was exhausted physically, emotionally, and mentally. With the cardiac catheterization ordeal over, interrupted plans to start our family was priority one, again.

Josh, my lawyer, had said early on, "You're my boss. I work for you." Despite everything, my plan was to call him, pay my bill for his time, and have him ask for an apology from my surgeon for hanging up, abandoning me, when all I asked for was medical treatment.

Years later, I came to think of the whole fiasco in terms of other professions. If a car mechanic accidentally cracked the windshield while working on a vehicle, not only would it be repaired, quickly and for free, those with the expertise necessary wouldn't refuse to get involved.

Within days of the procedure, I returned to work. It felt good to have a reason to dress in business clothes, high heels, and wear make-up again. A flight of stairs to the second floor revealed a mammoth open room with five hundred employees, their desks, phones, and computer terminals all positioned to face the interior of the room. The walls were white and there were unending miles of generic beige carpeting. In the air was the smell of dust on glaring fluorescent lighting. Towering stacks of insurance policies covered employees' desks.

My desk phone rang, an irate agent. He said, "Tell that prick underwriter you work for that if he cancels Mr. William's auto policy, he'll pull all his business. I could lose a lot of commission: cars, boats, homeowners, life. He has everything insured with my agency."

"I'll pull their MVRs, motor vehicle reports." I typed in the policy number on the keyboard, then finger walked my right hand through the file folders in my desk drawer. The CRT (cathode ray tube) computer, with the fluorescent green text came to life. The parents were clean. It was the son.

On the 16-year-olds MVR I spotted the acronym. "The son has a DUI. I don't have the authority. You'll have to speak to the lead underwriter."

"Then why did you sign the letter?"

"That's my job. Guidelines, Bob. The monetary risks are too great. You know the drill: male, sixteen, and DUI? That's the potential for a multi-million-dollar loss to the company with his next accident."

He slammed his receiver down. I winced as I pulled the phone away from my ear. *We hold people accountable.*

Home from work, I tossed my purse and car keys onto the kitchen counter, changed into jeans and a T-shirt. The October air had a chill. I pulled on a pair of socks and a grey sweater. Before starting dinner, I knelt on the floor and gave tummy rubs to both of our dogs.

While the pot roast heated up the kitchen I stepped out onto the screened porch. A jade plant I'd bought at a garage sale earlier that summer needed water. The dogs followed. I threw a stick for them as I picked up a plastic watering can by the hose. In the distance, the sun was setting behind the trees. I pulled my sweater around my shoulders. I thought about the past few months. Shuddered. *Life is finally normal again. It's over.*

Sometime later, my attorney called. The news wasn't good. "Mary, I'm happy to charge you a flat fee. You did a lot of the leg work at the medical library, so my bill won't be too much. Your request for an apology has not been accepted. Specifically, the response was, 'Sue.'"

I was stunned. *No apology? After everything I went through.* My Catholic upbringing meant nonstop apologies, even when you weren't wrong. I blinked continuously, startled to realize the rules didn't apply to everyone. Josh wordlessly waited for my answer, then spoke, "Mary, it's your decision."

Disheartened, I said "Okay, file."

As the months passed, the legal aspect was unimportant. As far as I was concerned, it was for accountability purposes, like a report card grade. My mind was on someone else. March of 1988 marked five months since my cardiac catheterization. I was eighteen weeks pregnant: my own family. I was overjoyed.

We decided not to discover the baby's gender until birth. Still, I had it on good authority, from coworkers who represented old wives' tales from every region of the United States and beyond, that without any doubt whatsoever based upon profile, width, girth, and waddle that I carried a baby girl. Aaron and I picked a name.

Soon, I was greeted by my coworkers, "Good morning. How's Caitlyn today?" Then they started to think Caitlyn was only half of the story. Many declared, "You must be carrying twins." "One baby is hiding behind the other."

"No. It's only one. I'm short."

After work, rather than picking colors for the nursery or preparing for the new baby, I answered thickly stapled questionnaires, full of ridiculous and inappropriate questions, like, "Were you drinking alcohol at the time of the alleged injury?" As I was a surgical patient, unconscious, and under anesthesia, with sarcasm, I was tempted to reply, "Hell, yeah, me, the nurses, doctors we were all drunk off our asses. IVs of vodka, gin, and champagne. Sterile surgical trays full of appetizers of caviar, crackers and cheese, wheelchair races in the hallway." My pen poised over the questionnaire, I resisted the urge, answered, "No."

The deposition was worse. Aaron and I met with Josh. The three of us stood on a windy street corner, a biting snap of March air indicating winter's refusal to surrender to spring.

Towering cocoa-brown skyscrapers loomed upwards immediately from the sidewalk's edge. There was barely a speck of blue sky. Encircled by the tall buildings, we talked about the case. Josh said, "They will say anything to upset you. To make you cry. Their goal is to make you drop the lawsuit."

A solitary glimmer of light made its way through a crevice at the base of the soaring buildings. My eyes tried to trace the tunnel of brightness. *The sunlight must be coming from the nearby ocean.* I closed my eyes: imagined the feel of the cobalt waters, cresting waves in the vastness, the sugary, coquina-embedded sand between my toes, golden dunes of shoreline, sea oats swaying in the breeze, the enormous ocean's sky. When I opened my eyes, I shook off an uneasy sense of *déjà vu.*

My deposition took five hours that day. I was asked over a hundred questions. The small, rectangular room had naked walls. The solitary window revealed a brick wall. The glass was cracked.

The oblong, 12-foot, glaringly polished mahogany table eclipsed the room with barely a walking path around its perimeter. Barely-out-of-law-school Josh and I sat on one side; across from us were six attorneys. They all wore expensive, three-piece, pin-striped suits. I wore a red-and-white cotton maternity dress with a white cotton-lace collar. From behind a wall of opened leather briefcases, conflicting cloying odors of their after-shave filled the room.

Josh was my David against their Goliath. As the only one not wearing a suit, I felt as insignificant as a tiny pebble zooming helplessly through space at a target too large.

They didn't allow Aaron in the room. I was on my own with my unborn child, Caitlyn. The bulk of their questioning was about my family. They wanted to know precise details about my father's death from cancer—whether he suffered, level of pain—my parent's education, where they attended high school, and their past employers. They required the same information about my sibling as well as her husband's military service and health. They asked about my gynecological records, questioned the existence of my child at my fifth month of pregnancy. "Will the fetus be aborted?" The lawyer pointed his high-priced gold pen, like a dagger, at my baby, Caitlyn. I was stunned by their cruelty.

Josh squeezed my hand under the table, leaned in, whispered, "This is the worst of it."

I barely gave a nod, with an intense gaze to confirm our earlier conversation.

Towards opposing counsel, I simply said, "No," my jaw cement. *You're not going to make me cry.*

The months flew by. Summer arrived along with my due date. When my belly button popped out like the prepackaged thermometer in the better brand of Thanksgiving turkeys, I knew my little Caitlyn was arriving soon. Days before my due date my blood pressure shot up. My OB said, "You have pre-eclampsia. If you don't have the baby within 24 hours, I'll meet you in the hospital at six a.m. to induce labor. When the day passed and no Caitlyn, Aaron and I arrived at the hospital as instructed.

The doctor said, "We'll put an IV line in with a drug that will initiate contractions. The good news: your baby will be born within three hours, four tops. The bad news: you'll be in hard labor those few hours, there's no gradual build-up of contractions. Ask for an epidural when pain becomes too severe."

Fifteen hours later I requested the injection. As I sat on the edge of the bed with the gown pulled away from my lower back, the anesthesiologist briefly questioned the portion of my scoliosis scar he could see. He was unable to insert the needle. "I must have hit the fusion bone between your vertebrae. I'll try another location." He made six attempts. The needle wouldn't penetrate anywhere. Finally, he asked, "Do you know which levels are fused?"

"Yes, from T7 to L4, nine levels."

"Nine levels? You're not eligible for an epidural. Didn't your OB tell you that? You're wasting my time." I heard the clunk of the needle as he hurled it into the metal basin on my bed. He stormed out. The door closed.

My original OB had been a newly graduated young obstetrician, he said, "You can't have an epidural. You have too much fusion mass." He had read my scoliosis surgical report.

My coworkers had advised otherwise. "He's nuts. Of course, there's space. It's only the width of a needle. You need someone more experienced."

I switched doctors. The middle-aged, seasoned OB laughed out loud when he heard his colleague's warning. "Well of course you can have an epidural." He continued, "No, I don't need to read your records. I know what scoliosis surgery entails." I realized afterwards that he must have assumed fusion was at one or two levels. Plus, my gown wasn't fully opened, or the anesthesiologist would have seen the entire 18-inch scar.

We had not planned for a natural childbirth. Aaron stayed every minute, not even a meal break. Throughout the night, we both begged the doctor to perform a C-section. He declined. Sometime around 4:00 a.m. my husband called a local DJ and requested they play *The Lion Sleeps Tonight.* The DJ announced on air, "This one is for Mary. She's been in labor for over twenty hours, going to have a baby!" The lyrics were a comfort.

When the morning shift arrived, nurses from the prior day were surprised to see I was still in labor. They didn't hide huddled conversations, "She's still only nine centimeters." "She can't take much more of this." "She hasn't slept in 48 hours. How will she be able to care for a newborn?" They had a plan. We agreed. The four nurses—two on each side—pushed downward gently with their combined body weight, from the breast-side slope of my belly towards my feet. One went running for my obstetrician.

My OB briskly walked in, instructed to push. Swoosh...the baby was born. My doctor held up the umbilical-tethered, bloody, wailing, waxy newborn. I laughed with pure delight, shouted, "It's a boy!" "It's a boy?" Over my protruding belly, looked, *Where's Caitlyn? Twins?*

There was no Caitlyn.

Cameron had arrived.

Four days later, the baby and I were released from the hospital. In the wee hours of our first night home, I rocked our beautiful son. My life was complete. *Some dreams do come true.* I was ecstatically happy.

That first month Cameron cried nonstop, day and night. He only slept from 3:00 a.m. to 5:00 a.m. I turned into a sleep-deprived-zombie. The slightest noise woke him, even the sound of the light switch turning off as I tip-toed out of his room.

The phone rang. I scrambled to pick up the receiver before it woke my son from his first afternoon nap since coming home from the hospital. It was Josh. "We need to talk about a lawsuit against the manufacturer of the catheter."

"I haven't had any sleep. Do we have to talk about this now?"

"That catheter shouldn't have crumbled. There's a possibility it was defective. Also, I found litigation where other hospitals were re-using central lines from patient to patient. I also think we have a case against Dr. Mayberry for not referring you to a specialist when it was first discovered."

I shouted, "Dr. Mayberry? No. I'm done with all this legal mess. Drop it."

"Are you certain? This is your health and well-being we're talking about."

"Josh, my pregnancy should have been the happiest days of my life. I'm 31 years old. I've waited for years to have children. Don't laugh. My older coworkers claim Cameron cries so much now because of all my blubbering during my pregnancy. Silly, I know. Whether related or not, I need to shift gears to the future, and take care of my son."

"All right, then. If that's your decision, I wish you all the best."

My chronic lumbar pain, which had mysteriously gone on hiatus during my pregnancy, returned with a vengeance during my maternity leave. I couldn't carry my infant son, all seven pounds of him, without a searing sensation. I used his small light-weight umbrella stroller for trips down our long dirt driveway to the mailbox. Soon, his little stroller was the only way I could move him from room-to-room inside our 900-square-foot home. That saved my back for the other 4,000 times a day I absolutely had to lift my infant son.

Picking up friends' babies or toddlers wasn't painful until after my scoliosis surgery. I had questioned Dr. Ribby, before becoming pregnant with Cameron. "Isn't this a symptom? Aren't you concerned?"

He said, "You don't have to pick up a child to love them." It seemed like an odd response. My scoliosis surgery was never implicated, and I didn't know he was a close friend of the referring physician, Dr. Fixit.

In desperation, I returned to my acupuncturist, Michael. He had switched locations. I looked up the steep set of exterior steps to his second-floor office with dread. I carried Cameron, each step like a dagger in my lower back. Each visit offered some relief.

When my mother offered to help around the house, I was thrilled. When she arrived that first day, I asked her to hold the baby while I vacuumed. In her 70s she was hesitant. "No. I don't want to drop him."

"Sit on the couch with him." She held him awkwardly like an overripe pumpkin ready to explode. Within minutes she signaled to stop. "It's too dangerous, he might fall. I came to help you. Turn off the vacuum. Sit. Let's talk." She patted the couch.

When Cameron fell asleep cradled in my arms, I said, "Mom I'm going to put him down, and take a nap, too."

Within five minutes, as soon as I dozed off, she shook my shoulder. "I want to do a load of laundry for you, but your machine isn't like mine. Show me how to use it."

Bleary-eyed and sleepy, I said, "Thanks. Skip it. I'll do the laundry later. I really need some sleep."

"I want to help you. I can hang it up outside to dry. Where are your clothespins?"

"We use a dryer."

"I've never owned a dryer in my entire life. That makes your clothes wear out quicker. Look at the lint."

"Mom, please. I'm exhausted. Everyone has a dryer."

"I gave up my bridge games for you."

"You play bridge one day a week. Keep going to bridge and come here a different day."

"The other bridge players said I needed to quit coming for two months, so I could help my daughter with the baby."

"You know helping is sometimes doing nothing. Can't you read a magazine, or watch TV, while Cameron and I sleep?"

The dark shadow on her face indicated *Brace for impact!* "Well, I guess since you have one of those fancy dryers you don't need your mother anymore. I don't like your attitude. I'm leaving."

"Mom! Stop. Please." The door slammed shut. Cameron woke crying.

It must have been a Sunday. Aaron was glued to a baseball game on the TV in the bedroom. I was rocking Cameron while we sat on the blue rocker-recliner in the adjacent living room. I sneezed. There was a piercing sound of a bone breaking.

My husband ran out of the bedroom, immediately at my side. He shouted with alarm, "What was that noise? It was so loud."

I froze, afraid to move. I could feel the color drain from my face. "It came from my back. Hold the baby." Gingerly, I handed him our son.

Cautiously, I stood up. Aaron steadied my elbow while he cradled Cameron in the crook of his left arm. "Are you okay? Are you sure it was your back?"

"Yes. Inside … I felt it … move?"

I took a few hesitant steps, "I think all is okay."

We both dismissed it as some quasi, tight-muscle, long-labor, bone-cracking thing. I was at a loss for words to describe the sensation. It was as if, deep inside my body, bones had shifted. The event was soon forgotten.

Years later, I learned the truth, the sound from that sneeze was my back breaking.

In fall of 1988 Cameron finally slept through the night. Like a spy on a mission, I tip-toed along the perimeter of his room, checked for the three telltale signs: *Drooled out pacifier stuck on his lower lip? Check. And then saliva-pasted onto his chin? Check. Lastly, plunge of plug, off Baby Chin Mountain? We have confirmation. Cam is finally, truly, sound asleep. Hallelujah!*

I headed towards my bedroom, noticed the kitchen window was cracked open. October in northern Florida ushered in the first cool, no air-conditioning-required, temperatures. With my arms widely stretched across the large frame, it moved. Inside the windowsill, along the entire three-foot width, and at least a foot up both sides, was a skinny black snake. I screamed. I ran to the adjoining bedroom where Aaron's response was to grab my pillow and cover his head as he rolled over. I jumped onto the bed, ripped my pillow off his head, and shook his shoulders, screaming, "Snake!"

He rolled. Too late, my feet became entangled in the blanket. When he sprang upright, we both fell off the bed, him full-tackle landing on my foot.

The sound of the bone breaking in my toe was unmistakable. *Like the sneeze? Not as loud?*

Wide awake, he jumped up, "What's happening?"

I hopped on one foot, while holding the injured one. A new layer of fear struck. *With all this commotion, why isn't Cameron awake? Crying?*

In complete panic I babbled: "Save the baby! Snake! Toe broke! Get baby! Find snake!" I grabbed his hand and dragged him to the adjoining kitchen. By then, the upper half of the snake's body had emerged from the window frame, suspended mid-air, in our direction. When the snake saw us, its tongue-darting, serpentine body retreated backwards inside the window frame, exactly where it had been a few moments before. Aaron saw the movement, leapt across the kitchen floor, and slammed the storm casement shut to trap the snake. Then he went outside and pried off the bent screen, to release the frightened creature into the night.

My husband soon fell asleep. I was wide awake. I checked on Cameron every few minutes. The irony of any squeak of a noise waking him versus the snake encounter made me laugh out loud. I asked my infant son, "That's it? Now you're asleep? None of this woke you?" I motioned with broad circles.

Cameron responded with happy, bubbly-baby noises and rolled over.

The next day an x-ray confirmed my toe was broken. With the injury taped, and even darker circles under my eyes from yet another sleepless night, I limped around the house on my heel as I pushed the baby from room-to-room in his umbrella stroller. The next night we resumed our old routine. Cameron was awake until 3 a.m., fell asleep for only two hours, and then was wide awake again at 5 a.m. My window of opportunity for sleep had closed.

As far as living out in the country, the snake coming through the broken screen was the last straw. My team of experts, wiser, mature coworkers, many of whom also lived in rural areas, unanimously chimed in. "The snake smelled your breast milk on the baby. It was heading to your son's crib."

That was it. Within months the three of us moved to the nearby college town. Our 1,600 square-foot home was a pluck of rural in the middle of suburbia. Some neighbors had grassy lawns. Others opted for all-natural wooded lots. Driveways varied—dirt, lime rock, black asphalt, or cement. Nearby, a new library was being built.

At our cluster of rural mailboxes, pushing my son in his stroller, I met one of our new neighbors. He looked familiar. It had been 12 years. It was my former organic chemistry classmate from 1976. His innocent comment, that my scoliosis was "obvious," had sealed my fate. While we chatted, I said, "I took your advice. I had my scoliosis fixed. You were mistaken about only needing a back brace, though."

He beamed, and said, "See. I told you so. Now you'll never have pain, again."

"Actually, it's been much worse since my scoliosis surgery."

He frowned, "Well, that doesn't make sense."

Neither of us knew: my scoliosis had not been fixed.

August 1990

Two years had passed. I thought we would have a normal life. Toddler Cameron rode his tricycle along our circular driveway. He and I tossed a ball in the yard by the picnic table. I gave him horseback rides in the house. We always laughed, played hide-n-seek, countless laps as we chased each other from kitchen, living room, to bedrooms. On excursions to the grocery store, I taught him colors by pointing at canned food items. Husband, child, home and two dogs; add the white-picket fence and we were the quintessential image of a happy family.

Summer of 1990, I turned 33 and Cameron turned two. I joined a gym with a daycare facility. After a workout, one day, I parked the car in our circular drive, opened the back door, unfastened my son's car seat, picked him up, and deposited him onto the black asphalt. He ran ahead across the lawn.

As I followed him, my entire right leg went numb. I fell flat on my face. Startled, I lay there a moment, dazed, brushed the gravel dirt off my cheeks. Sitting upright on my heels, "Cameron, come back." I looked around the ground. *Did I trip? On what?* I scanned the ground. Cameron scampered over, mimicked, attempted to squat, but rolled backwards off-balance. We both laughed. He said, "Mommy, what'cha doing? Draw chalk time?"

The leg numbness episodes continued. I fell in the grocery store, barely caught an endcap before an avalanche of cereal boxes tumbled onto the floor. Other shoppers stared, I felt embarrassed. Days later, at home, kneeling and leaning over the tub to bathe Cameron, my right leg gave out. I fell against the tub. My concern became full blown fear.

Dr. Mayberry ordered an x-ray. He and the Radiologist both deemed it "Inconclusive." Throughout the rest of my life, when I tried to make sense of my memories, feelings, and data from these events of August, 1990, I was surprised to see that the first report, from mid-August, had correctly identified the problem: "There is 1 cm of anterior subluxation of L4 on L5."

> "AP AND LATERAL VIEWS …
> WITHOUT PRIOR STUDY FOR
> COMPARISON.
>
> There is 1 cm of anterior subluxation
> of L4 on L5. A short small tubular
> radiopaque density is seen projected at the
> end of the eighth left rib. This may represent
> something outside the patient."

Their commentary, "without prior study for comparison," caused great alarm. Absolutely I knew the subluxation was a new discovery. I'd had over a dozen spine x-rays over the years. I called the facility repeatedly, begged them to compare my new film to my old x-rays. They finally agreed. Their revised report didn't indicate any urgency. Still, I was uneasy. I didn't know, to have a vertebra, not a disc—an actual vertebra—slip out of place was not normal. Not without a trauma.

> "STUDY FOR COMPARISON
> (ADDENDUM)
>
> The film dated 1986 reveals no
> evidence of slippage of L4 on L5 and
> therefore this has occurred since 1986.
>
> IMPRESSION: IT IS BELIEVED
> THAT THIS SLIPPAGE IS ON A
> DEGENERATIVE BASIS."

Two weeks later, at the end of August, our scheduled out-of-state family vacation to visit relatives arrived. I was still falling with episodes of leg numbness. Aaron suggested, "Stay home. We'll go without you. Rest up. I bet without an active toddler to chase around your leg will feel better."

While the boys were out of town, that Saturday, I took a short drive to a nearby garage sale. They were selling a cane, portable commode, a walker, and a wheelchair. Again, I had an uneasy feeling. On an impulse, I bought the cane.

On the car radio while driving home, local news erupted with the discovery of a third brutally murdered college student. The first two had been discovered the day before. The announcer reported, "...a serial killer on the loose." As the day wore on and details emerged of vicious mutilation, terrified friends called friends. Neighbors gathered in front yards. I called my mother, no answer. *She must be at the grocery store.*

That Monday morning parents protectively circled their children at school bus stops. Two more students were murdered that day. I repeatedly called my mother, again, no answer. She didn't live far from any of the three crime scenes. Worried, I drove over to her place. Before I pulled out from our circular driveway, I practiced braking with my left foot in case my right leg went numb while driving.

After knocking and then banging on her door, I stepped backwards and looked around, *all okay.* I rotated through my key ring, found hers. Cautiously, I pushed the door wide open, without entering. Past the living room, directly in my line of view, she sat at the kitchen table, hands in prayer position as she leaned on her elbows, her eyes closed. She didn't answer when I called out to her. As I walked over, I noticed our local paper on the table with the headline.

"Are you okay? Didn't you hear the knocking? I've been calling you. Didn't you hear the phone? You know what happened?" I gestured towards the paper. "Two more today, Mom, this is really scary."

She refused to come to my house. *She's safe. She always keeps her doors locked.* My leg was going numb. I didn't want to add to her distress, so kept my reason for leaving to myself. She was still staring out the window with a faraway look when I left.

The boys returned from vacation. My symptoms worsened. I returned to my family doctor. "I'm falling every day now. I can't walk at all without the cane."

Dr. Mayberry said, "A new diagnostic test has been invented. They're saying it's better than a standard x-ray. It's called a magnetic resonance imaging machine, MRI for short. The magnet is extremely powerful. Despite walls, it could cause metal instruments in adjoining rooms to go flying. They'll never be housed inside hospitals for that reason.

"You're in luck, the first ever MRI in our fair city has arrived. It's housed inside an 18-wheeler truck parked behind Community Hospital. You're going to be one of the first patients ever, in our county, to have one of these highfalutin tests."

When my husband and I arrived for the MRI, I asked, "My doctor said it's a strong magnet. I have Harrington rods from a scoliosis surgery? Is that okay?"

The receptionist double-shoulder shrugged. "It's only a fancy x-ray." I repeated my question to the MRI tech. He answered, "That shouldn't make any difference." When he showed us the long cylinder and explained my face and entire body would only be a few inches from the walls of the machine I was scared. Aaron offered, and the tech approved, for him to stand outside the machine. I stretched my right arm as far as I could over my head. Aaron reached in until our fingertips barely touched.

The noise inside sounded like a thousand jackhammers. Soon my stomach felt like it was on fire. There were no microphones inside the machines in those days. When the test was over, I asked the tech. "Is the burning sensation normal?"

Without looking up from his clipboard, he said, "No one else has complained."

Not a complaint, only reporting what I experienced. My thoughts became a loud sigh.

At the follow-up appointment Dr. Mayberry said, "The test results were invalid. Your hardware caused distortion. I plumb forgot you still have those darn Harrington rods, too bad. I'm stumped. I'm going to have to refer you to a neurosurgeon. Let's rule out your spine, just in case."

When my appointment date arrived, the neurosurgeon closed the exam room door slowly, her back to us. When she finally faced us, she looked angry, snapped my x-ray from my hand, and flung it up on the pre-lit monitor. Red-faced, hands on her hips, she roared, "If you think for one minute, I'm going to lift a finger to help the type of patient who sues doctors, you can forget it. No one in this city will take you as a patient."

Speechless, neither of us said anything. I couldn't think fast enough to assemble the words to inform her of her misinformation. She barked, "Go to Minnesota. You need to see a scoliosis specialist." Then shouted at us. "Get out! Get out of my office! Right now!" She flung the cubicle door open so hard the metal handle left a mark on the wall.

As we walked out the young receptionist looked up from her desk, wide-eyed. She must have overheard. The surgeon waved us on. "Don't worry about the bill."

No bill, no proof of visit? Haven't we done this before?

My insurance company was billed for the "forty-five-minute extended visit" of five-minute duration. I paid my co-pay, later obtained her full-page report.

> "There is 1 cm anterior subluxation of L4 on L5. ... No change in bowel habits is reported, but the patient feels that she does not empty her bladder completely."

Briefly, I entertained her suggestion of going to Minnesota. But daycare hours didn't cover Aaron's evening shifts. None of the extended family were willing or available to take care of our son. That turned out to be a blessing.

The bladder difficulties worsened. I struggled to urinate, even with a full bladder. Eventually, I discovered that pushing hard on my stomach with two open palms initiated a weak stream. *Must be a bladder infection, what else at my age?* The increasing frequency of leg numbness and falling episodes took priority.

Then a mystery third symptom surfaced: When attempting to pull a mixing bowl off the top shelf in the kitchen, I was unable to lift myself up on tippy toe. No matter how hard I tried, the muscles in both calves seized. With each passing day, my fears multiplied.

Even with the garage sale cane, it became an enormous struggle to walk down the twenty-foot hallway from the master bedroom to the family room, let alone to continue onward to the rest of the house.

There were new sensations, razor sharp inside my right leg. It felt like a long rubber band had been pulled as tight as possible, and then scraped up-and-down, like a barber sharpening his blade in a Western movie.

In despair, I made an appointment to see my acupuncturist. I had seen him off and on for three years, but only for pain management. Before the insertion of the needles, Michael checked all my pulses. Chinese medicine believes there is more than one. He frowned, and repeated his exam, several times. "Mary, there is serious problem. There is almost no *chi, life force,* in your body. You need to go to a hospital emergency room immediately."

"Michael? Are you kidding? You grew up in this country, you know I can't walk into an American hospital and tell them my *chi* is blocked."

"Yes, of course." He held his palms together, closed his eyes, and bowed his head, for a moment. When he looked up, he continued, "I'm sure one of their standardized tests will reveal the problem. Please, go, immediately."

My husband and I arrived at the ER. I was unable to walk the two-hundred feet from the parking lot to the entrance. Not without my entire leg going numb and falling flat on my face. While I waited in the car, Aaron broke the rules about wheelchairs being removed from the hospital and snuck one out.

Hours later, when it was our turn, I told the ER doctor, "...cramp-like numbness, constantly falling, razor-sharp sensation in my leg, and difficulty walking." I handed him the x-ray Dr. Mayberry had ordered weeks earlier.

The emergency room doctor took a quick look, sent us home. "I'm comfortable letting your family physician handle this. Pain is not an emergency."

I was afraid to mention the neurosurgeon, without disclosing why I was thrown out. *Would they refuse care, too?* Then I remembered Michael's comments, and said, "Don't you want to run a test?"

"Oh no, that's not necessary."

We left the hospital and returned home. Within days my doubts escalated: Michael's words about blocked *chi*. I trusted him more than anyone else at that point. My husband suggested, "Let's return. There'll be a different shift. A different doctor might order a test."

We returned, again, in a wheelchair. I was in a total state of dry-mouth panic. In the cubicle, ER doctor #2 skimmed my film, said, "Here's a referral for our orthopedic department. You've had some extensive spine reconstruction. You should have it checked out." He glanced through the opened door at someone, pointed to his watch, and rubbed his stomach in a circular motion.

I can't walk and he's worried about lunch? A deep hopeless sigh erupted from my lips.

As we left the hospital, I looked down at his referral. The appointment was over a month away, nearly Halloween.

In the car heading home, I cried inaudibly at first, and then my emotions erupted into full-blown, uncontrollable, sobbing. Aaron asked, "What's the matter?"

"A...month...from...now...is...too...late. The words bubbled up from my gut. As if my body knew what my brain couldn't understand.

"Your sister said it's nothing to worry about."

"I know. She said, 'Quit bothering them at the ER with a leg cramp.' She's wrong. I'm falling. Every. Single. Day. Now, I can't go up on tippy toes? This isn't normal. Why doesn't anyone believe me?"

"They'll see you in October, can't you wait?"

"No! Don't you understand? I don't have a month! I'm out of time!" I screamed, then burst into tears. I felt the truth of my words with every fiber of my being.

"Okay, okay." Aaron slammed on the brakes and made a screeching, sharp U-turn. My head bumped against the side window.

To this day, like viewing a snapshot, I know exactly the street we were on and where we turned that day. We were half-way home. There was a fire station on my left, a small strip shopping center on my right, a traffic light swung in the breeze. I think the worst moments of our lives are frozen, black-and-white photographs in memory.

For the third time that week and the second visit that day, my husband wheeled me into the hospital. The same nurse was at the triage counter. When our turn came up, I blurted out, "I can't walk! Please I'm begging! Help me!"

The triage nurse replied, tartly, "You were already seen today, plus a few days ago. You can walk. I saw you stand up and walk over to the water fountain." Her unspoken words screamed in my mind, *Faking it, lady.*

I was dumbfounded. *No one was listening.* Years later, like a trauma survivor, searching to alter the events, I wondered, *what if I'd said, furthest distance? Were those the magic words to make her believe me?* She continued, "This is an emergency room. We need the space for patients with *real* emergencies, not a leg cramp. We're not admitting you. You both need to leave immediately." She seemed to be reaching under the counter.

Within a minute, two burly, bouncer-looking, six-foot plus security guards with bulging biceps showed up to escort us out of the hospital. Aaron lost his temper. He flung waiting room chairs, shouted, "You're going to need more than two people to throw me out of here." With his hands on his hips,

"Pick me up and carry me out! Pick up my wife—wheelchair and all—and carry her out! She. Can't. Fucking. Walk! What don't you understand? I'm calling the newspapers. I'm calling the TV stations. You can use that for your fucking commercials about being 'The Helpful Hospital.'"

The department head of the ER came running. He ushered us into a small room. I said, "A month from now will be too late. This has been going on since August. Please, I'm begging you. I need to be seen by a specialist, right away. I have a two-year-old son. I'm falling every single day...can't go up on tippy toe. This can't be normal. I'm only 33 years old."

With firm authority he answered. "You're right. I can help you. Give me a few minutes." My fears about the security guards or police showing up to escort us out of the hospital weren't realized. In less than five minutes, he returned. "I've talked to our most experienced orthopedic surgeon. He's agreed to fit you in tomorrow morning, before his first patient of the day."

He handed us the appointment card: 7:45 a.m. September 17th, 1990—it had been three weeks since the neurosurgeon threw us out of her office.

Dr. BrownEyes

The next morning Aaron wheeled me into the cubicle of an examination room. Dejected, I clutched the x-ray from August. Aaron sat on the only chair.

A deeply tanned young man with sun-bleached blonde hair, wearing a highly starched white jacket, entered. It was easy to imagine him playing volleyball on the beach the prior weekend. There was a bounce in his voice as he introduced himself. "I'm Dr. So-and-so's surgical resident."

The word "resident" brought back the memory of my debut surgeon, Dr. Unknown, 1977, his students laughing. I questioned the arrival of his classmates. My worries were thankfully abated when he reassured it was only him. Still, I was anxious about another brush-off, like the neurosurgeon appointment. *Dear God please show him what I'm feeling.*

Dr. BeachBoy was over six-feet tall and most notably had a sincere smile as he greeted us and shook our hands. His eyes were friendly, reassuring. Clearly, he wasn't going to rush my appointment. I felt a sense of relief. He said, "Since this is a teaching hospital, I'll talk to you first and then present my diagnosis to the Attending. He'll then perform his own exam, which should confirm my findings." Taking my film from August, Dr. BeachBoy sat down on rotating stool with stainless-steel legs. He flicked the switch on the wall-mounted viewer, leaned in, and with a jovial tone of voice, said, "Let's see what we have here, Mrs. Adams."

I zoomed in on his every micro-movement. There was a subtle jerking backwards, then a stiffened spine. He rotated towards me, with a granite face, his tone of voice gravel, deadly serious. With rushed words, he asked, "Have you been in a car accident recently?"

"No."

"Anything serious, like a sky-diving accident?"

"No."

"A blunt-force injury? A fall down a flight of stairs?"

"No."

He partially turned back to the monitor, audibly exhaled, while he nervously drummed his fingers on the counter. "I see you have Harrington rods. When was your scoliosis surgery?"

"Seven years ago, 1983."

"I'll be right back." He bolted upright off the stool so fast he sent it spinning. "Dr. BrownEyes needs to see this." He snatched the film, left the monitor light on, flung open the heavy metal door, as he rushed out. My husband and I gave each other a wordless glance. Aaron responded to my furrowed eyebrows, with a shrug of his shoulders. Before we could verbalize our thoughts, Dr. BeachBoy returned with an equally tall, slightly older, brown-eyed doctor wearing glasses. He extended his right hand for a warm handshake. With his other hand, he held my x-ray. He, too, seemed genuinely concerned for my health and well-being. I was so thankful this wasn't going to be like the ER or the neurosurgeon who threw us out.

Clearly, the brown-eyed doctor was the superior to the sun-bleached blonde, whom he called by his last name without using the preface, "Doctor." Dr. BrownEyes gave orders. "Turn off the overheads, BeachBoy. We need the best possible lighting in here." He clipped my x-ray onto the still-lit monitor and sat on the stool. He was the seventh doctor to look at the exact same image.

The glare from the monitor cast an eerie yellow glow, like a sepia picture from the 1800s. There was complete silence as Dr. BrownEyes leaned in and positioned his face as close as possible. He lifted and lowered his glasses repeatedly as he stared at an item an inch from his nose. Less than a minute later, he turned, motioned for BeachBoy to turn on the overhead lights, and instructed, "Escort our patient down to the Radiology Department. Wait there with her for the film to be developed. Then hand-carry it here."

The brown-eyed doctor swiveled his stool, reached across the counter for the ivory wall phone hanging nearby, and picked up the receiver. As the overly stretched, cord, dangled, he punched out an extension "This is Dr. BrownEyes, Chief of the Orthopedic Department. I need to speak with the Radiology Department Chief, priority one." A slight pause, then he continued, "I'm sending down my patient, Mary Adams, accompanied by my resident.

"She has had extensive spinal fusion with instrumentation for scoliosis. I need multiple views of the lumbar spine. There is significant slippage at the L4/L5, suspected impingement.

Did he say, 'My patient?' Thank God.

"My resident will be waiting to hand carry the film for me to read. I need it without delay. Your radiologist will have to file his report later." Dr. BrownEyes hung up, sprung off the seat, and with one step had his hand on the doorknob. Over his shoulder, he commanded, "BeachBoy, we'll reconvene here in fifteen minutes."

Somewhere far away I heard my trembling voice ask, "Doctor, is there a problem with the x-ray I brought?"

Dr. BrownEyes stopped, turned. With a soft smile, his words were reassuring, "No. I need to know if the slippage has advanced since last month. Plus, as a surgeon, I need the best quality diagnostic tests and our x-ray equipment is cutting edge."

When BeachBoy and I returned from Radiology, Aaron said, "Hey, guess what? The former governor of Florida is in the next cubicle. You bumped him for Dr. BrownEyes' first appointment of the day."

BeachBoy clipped the new film alongside the one from August. Dr. BrownEyes entered, and with a nod to us, immediately strode over to the monitor, sat down, and rolled his stool closer. With the two films side-by-side, he used the sharpened point of a pencil as he drew a sideways L-shape on my new x-ray. He looked up at BeachBoy, "You're correct, Doctor. That's a one-centimeter slippage of the vertebra, spondylolisthesis." With a puckered-lip exhalation, he continued, "Good catch. It was appropriate to interrupt the other exam." He pointed to the film I had brought. "It was there in August, difficult to visualize due to her fusion mass and hardware."

Dr. BrownEyes swiveled his stool. He squared off both his shoulders, looked directly into my eyes and said, "Okay then, Mrs. Adams, let's start with some questions about your scoliosis surgery."

When I answered his first question, "Where?" Dr. BeachBoy interjected, "Oh good! It wasn't us." Dr. BrownEyes raised his eyebrows, with a reprimanding stare.

The surgeon continued, "And the Harrington rods have been in place for seven years now, since 1983? Do you know you have an extra lumbar vertebra in your spine? You have six rather than five?"

"Yes, and it's hemi-sacralized, still attached to the hip bone. No doubt, it's an in-utero birth defect. My mother would have been about a month pregnant when it developed or, rather, failed to separate." I heard the tone of my clinical responses. I'd reverted to cerebral to ignore my emotions.

Dr. BrownEyes said, "Actually, it failed to separate from the sacrum, the bone below the spine. Do you know why that birth-defect wasn't included in the fusion?"

"Prior to surgery, Dr. Fixit said, 'that vertebra is deformed and unstable. It must be included in your fusion.' I assumed it had been. I kept telling him for years that my back pain was much worse. Three years post-op, in 1986, I found out that it wasn't. Dr. Fixit said, 'Surgeons often alter their plans during surgery."

I felt like I had divided into two people. One person: distant, factual, student mode. I scrambled to stuff emotions. *Why all the questions about my scoli surgery?* I was keenly aware my heart was beating louder with each passing minute.

Dr. BrownEyes agreed. "Technically that's true. There is no test in the world as revealing as when a surgeon has a patient opened. However, that appears to have been a questionable decision. Mrs. Adams, may I call you Mary?"

"Yes."

"And you've had no other surgeries since then?

"No." My stomach was doing summersaults. The expression on his face confirmed my worst fears. He adjusted his glasses, seemed to already know my answer to his next question. "Mary, are you having trouble urinating?"

"Well, yes. I mean no. Yes. Trouble starting. I need to push hard with both hands on my stomach." I knew how ridiculous I sounded. My fears escalated. "How do you know that? My leg goes numb, and I fall down a lot." Stuttering kicked in as I continued, "...and now, now, na, na, now, I can't stand on tippy toe. That has nothing to do with my bladder. It must be an infection. What else?"

Reaching backwards towards a drawer, Dr. BrownEyes pulled out a triangle-shaped rubber hammer like the ones I'd seen on TV, and asked, "Has anyone used one of these on you?"

"No."

Dr. BeachBoy gasped, "Not even our ER?"

"No."

The two surgeons gave each other a quick look. Dr. BrownEyes rotated his stool, calmly instructed, "Make a note of that, please. Ortho needs to do some cross-training with the ER staff about the importance of a simple reflex hammer test."

Dr. BrownEyes said, with the friendliest and most re-assuring of voices, "Mary, let's do a little exam. First, let's get you out of this wheelchair."

Aaron started to stand up. "Here's my chair. She's having trouble walking. It was the fastest way to get her into the hospital. Leg cramp."

Dr. BrownEyes, "That's not necessary. I'm sure the department has more than one. To his resident, "Check the hall and remove this wheelchair."

Once I sat down, Dr. BrownEyes rolled his stool over, lightly, but firmly struck my left knee with the hammer. My lower leg slowly kicked upwards. He reached over, repeated the test on my right knee. My leg didn't move. He shifted the hammer, slightly, several more attempts. Nothing. No movement. He stood up, moved to my right side, and crouched down before repeating the test. At one spot, there was barely a slight twinge from my leg. He looked up at Dr.

BeachBoy, nodded affirmative, while he said out loud, "Cauda equina syndrome, CES."

His diagnosis meant nothing to me. I tried to analyze. *What could affect both my bladder and my leg?* My eyes teared up, and the reverberation of my own question hit the part of my throbbing brain with the answer. *Oh my God! This can't be happening.*

Dr. BrownEyes stood up, reached backwards and gently placed the little hammer on the counter. He sat down and wheeled his stool over. At that moment everything faded away. It was as if we were the only two people in the room, in the entire hospital, or orbiting in outer space. I held my breath, waited for his official decree.

"Mary, your spinal cord is being severed. Your entire spinal column has slid off the last vertebra. You need emergency surgery, otherwise you'll become paralyzed within days."

Angry. Horrified. Speechless. I glared at this new doctor with his terrible prediction. *Was he another Dr. Panic? The doctor with the false, "You need a lung removed," diagnosis?* Then my lower lip quivered. *Or is he a doctor with the expertise I require?* I managed a coarse whisper, "How did this happen?"

"Mary, that's a good question. Likely, it started with a stress fracture. I don't know the details about the past, but I do know without surgery, you will become paralyzed soon."

Memories tumbled from my scoliosis surgery. A new wave of panic hit: *The catheters.* I looked at Dr. BrownEyes. "No, I can't have an operation."

The surgeon wasn't offended. He didn't take my refusal personally. Without judgment and a sincere voice, he responded, "How can I alleviate your concerns? Why can't you have surgery?"

My jaw tightened. *Would he throw us out like the neurosurgeon? I'll have to take my chances.* "I have a fragmented central line from my 1983 scoliosis surgery. Two pieces were left, embedded near the tricuspid valve of my heart. In addition, there are four pieces, two each, in my lungs. Wouldn't a new central line dislodge the pieces still in my heart?"

Dr. BrownEyes unruffled questioned, "I take it you've had a cardiac catheterization?"

"Yes. Here. Three years ago, in 1987."

His eyebrows shot up, "Not seven years ago in 1983 when you had your scoli surgery? Usually they're removed immediately, once inadvertently cut."

"The catheter wasn't discovered until 1987."

"Who did the procedure here?"

"Dr. Ritz."

"He couldn't retrieve the entire piece?"

"No, it crumbled when they pulled."

"He's an expert. If he couldn't remove it, no one could. Mary, is there anything else?"

"I'm a stay-at-home mom. I have a two-year-old son. I can't have surgery. Who will care for him?"

Dr. BrownEyes narrowed his eyes, and leaned in, "Mary, without any doubt, paralysis is certain. Then, who will raise your son?"

I felt as if I were in a free-fall jump out of an airplane without a parachute. My thoughts spun. *This will be permanent. How do I give up without a fight? I have no choice. No choice. I must do this for Cameron. I can't have another surgery. I have a son. I can't give up. Oh God, should I trust this doctor? What if he's wrong and more mistakes occur?*

Hopeless tears dripped off my chin. As I looked at the floor I whispered, "Okay." I bit my bottom lip and squeezed my eyes shut. When I opened them, there were three sets of men's shoes. I recognized my husband's, ankles crossed, foot bouncing in nervousness.

The surgeon turned to Dr. BeachBoy, "First of all, you're going to need a lot more paper than that." He pointed to the resident's scrawl along the two vertical edges of the clip-boarded paper he'd been writing on. Dr. BrownEyes pulled out a wallet-size spiral notebook from a drawer behind him, handed it to his resident, "Are you ready? Let me know if I talk too fast, or if you need a repeat."

Dr. BeachBoy nodded in agreement.

"First, put in a call to the cardiology and pulmonary boys. Let's obtain their opinions about the catheter. Contact Records. I want the cardiac cath report and cine film from "87. I'll review it personally.

"Page the OR, we need a theatre immediately. Phone Admissions and tell them emergency surgery. They'll have to catch up with their paperwork post-op."

Dr. BeachBoy interrupted, tilted his head towards the wall. "What about our 8 a.m. patient?"

"He's gone. I met with him while you went to Radiology. I decided you could skip that case, due to this situation." He motioned for Dr. BeachBoy to continue writing. "Urology needs to perform a neurogenic bladder exam. Have Radiology perform a myelogram. Oh, and call my secretary. Clear my appointments for the rest of today."

Dr. BeachBoy asked, "No MRI?"

"She has stainless-steel Harrington rods."

"Oh right. I forgot."

"Your patients can't afford for you to overlook critical details like that, Doctor."

Another wave of angst hit, all I could mutter was, "MRI?"

Dr. BrownEyes said, "Mary, you're not a candidate. It's an incredibly powerful magnet which can loosen hardware causing substantial injury."

The color drained from my face. "My family doctor ordered an MRI a month ago. The results were blurred. My stomach felt like it was burning."

Dr. BeachBoy said, "That's the metal heating up. Didn't they know about your rods?"

"Yes, I told them."

The surgeon's eyebrows knitted. He frowned. "I'm an orthopedic surgeon. This is my field of expertise. I'll look for any damage while we have you open."

My whole body sagged.

Dr. BrownEyes gestured to his resident. "Have our Communication Officer notify them. They must screen for stainless steel metal before running these new MRI tests."

My thoughts clicked *Too late to worry about.* I shifted gears to the immediate future. "Myelogram?"

"It's a diagnostic test that was used prior to the MRI being invented. Dye is injected into your spinal cord fluid and tracked via a fluoroscope. Afterwards, patients lie flat for twenty-four hours. Otherwise, the dye goes into your brain, causing the worst migraine. Let's go."

"No!" I barely recognized my own voice.

I noticed the floor's tile had squiggly, light grey lines in the repeated pattern. It was impeccably clean, even the corners. The nine-by-five-foot cubicle of an exam room felt as if there was no oxygen to inhale.

"I want to go home. I must see my son. I must explain why I won't be there tomorrow. I can't vanish."

"That's not a good idea—"

"I must see my son! Please! Doctor?"

The surgeon leaned back, planted his hands firmly on his knees, "Be here at seven a.m. tomorrow morning. The tests alone will take several hours."

To the resident Dr. BrownEyes said, "In that case I want a specific neurosurgeon, call Dr. Fearless and have him clear his board for tomorrow."

The sheets of Dr. BeachBoy's notebook whirled as Dr. BrownEyes continued. "Mary, even after we take the pressure off your spinal cord, Urology might need to perform a separate surgery if tests confirm nerve damage to your bladder."

"Did you say 'surgeries', more than one?"

"Technically, yes, we will be performing three surgeries in a row on you. I'll remove your Harrington rods. Neuro scrubs in to take pressure off your spinal cord. Ortho returns. We can't slide that vertebra into place; we can prevent it from slipping further by extending your current fusion."

He turned to his resident, "On second thought, make the myelogram the last test immediately prior to surgery. That way surgery itself will incorporate the 24-hour lying down requirement."

Even after that flurry of information, Dr. BrownEyes understood I had feelings and was a human being. "Mary is there anything else before I leave? I won't see you until late tomorrow, only a few minutes prior to surgery."

Should I trust him? Do I have a choice? My gut settled. I prepared for battle.

"Yes, Doctor. There is one more thing. "Promise there won't be any foreign objects left behind. Would you do that for me, Doctor?"

"Yes. I promise you. And now I have a question. Is going home non-negotiable? Even a minor fender-bender could paralyze you."

"I need to see my son."

"All right, if that's your decision." Dr. BrownEyes stood up and started to leave. He turned. "Don't pick up your son or anything more than the weight of a cup of coffee."

I nodded confirmation. He left.

I said, "Dr. BeachBoy, please write down all those diagnoses. I want to look them up in my medical dictionary."

The resident handed over the list. "We don't often have a patient who self-educates. It makes things a lot easier on us. Let's talk about post-surgical care for a moment. You'll receive physical therapy, of course. A hospital social worker will provide referrals for family counseling, to help everyone adjust, as well as recommendations for additional schooling to help you become employable again—"

"Finish my bachelor's degree?"

"Sure. I don't see why not."

Dr. BeachBoy left. I looked down at the words on a small piece of lined paper with a spiral tear at the top: *spondylolisthesis, one-centimeter slippage, laminectomy, cauda equina syndrome, neurogenic bladder, Babinski signs declining.*

There was too much information to absorb: The MRI mistake, the surgeon's fusion error, catheter souvenirs, foreign medical words.

The shrinking room felt distorted. My mouth was dry. Across the cubicle my husband appeared miles away. My thoughts shifted to my toddler son: *Will I be able to take care of him?* I blurted out what for me, was more of a question than a statement. "We can't have any more children?"

Aaron shrugged, "Okay."

Chamomile Tea

Once home, I fell to my knees in the kitchen and tightly hugged my twenty-pound toddler, heeding Dr. BrownEyes' warning not to lift him. "Cameron, come to the backyard," I said. "Mommy needs to talk to you." I held his hand tightly and led him out the door. *Outside. Air. I need to be among the trees for this difficult conversation.* I sat on the bench of our wooden picnic table and patted the top, motioning for him to climb up.

How would I be able to explain the situation without scaring him? Am I going to die? Did I come home to say goodbye? I had to reassure him, and myself, that everything would be okay. The rays of the setting sun filtered through the laurel oak trees that towered eighty feet above us and blended with the woodland plants behind our house into a wall of greenery. Cameron dawdled, kicking a twig, rolling onto his stomach on the bench, distracted by a beetle as it struggled through the blades of grass.

I rubbed my fingers across the ridges of the coarse-grained, cedar-stained wood of the table as the previous year morphed into a kaleidoscope of images in my mind. I remembered how one-year-old Cameron hated his highchair. One day, he had rocked in it so forcefully that he had flown out of the seat. From a few feet away, seeing him airborne, I had dived under my flying daredevil, sliding across the kitchen floor on my shoulder like a major-league baseball player's split-second attempt to prevent a run at home plate. I grabbed him by his armpits, my straight arms extended towards the ceiling, his head inches away from hitting the wall.

In those few seconds as his feet dangled over my face he giggled, then laughed, gleefully announcing, "Fun! Mommy! Do again!"

"No!" I had shouted. "This isn't funny!"

What if I hadn't been here? I knew that Aaron would be a good father. He loved Cameron dearly. No doubt, there would be plenty of sports. My husband had read baseball statistics to my pregnant belly before our baby was born.

My thoughts returned to the present moment. Cameron stood up to jump off the bench. The sunlight glistened through curly ringlets of his golden-blonde hair. "Come on, Cameron, quit goofing around and sit up here on the tabletop. Big people talk." He climbed onto the tabletop, toddler wiggling all the way.

Our souls must connect. I looked directly into his eyes and held both of his little shoulders. "Mommy has a bad boo-boo. Mommy needs to go to a great big building called a hospital. Daddy will bring you to visit. Mommy loves you. I will be home in seven seepy nights," I explained using his word for "sleep." He hadn't quite mastered the "L" sound yet. I spread the fingers of my two hands wide and counted off the seven days for him.

"When Mommy comes home, she will be fragile. Do you remember what I told you about Mommy's flowers and doggies' ears? That they're fragile? Mommy will be like that, too. I won't be able to give you horsey back rides for a while."

Cameron had stopped jiggling, and his eyes grew wide. His lower lip began to quiver, and he wailed. "No! Don't go, Mommy!" He flung himself off the table into my arms.

I held him close until he protested and squirmed away. I firmly held his shoulders and looked him squarely in the eyes. "I love you, Cameron. Don't ever forget that. I will come home. I promise you."

What if that's not the truth? The wind kicked up, and dried fallen leaves from the crape myrtle blew across the grass. I stood up, squared my shoulders against the oncoming storm, and shouted at the sky. "I will live to defy this day."

Cameron's face puckered a toddler's confused frown.

My body softened to mommy-mode. "It's going to rain, Sweetie. Want to play with your cars in your bedroom? Put together a puzzle, or read a book? Mommy's going to play with you every minute until bedtime."

That night I couldn't sleep, slipped on my bathrobe, and headed to the kitchen. With a cup of steaming-hot chamomile tea I curled up on a living room chair. The only light was the glow from the end table lamp.

My medical books along with my medical records were piled on both the end table and my lap. Medical textbooks were always available from the Friends of the Library sales. I had gathered quite a few over the years.

The old x-ray reports indicated that the curve had kept increasing after surgery from 42 to 47-degrees. *Didn't anyone catch this in 1983?*

Then I noticed his pre-op notes contradicted the surgical report. *Did Dr. Fixit fuse to the wrong level?*

> "This will need to be a spinal fusion down to L5 and for all practical purposes down to the sacrum."

> "… a spinal fusion was performed from T-7, to L-4 …"

After the 1983 scoliosis surgery Dr. Fixit attributed my escalating pain to "The girl has tension headaches," despite symptoms while standing and walking.

> "Mary is having an increasing amount of back pain. She has trouble standing or shopping. There is movement at L4-L5."

Then three years post-op in 1986.

> "This problem is the result of the load being carried on just one lumbar disc. There is no motion at L5 and S1. She should put up with it as best she can … if necessary … surgery would involve fusing to the sacrum."

I scanned the handwritten note from earlier in the day, from the brown-eyed doctor.

> "Post-surgical spondylolisthesis (vertebra slippage) L4-L5.
>
> Fusion L4, L5, S1"

Despite the records I read that night and in the upcoming years, it took decades to truly understand what had happened. Due to my primary birth defect, the biological fusion of my last vertebra, which caused my scoliosis, and the 9-level surgical fusion above it, that solitary unfused level between L4 and L5 took all the stress of my movements.

It was as if someone built a skyscraper and forgot to pour cement between the fourth and fifth floors. Of course, with time, the "unfused," no-cement level, would break and topple from there.

On that night, my papers slid off my lap onto the floor. *What's going to happen tomorrow? The books will have the answer.* I alternated between the books and the medical dictionary. Looked up the words on the list:

Spondylolisthesis: Of all the devilish exhibits in the back's chamber of horrors, ... there is no way the spine can be brought back to its proper alignment....

Sacrum: Base of the spine.

Babinski Declining: "Indicative of a spinal cord injury."

Cauda Equina Syndrome: A medical emergency. Paralysis is imminent ... these nerves control bladder, bowel, sexual, and leg function." My dictionary dropped to the carpeting with a soft thud.

I wrapped my shaking hands around the mug of chamomile tea. The drink, like my body, was ice cold.

What are they going to do to me tomorrow?

Victory Lap

Early the next morning I was admitted to the hospital. There was a flurry of departments to visit. Several hours passed. I was dropped off at the Urology Department in the basement, to test my bladder.

A nurse explained the procedure. It must have been routine for them. I was incredulous when I heard what the test entailed.

"Have you had a Foley catheter before?"

"Yes, in 1983 for my scoliosis surgery."

"This isn't going to be fun. Urinary catheters are typically inserted when a patient is unconscious." I nodded. She continued, "Don't worry. You'll be seated and securely fastened." I saw an odd, open, U-shaped chair behind her. She continued, "You'll be tied down, at your waist, your arms, and your legs. Most patients are afraid of falling out. You won't. I promise you. We then rotate the chair upside down and fill your bladder with water. Once at maximum capacity, we'll turn the chair upright. Then our monitors record the volume and rate of flow to determine if bladder function is impaired."

My panicked brain couldn't decipher her words.

The nurse asked, "How long ago was your car accident?"

"I've not been in a car accident."

She looked up from her clipboard, "Did you fall off a balcony?"

"No."

She raised her eyebrows, eyed me, and asked nonchalantly, "A gunshot wound?"

"No."

"Well, what type of traumatic injury occurred?"

"None. I had a scoliosis surgery seven years ago."

"That wouldn't cause a spinal cord injury." She bent her head, continued to write.

"I didn't think so either."

After the Urology Department I was taken for the last test prior to the surgery: the myelogram. When finished, my gurney was wheeled into the hallway. I awaited transport.

It was early afternoon by then. Alone, afraid, I stared at the static, unending beige ceiling tiles, looking for any hint of color to differentiate one from another. Within minutes a man in a white lab coat appeared. Politely, he said, "Ma'am here's your wheelchair." He looked down at a clipboard. "I'm taking you to the OR."

"I'm not allowed to stand due to the myelogram dye."

"Wheelchair, Ma'am. No standing involved. You'll be sitting."

"No. My surgeon said not to sit either."

"Well, of course, you can sit." He looked at his watch, "I've got other patients to collect." He pushed the wheelchair closer and motioned.

"My surgeon said I had to remain lying down for twenty-four hours or the dye would go into my brain."

"Well, I don't know who your surgeon is Ma'am, must be one of them new college boy residents. The real world is way different from book learning. Let's get you into this wheelchair."

At first my mind registered his white lab coat as the equivalent of my surgeon. I almost obeyed him. Then a split-second neuron fired inside my brain. I decided to trust Dr. BrownEyes. "No."

"We can't have gurneys blocking the hallway. That's against the rules Ma'am." With that information he snatched my wrist with both of his hands and tried pulling.

I snapped, yelled at him, "No! Don't touch me!"

He threw his hands up in the air, muttered, left.

Afraid to even move my head, I rotated my eyes in a circle: towards my feet, left, then right to the wall: *white, white, white. How long will I be in this hallway?* On my second rotation, when my eyes looked upwards again, there were the clearest blue eyes and a sun-tanned smiling face looking down.

"I'm so relieved to see you, Doctor."

With his typical, cheerful, and upbeat voice Dr. BeachBoy, wearing a surgical gown, cap, and mask under his chin, said, "There you are Mrs. Adams. We have our teams assembled in the OR. Dr. BrownEyes sent me to look for you. Guess we've had a communication glitch. An orderly should have brought you to us." With those words, he wheeled my gurney through a few hallways and into the darkened operating room.

There were a dozen people, all latex-gloved, masked, capped, and wearing surgical paper booties. Staff carefully transferred my body to the operating table. Dr. BrownEyes emerged from the clustered conversations. He briskly walked over with bent elbows, his arms, upright in a sterile position. Over his shoulder, he said, "Mary, your myelogram is showing a 98% blockage. Are you ready? We barely caught this in time."

"Yes."

A voice from the darkness, asked, "What about Dr. BeachBoy? Should we wait?"

"No. He has to re-scrub." Dr. BrownEyes said to the anesthetist, "Proceed."

With the mask over my nose and mouth, my voice counted off, "100, 99, 98...." as I drifted into blackness.

When I woke up, I was in a hospital room. To my left a roommate; beyond her, a window revealed a crisp September sky. Chunky clouds lingered. I became aware of the texture of the sheets. *I'm alive.*

Like my scoliosis surgery, I was tethered in all directions. A Foley catheter extracted urine, IVs in both arms, and another port drained blood from the site of the incision. Both of my legs, from the ankle to the knee, were encased in large, cloudy-plastic compression boots that inflated and deflated as a machine pumped. A nurse said, "To prevent blood clots. Bed rolls? Oh, no. That's old school. Where did you have surgery?" I strained to see my tippy toes barely sticking out. In response to my brain's question, they moved. *Thank you, Jesus.*

Later that morning, Dr. BrownEyes entered my room. Smiling, he said, "The laminectomy was a complete success. Impending paralysis has been reversed. Any questions before I continue?"

"Yes, inside my legs it feels like I'm being struck by lightning, electrocuted, repeatedly. Is that from the boots?"

"No. What you're describing are the nerves in your legs coming back to life. They had been compressed due to the impingement. This is good news." Before I could ask, he anticipated my next question: "The sensation will go away."

Dr. BrownEyes pulled up a chair, sat down. "However, we had an unexpected finding."

"Oh right, did the MRI loosen my Harrington rods?" I already knew there was some complication. My sister had called that morning with the news: "You were in surgery eleven hours, not the anticipated four."

"A bit more than that, I'm afraid. Our pre-op plan was to fuse you at two levels. However, when we opened you up, we discovered gross mobility. Your fusion from 1983 completely failed, at seven levels."

"Doctor that makes no sense, I've had plenty of x-rays following that surgery. There was 'fusion mass', nine levels, from T7 to L4."

"Yes, the marrow solidified, however, did not bridge the vertebrae at those levels. Motion segments aren't always obvious on film. We had to re-do the fusion from your scoliosis surgery."

"Is that why surgery lasted eleven hours?"

"Yes. We also fused nine levels, but from T10 to the sacrum, inclusive of the extra lumbar, birth-defect vertebra. Fusing the weak link should finally offer you some pain relief. Well, at least for that one specific area." He thoughtfully waited until I caught on.

Words from my light bulb moment erupted from my mouth. "Oh Doctor! You had to put in more hardware because of the long-spine fusion?"

"Yes, Mary, there was no choice. It's like those we removed. Rather than hooks they're secured with screws, a much more stable system for an adult spine."

"Doctor, how is it possible in seven years this was not discovered earlier?"

With a slight exhalation, he said, "That's a very good question."

Then I remembered, "Was there any harm from the MRI?"

"I'll put it to you this way, we're fortunate you were in surgery relatively soon after that test."

My brain was spinning with information overload.

He stood up, "I'll return later in the day. The nursing staff has clear instructions on your care. In a few days, I want you up, moving around."

"Wait. No bed rest, for ten days, like my scoliosis surgery in1983?"

"No, research has proven bed rest contributes to muscle atrophy. Do you have any other questions?"

"No."

"I'll be in to see you later. If you think of anything else, we'll talk about it then." As he exited, Dr. BrownEyes turned slightly and said, "I personally counted all the instruments, before and after surgery. Then I had my staff count, twice. You'll have no souvenirs this time."

"Thank you, Doctor."

Within days my hospital room filled with a rainbow of color from all the flowers and latex balloons. Friends and family arrived. On each visit, I hugged Cameron. *I made it, everything will be okay now.* Within days, I was walking a few steps in my room, then the hallway with my walker.

I quickly advanced to solo victory laps on my floor. The nursing staff cheered as I passed their station. "Way to go." "You're doing great." "A year from now, you'll be running a marathon." I beamed with joy.

With happiness to spare I called out and waved, "Hello," to other patients as I ambled past, pushing my walker. Almost all returned my wave, except for one elderly, frail, grey-haired woman. On my next trip I noticed her crying softly. She didn't have any visitors. At her hallway doorway, I asked, "Would you like some company?"

"Why, yes, dear, that would be nice. My family lives out of town. I've had multiple surgeries on my hips."

We shared our reasons for being patients, my second spine surgery and her third hip replacement. She'd had several complications, from infection to hardware failure. She was clutching an old, worn-out teddy bear, and asked, "Sweetie, would you mind holding my hand?" Her chilly, bony-thin appendage with protruding veins, felt foreign to my touch.

"Oh, thank you. That's the hardest thing about being alone without family or visitors, the loss of a loving touch. I do have Franklin here." She cradled the stuffed animal. "He helps with the loneliness. You're too young to have these problems." She squeezed my hand. "Do you have a stuffed animal to cuddle, for the lonely days."

"My family and friends visit."

"The day will come, when they'll all tire of your medical problems."

Doesn't she realize? All of mine are gone.

She continued, "And may I give you some more free advice, my dear?"

"Sure."

"You need to cry. You've been through a ghastly ordeal. I can see you're holding everything inside. I know you had to be brave, but now you need to let go."

"I'm okay."

As she reached over and squeezed the back of my hand, I flinched. With her watery-blue eyes she looked over the top of her silver-rimmed glasses. "If you don't cry on the outside, Sweetie, you'll drown on the inside. I know."

"I don't need to cry. I'm okay. Really, I am. Everything is fine now." I realized the handholding was for me, not her.

One-week post-op, I again pushed my walker down the hallway to visit my new hospital buddy. In her room, I leaned, half-seated against the edge of her bed, while we laughed and chatted. Suddenly there was a lightning bolt sharp sensation deep inside my lower back.

Immediately nauseated, I started to sweat profusely. In minutes my entire face and hair were dripping wet. "I have to leave, my back ...." As I attempted to stand up, I shrieked with a stabbing, ripping sensation. My new friend didn't hesitate, she rang for the nurse. In those few minutes, before the nurse arrived, my hospital gown was soaked from sweat. Even with the nurse's help I couldn't walk. She quickly returned with a wheelchair, wheeled me to my room. "The head nurse has made a STAT call to your surgeon. He'll respond quickly. He's adamant about the post-surgical care of his patients. Not all surgeons are like that."

After she left, I remained motionless. I tried to breathe as shallowly as possible. Thankfully, the nursing staff and Dr. BrownEyes took my sudden onset of symptoms seriously. Within minutes the floor's head nurse came into my room, introduced herself. "Dr. BrownEyes doesn't want you moved. Radiology is bringing up a portable x-ray machine and a technician, to your room."

Within fifteen minutes the tests were finished. My roommate complained bitterly to staff. "Remove that noisy machine. What makes her so special?" I ignored her.

Soon Dr. BrownEyes trudged into my room. I was relieved that he came in person. Then wondered, *Is the news too serious to be relayed by a nurse?*

My mind scrambled to decipher a peculiar look on his face. His skin color was an ashen-grey. When he removed his glasses for a moment to rub his eyes, they looked glossy.

"Mary, may I sit on the edge of your bed?" As he has not done this in the past seven days, it felt both comforting and alarming. He sat near my feet and crossed his long grasshopper legs, his lab coat trailed over his grey pants. His shoes were impeccably clean, their soles well-worn, no doubt from hours standing in the operating room.

"Mary, we have a complication. The x-rays are showing a malfunction of the hardware we installed. The rods have broken free from the screws. We must take you into surgery immediately. They are preparing the OR as we speak." I bit my bottom lip. He continued, "As we are a teaching hospital, and your case is unusual, we had filmed your surgery. A dozen of us, including department heads, have reviewed this film with specific attention to the instrumentation.

"Consensus among all of us is the same. It appears each step was flawless. There were no surgical errors." He paused. Leaned forward, closed his eyes for a split second, and rubbed his forehead with his fingertips. I noticed the cursive royal blue embroidery of his name on his glaring white, starch-stiffened lab coat. A dangling loose thread, from the last letter of the abbreviation "Dr." had come undone.

He continued, "As we are at a loss for an explanation, on a hunch, I put in an emergency call to the manufacturer of the stainless-steel rods. My suspicions have been confirmed. They checked the serial numbers. A defective batch was shipped to us. They're flying in a rep to pick up the hardware we remove from your body."

His last words were surreal.

With thumb and ring-finger widely stretched, Dr. BrownEyes adjusted his glasses from the bottom rim of their frames. He bent his neck forward, rested tight fingertips over his mouth. In an instant, he straightened his shoulders, stood up. "Alright, let's proceed."

"Now? Wait! I need to call my husband." Frightened, I nervously rattled off irrelevant information. "His mother flew in last night. I asked him to take vacation days to stay home with our son. She flew up to help him. He called. They're going out to breakfast. Take Cameron to the playground, the good one by the mall, then here to visit." I peeked at the wall clock, "They'll be here in fifteen minutes. Can't we wait?"

A gurney appeared. There were five or six grim-looking employees, all staring at the floor, including Dr. BeachBoy.

"No. Mary, we can't wait."

"I'll call the house. Leave a message on the answering machine."

"No. This is urgent. Your spinal cord is in jeopardy."

The head nurse walked over to my bed. "I can assure you; I'll personally advise your family of the situation when they arrive."

Dr. BrownEyes continued, "These people are hand-picked. They'll ensure your safety while being transferred to the operating room and stay with you until the surgical team takes over."

I felt comforted. *He remembered.* I had told him about the orderly, after the myelogram.

Dr. BrownEyes waved in the rest of the staff. Without making a sound, they entered. To them, he said, "The OR is on stand-by waiting for us. My other surgeries have been cancelled for the day. Security is holding the staff elevator for direct transport. I'm leaving now to scrub in with the surgical team. I'll meet you in the OR. Don't bump anything or jostle her."

As he strode out, staff circled my hospital bed. The head nurse decisively ordered, "On three, people." She counted off, "Okay, one, two, three. Lift." They transferred my body to the gurney.

The second emergency surgery was a success, but the recovery plan was greatly altered. Dr. BrownEyes said, "You'll have to stay in the hospital a couple more weeks. We had to upgrade to a more complex hardware system. In addition to two vertical rods, we used three horizontal stabilization rods along with larger screws."

"Was this another eighteen-inch incision?"

"Yes, I'm afraid so."

I never saw the elderly woman again. *Was she discharged? Moved elsewhere in the hospital? Or was I on a different floor?* Her predictions started to unfold. There were fewer visitors. My mother was the first to bail. She said, "I can't visit you here anymore. It's too hard for me to pull my girdle on and off. I'll be at your house the day you get home from the hospital." She gently kissed my forehead and left.

When I questioned my sister Judy, she said, "Mom can't handle seeing you in the hospital. It really upsets her."

Evenings and nights were the worst. I couldn't sleep with the beeping machines and hallway lights. I would drift in and out of awareness, *where am I? Why am I here?* Extreme sweating—my hair sopping wet as if I had showered—

alternated with non-stop chills, and uncontrollable shaking. I appreciated the nurses who came in every few hours to change my gown and sheets.

It was 2:30 a.m. I was wide awake, lonely, confused. *Why did this happen to me? Why all these surgeries?* In despair I called my sister. "I have work in the morning! Don't call me in the middle of the night!" She hung up. I burst into tears, and at that moment a nurse walked into my room. "Oh! Wow! You're soaked through, again. We almost need a bucket to ring out your gown and sheets they're so wet. Let's get you into a dry gown. That will help you stop shaking.

"Why am I sweating like this? Am I dying?"

"No. All your labs and vitals look good. I'll admit it's not typical. I've been a nurse for twenty years. It's rare, but I have encountered this before. I have a theory. It's your personal physiology. Your metabolism is revved up from the trauma of your surgeries. Your body doesn't know the difference between a skilled surgeon and being knifed in an alley. Your body is trying to heal as quickly as possible."

My teeth chattered. "Is it going to stop?"

"Yes. You know what you need? A non-hospital related object to see and touch. I've been working on my family scrapbook and brought it in to show my coworkers. Would you like to look through it, even though you won't know anyone? It'll take your mind off things."

"Yes. That sounds wonderful. Thank you."

The thick, dainty-daisy, fabric-covered, photo album had a cupid-shaped peephole cover revealing a loving family. The coarse texture against my fingertips and colorful floral pattern seemed to reset all my senses. There were pages of smiling faces, picnics, birthdays, and holidays. I even found comfort in the shininess and feel of the smooth, clear plastic sheets. I started to hand the album back to her, she said, "Keep it for my full shift. I need to check on my other patients. Would you like to chat later if I have time?"

"Yes, that would be really nice."

When she returned, she pulled up a chair and sat. "Do you mind me asking, how did you end up being a patient here? Your chart is showing some extremely serious injuries."

"I don't know why I'm here. My scoliosis surgery from 1983…problems." With those words, the memory of the SICU morphine overdose came into my thoughts. When I finished telling her, I felt the warmth of a compassionate human. Her eyes narrowed. Lips tightened. I noticed her subtle movements and was afraid I offended her.

With a deep, long, drawn-out sigh, she commented. "I'm familiar with what you described."

"Did the overdose cause loss of vision? I kept touching my eyes, they were open. I'm sure of it."

"No. You were that close to death. Hearing is the last of our senses to stop functioning. I'm so sorry that happened to you. I've worked in hospitals like that. Nothing in your medical records will acknowledge their error. You're a real survivor." She blinked her eyes. "I have to look in on my other patients." She handed her photo album over to me, again. "As you look through the pictures, imagine being at those occasions. It'll help to shift your thoughts to the future, rather than the past."

That photo album, her wisdom, and consolation over past events, was a pivotal point in my recovery.

The next morning, daylight, curtains open. Sparkling clean windows revealed a gloriously blue sky.

Aaron brought two-year old Cameron for daily visits—moving my IVs, EKG, and Foley lines—so my son would cuddle in the crook of my arm, after a side-swiped kiss. Each day my son brought another one of his stuffed animals: his teddy bear, turtle, and dog were a huge comfort, especially when I was alone. They had the *essence* of his scent, his bedroom, and home.

I knew everything would be okay. I was Cam's mom. *He needs me. I can do this for him.*

Smoke Signals

Soon after that night a nurse changing bandages on my incision exclaimed, "That's odd. You have a first-degree burn along both sides of your entire incision. Everywhere the tape touched your skin. If I didn't know better, I'd say that was an allergic reaction."

"Tape?"

"The muscle underneath was sutured with dissolving thread. The skin was closed using sticky adhesive strips."

"My back has been incredibly itchy. Could it be—."

"No. It's not the tape. I'll have Dr. BeachBoy write for something." She replaced the sticky latex strips.

When I broke out in massive hives, the staff assumed it was an allergic reaction to the "something" drug, so they added a second medication. When I started wheezing, they added a third drug, to off-set what they assumed were the side effects from the second drug. The hives, itching, and wheezing intensified. Staff continued to re-apply the adhesive latex strips.

Dr. BrownEyes had a different take on things. "We have to trust what we see, more than what we know." He stapled the length of my incision. No more sticky strips.

All my symptoms disappeared. *Was I allergic to the tape?* When I discontinued the three unnecessary drugs, their actual side-effects dissipated, too.

When a weekend nurse came on shift, she listened for bowel sounds with her stethoscope. It had been a week since the second emergency surgery. She paged through my chart. "Why aren't you on a stool softener? Your resident doesn't have any orders written."

"They give me a handful of pills. I take them. I don't ask questions. Now that you mention it, for my surgery in 1983, staff made a big deal about the importance of a stool softener."

"Didn't anyone tell you the effect of narcotics on the bowels?"

"No."

"This could be a problem."

That turned out to be the understatement of the year. When the cramping and spasms started, it felt like hard labor during childbirth. I was in anguish. The same nurse told me, "Your bowels are impacted. We're coming up on the 3 p.m. shift in a few hours. The next shift will have to handle this. And they'll have to do rounds first. So, it might take a while."

By 6:00 p.m. I was convinced I was giving birth to an elephant. I think the dejected nurse who arrived had drawn the short straw. She told me, "The fecal material has dried up inside of you like cement. There is only one way to remove it. I'll have to dig it out with my fingers."

"You can't be serious."

"It's that or an emergency surgery to open up that section of your bowel."

Despite the monstrous embarrassment, I agreed. "Take me off all the narcotics. I'll tough it out." I felt exasperated that a simple oversight could potentially result in a third emergency surgery.

Days passed. I had strange cravings after going off the narcotics. I fantasized about attaching my IV to an industrial-sized coffee machine. The craving for caffeine seemed odd, until I remembered an organic chemistry class from my pre-pharmacy college days: *morphine, caffeine, and nicotine are all alkaloids, in the same "feel-good" chemical family.*

An unknown resident entered my room. When he leaned over me with his stethoscope, I spotted a pack of cigarettes inside his opened lab coat. I motioned, "Hey, can I bum a cigarette from you?"

He seemed embarrassed, hurriedly pulled his jacket tightly closed. "You'll have to ask your surgeon."

As my former addiction called to me, it was ironic that the odor of those scores of burning chemicals, which had repulsed me as a non-smoker, now beckoned like an evil genie in a bottle. I obsessed over the memory: the touch of the smooth plastic wrapper, the sound of crinkling cellophane when opening a new pack, the acrid smell of a match on a closed matchbook cover.

Later the same day, I asked Dr. BrownEyes. "It's okay if I smoke one cigarette, right?"

"No."

"Why not?"

"Research has proven that nicotine inhibits fusion mass from healing."

I imagined igniting the straw from my iced tea as I took it out of my glass. "I don't need science right now."

"Mary, you have a history of a failed fusion. We can't take any chances."

"On the day prior to my surgery in 1983 I smoked an entire pack while a patient in the hospital. Their staff said it didn't matter as I had already donated my own blood."

"There appear to be several irregularities with your original scoliosis surgery." I saw his grin as he watched me holding the straw between the first two fingers of my right hand, as if a cigarette.

"I've got it!" I snapped my fingers and pointed at him. "Second-hand smoke isn't a problem, okay to hang out in one of the waiting rooms for a while?"

"We didn't used to think so, but the latest studies—."

"Oh, come on! You know half of your staff smoke, right? Even on this floor in the employee lounge. You can smell the smoke all the way down the hallway."

I came up with one last-ditch plea. "You know, Doctor, patient morale is integral to healing." My eyebrows arched up, pleading.

Dr. BrownEyes said, "You win. Let's go."

"Where?"

"To the employee lounge, I'll give you ten minutes. Inhale as much second-hand smoke as you like. Only this once, Mary, don't ask me again."

"Thank you so much, Doctor!"

Dr. BrownEyes pushed my wheelchair down the hall. "Give me a second. Staff needs to be informed, first." When he wheeled me in, he seemed to linger. *Inhaling, Doctor?* I chuckled to myself. My surgeon then introduced me to a mature woman with a stern look. "Mary, this is Nurse Anna. She has strict orders. She'll take you to your room in ten, not eleven, ten minutes."

He left. More than twenty employees packed the tiny room. The staffs' uniforms represented every profession possible, from doctor, to nurse, and even a respiratory therapist—wait, that was *my* respiratory therapist—in their LA smog of an employee lounge. My eyes teared. The cloud of smoke was intense. I was in druggie heaven. Without any shame, I tilted my head backwards, nostrils flared, as I inhaled as much smoke as possible. Then a light bulb moment: *Oh, someone here will let me bum an entire cigarette. Hal-le-lu-jah! Hallelujah! Hallelujah!* In my imagination I heard the Mormon Tabernacle Choir.

I scanned their faces: Mr. Hardcore Professional, Ms. Seasoned Social-Worker, and Mr. Wouldn't Share. Then I spotted a young, naïve face—a student's uniform. I rolled my wheelchair up to her and sincerely asked.

The entire room exploded in laughter, and in unison responded. "NO, Ms. Adams!"

Nurse Anna walked over, patted my shoulder, "Sorry, dear, Dr. BrownEyes warned us you would try to bum a cigarette." She squinted at her watch. "He said he smoked as an undergrad. He totally understands the addiction. You have eight minutes left."

Almost a month had passed since I'd been admitted at the end of September. Halloween approached. My sister, Judy, shopped for me, bought a white rabbit outfit for Cameron. Aaron was disappointed, "What, no superhero costume?"

Soon to be discharged, my happiness permeated the hospital room. It was as if the shiny metal handrails on my bed, glass in the windowpane, and even floor and ceiling tiles responded to an unknown frequency and softly vibrated with the power of the phrase, *I'm going home.*

I closed my eyes as I imagined the absolute joy of walking into my home, the comfort of my husband's arms holding me tight at night, drifting off to sleep in our own bed, our colorful sheets. I beamed when I imagined my son, Cameron, in his normal environment—toy cars, toddler books, and stuffed animals—not watching him climb the metal rails of a hospital bed to visit me. I'd missed my dogs, too. I'd be able to pet them. I couldn't stop smiling.

The day prior to my release, Dr. BrownEyes entered my room, pulled up a chair, and sat beside my bed. Usually, he stood when on rounds. "We need to go over your discharge instructions. They're quite lengthy. Mary, I'm afraid you're in for a very long recovery. You should write these down." He motioned to my note-taking system.

I reeled in the string of yarn, like a fishing line, tied to my bedrail. The pink strand was attached to the full-sized spiral-bound notebook, along with a pen, that Judy had bought and tied up for me. She suggested I write down physician instructions and anything that came to mind. Later she teased the quantity. "What is this? War and Peace?"

My favorite Confucius quote, "Pale ink is better than the most retentive memory" came from a booklet on "Chinese Proverbs" that my father had passed down to me when in high school. As a teen I thought I was terribly clever to underline that quote—in pale blue ink.

Now 33 years old in October, 1990, I was more than content to write down my recovery instructions.

Dr. BrownEyes, said, "First, I see you're wearing your hard plastic back brace. You'll need to wear it 24 hours a day for the next nine months to a year. The second leg-brace attachment immobilizes your hip joint, making it impossible for you to sit. It's to remain locked for the upcoming six months.

"During the first three months of your convalescence, you're not to leave your home, except for your return visit here for staple removal, ten days from now." He looked intently at my face.

"I can't wait to walk into my house, to be with my family, in our home. So, that's fine with me."

He continued, "The first month you'll need 24-hour bed rest. You're not to leave your bedroom for any reason. I'm afraid that means the use of a bed pan for toiletry needs.

I frowned. *No, I don't think so.*

"The second month, with a walker, you'll be permitted into the other rooms of your house. The hip attachment must remain locked. If you tolerate that, I'll release you to attempt a few steps outside, only in your backyard, during your third month of confinement. Again, hip locked, with the use of a walker, and someone to help you."

My stomach dropped. *I thought I was okay.*

Dr. BrownEyes continued, "Beginning the fourth month, hopefully by the end of February or early March, you may leave your home, for brief outings. If more than twenty or thirty feet, have a family member push you in wheelchair. Make that a reclining wheelchair since you won't be able to sit upright for half a year. Don't push yourself, that's too much stress for your upper spine fusion."

In complete denial, and desperate for a toehold of hope about my recovery, I asked, "When can I drive again?"

"I appreciate your enthusiasm. However, it's critical for this fusion mass to heal. Driving isn't an option until April at the earliest. You won't be able to sit upright until then anyway, due to the locked hip attachment."

"Oh, right." *No sitting for six months?* I shook my head. *How am I going to do this?*

A nurse walked in. "Oh, sorry Doctor, I didn't know you were still here." She did an abrupt about-face and left.

The brief interruption gave me a moment to think. *I'm going home. That's all that matters. We'll figure out the rest later.* Uncertainty and fears returned: *How will I care for an active toddler? Bathe him? Take him to the playground?*

I asked, "How long before I can pick up my son?"

"Let's leave that open-ended for now."

"I'm confused. In 1983 we didn't immobilize my hip. They took marrow then. I returned to work in two months. And since I had an office job, I was seated eight hours a day. Why is this different?"

"We're a teaching hospital. We rely on statistics. Sitting puts phenomenal pressure on the lumbar spine. We're taking all precautions. You can't equate these surgeries to your original scoliosis surgery. That would be like comparing the Wright Brothers' first airplane to the space shuttle."

I didn't question him. He must have noticed my frown.

"Mary, don't forget, in addition to everything else your spine went through three complete sets of hardware in one week."

My thoughts ricocheted. "I don't need the bed pan. My bedroom is only ten feet from either bathroom."

"And that makes it twenty feet round-trip. That's too far a distance for you to walk for your condition."

"It will set a bad example for my son. He was potty trained before I went into the hospital, but, has...." My eyebrows arched up, begging for him to give in on this topic.

"All right, how can I disagree with that argument?" He chuckled, "As long as you don't remind me about the importance of patient morale." He stopped for a minute and wrote on his notepad. "You might need a hospital bed."

"I want to sleep in my own bed."

"All right. However, except for bathroom trips, I don't want you out of bed until Thanksgiving. This fusion must heal."

"Understood."

"Did the Urology Department contact you with the date of your neurogenic bladder surgery? You tested positive for nerve damage from your spinal cord trauma."

"Yes, January. They want to wait until I'm three months post-op from the spine surgeries."

Dr. BrownEyes stood, rested his hand on the back of the chair. "One more item. After the first month, I want you to wear a spinal stimulator over your brace. It places an electro-magnetic field through your body to promote bone growth. Although still an experimental device, your insurance company agreed to cover the bulk of the cost. Any questions before I leave?"

"Yes, when do I start physical therapy? Rehab? Job training? Dr. BeachBoy said additional schooling would train me for work less stressful than an office job. When do I start those things? Maybe, I could finally finish my bachelor's degree at UF."

"Dr. BeachBoy is a resident and he's still learning. There's no longer any need for those services. The second surgery has really set us back for recovery. I've written orders for one PT session, to teach you to navigate your walker over the threshold entry of your home." He handed me his business card. "Like I said, you're in for a long recovery. If you have any concerns whatsoever, please call me. This is my direct number."

I'm going home, that's all that matters. "Doctor, thank you, for everything you've done for me." I reached for an unread paperback book, vision too blurry to read, and tucked the card safely between the pages, confident it wouldn't be necessary.

"Dr. BeachBoy will be in later this afternoon. He'll provide you with the appropriate prescriptions for your discharge tomorrow." He shook my hand. "Good luck. I'll see you in ten days when I remove your staples, after that, not until January, prior to your bladder surgery."

Hours later, my husband arrived. I brought him up to speed on my recovery plan, while he spun through channels with the TV remote, looking for "the game."

"Aaron, are you listening? This is important."

"Yeah, I heard you."

Dr. BeachBoy entered, "You ready to go home?" To my husband, he fanned out five prescriptions like a fortune-teller's game of chance. With the first one, "This is for her narcotics. You can use our pharmacy downstairs, today. So, you'll have them for tomorrow." Aaron's eyes were glued to the TV behind the doctor. Dr. BeachBoy continued, "When you or other family members are unavailable, this one is for a nurse's aide, the third for a hospital bed—."

I interrupted, "Dr. BrownEyes said I could sleep in my own bed. I already discussed this with him."

"Of course, that's your call. I would want to sleep in my own bed, too. It's better to have the script, though. In case you want the hospital bed later. Then you won't have the delay of contacting us first. I don't want to forget any of your prescriptions this time." He winked. I knew he meant the forgotten stool softener orders.

"These last two Mary won't need until spring when her confinement ends. This one is for a reclining wheelchair so you or a family member can take her out of the house, for brief outings, not longer than thirty minutes, while pushing her. No walking yet. Lastly, here's the paperwork to obtain a disabled parking permit, for when she's able to sit upright again, and hopefully drive herself. Best wishes to both of you. My rotation at this hospital is up. I won't be here when you return."

Soon after, Aaron left. He gave me a peck on the cheek, "I'd better go, get things ready for your homecoming."

Later that evening there was a lot of laughter in my room. I was joking around with anyone who came in. The cleaning woman remarked, "I bet your family is going to have a great big party for you when you get home. There'll be tons of flowers, and balloons everywhere, like that homecoming parade downtown."

Young nurses' aides echoed the same comments. "I'm sure your husband is planning a big welcome home party." Another said, "They'll hide all the cars. Everyone will pile into one car, so you won't get suspicious. That's how my family surprised me when I had knee surgery."

Does staff know something I don't? After the last nurse left my room, I called my husband, "Hey, no surprise party tomorrow, immediate family only. Okay? All I want is to be able to walk into our home, lie on our bed. You filled the pain pill prescription, right?"

"Homerun!" he yelled. I pulled the phone away from my ear. I heard a full-volume baseball game on the TV in the background.

"Did you hear me?"

"Yeah, don't worry about it. Come on, I'm trying to watch the game. World Series. I took care of all of them."

We hung up. I paused and wondered, *all of them*? I picked up the receiver to dial back, then decided against interrupting the game again. *Right, it's October. Winter is coming. Months have passed since my first fall in August.*

133

My focus shifted to the solitary, last remaining vase of "to cheer you" half-dead, roses, on the stand across from the foot of my bed. Both housekeeping and the nurses had repeatedly asked for days, "Okay, to throw those out?"

"No, those were from my husband."

My last visitor that night was the nurse who'd lent me her family photo album. She carried an expensive looking crystal vase with a dozen vibrant red roses. The vase sparkled. "The other nurses and I took up a collection. We all decided you need a replacement." She tilted her head towards the ones from my husband. "Okay to toss now?"

"Well, okay."

"I bet there will be a whole house full of flowers when you arrive home tomorrow. We wanted you to have these, from the nursing staff. We all know the ordeal you've gone through. We collected too much money. Rather than multiple bouquets, harder to carry, I opted for a higher quality vase. A gift from all of us. Please know we're all cheering for you, and your best possible recovery."

"Thank you, they're so beautiful." I gushed, "They'll be the first thing I see when I wake up in my own bed tomorrow morning." I deeply appreciated their thoughtfulness.

She squeezed my hand before she left. "Keep fighting, no matter what happens."

"I'm going home. I'm all better now. There aren't any more battles to fight."

Her smile faded.

Homecoming Parade

The next day my husband arrived. I gushed about the gift from the nursing staff as he watched the game on TV. After we ate the subs he brought for lunch, he held the wheelchair until I was seated. With my cross-shoulder, overnight bag strapped around his body, he partially wheeled me into the hallway.

Over my shoulder, "Aaron, hand me the roses. I can carry them on my lap. Aren't they beautiful? I love the vase."

The TV blared. "...bases loaded."

"I'll take care of it."

Clunk. Behind me, I heard a heavy sound from the wastebasket in my room. "What was that noise?"

"Nothing...only the lunch wrappers." He cheered for his team on TV.

"Kind of loud to be paper...."

"We have to swing by the pharmacy downstairs to fill your prescription."

"I thought you did that yesterday. I'm not supposed to sit any longer than the drive home."

"Yeah, I didn't have time yesterday."

Once home, there was an unknown, beat-up car parked in our circular driveway. My mother's car, a Buick, had been the family joke for years. When she'd first moved to Florida from Ohio, and was not yet familiar with a Southern accent, she'd been involved in a minor car accident. While the sheriff was filling out his report, he asked her, "Ma'am is your car mow-beel (mobile)?" All she heard were the vowels, thinking he said Oldsmobile. She answered, "No Officer, it's a Buick."

"Whose car is that?" I asked.

"The nurse's aide I hired."

My husband parked in our circular driveway, sprang out, and brought me the walker. I slowly turned my body, grabbed the ceiling strap with two hands, and inched over to the edge of the seat. Aaron steadied my walker for me.

Once standing, I locked my hip attachment, as instructed at the hospital. The dozen steps to the front door looked like a mile. My gait was like a slow-moving tin soldier. I had to take one step with my left foot, then swing my rigid right leg, in a semi-circle, while holding onto the walker.

Aaron opened the front door. I focused on scaling the four-inch threshold. *Conquered!* I stood in the foyer of my home, exhaled, looked up with a self-satisfied smile, waited for the "Surprise! Welcome home!" shout as Cameron toddler galloped with arms outstretched, for a "Mommy's home!" hug and kiss reunion.

The house was barren, dark, and cold. No one. Not my son. Not my mother. No flowers. Not even our dogs.

A mute, lifeless, reclining wheelchair, stood in front of me. Alarmed, I wondered *Where is everyone? Why is this here?*

I took a few steps into the family room; movement from the end of the hallway made me think Cameron was in his bedroom. With complete joy I craned my neck, leaning heavily on the walker, to see him. A strange woman walked out of our adjacent bedroom. Rail thin, wearing faded, ripped jeans and a crumpled T-shirt.

Stunned, I finally found my voice. "Where is everyone? Where's Cameron? My mother?

Aaron yelled, "Surprise! I got you a wheelchair!"

I couldn't breathe. I felt sucker punched. He continued, "You said no surprise party. I dropped him off at a friend's house. I told your mother not to come, since it was 'too much girdle trouble' for her to visit you in the hospital."

"Oh!" I swallowed my disappointment. "What's with the wheelchair? You know I'm not allowed out of the house until February or March. That's four months from now."

Aaron shrugged, "You might as well get used to it now, Mary."

In that instant I knew. He was done with me. But, for my sanity I had to deny what I knew to be the truth.

By then the strange woman had joined us. She smelled of stale cigarettes, her T-shirt had cigarette burn holes. Her long, emotionless face was framed by waist-length stringy, greasy hair. Without saying a word, she positioned herself behind the wheelchair as if to push someone.

"Who's this woman?"

"Linda."

"Who's Linda? What's she doing in our bedroom?"

"Hey, calm down. She's the nurse I hired. I told her to make your bed before you arrived."

My thoughts spun. *She looks like a vagrant. He left a stranger alone in our home, while we were in the hospital for hours. Did he give her a key? Was he here with her?* I ignored my thoughts, said, "My bed …?"

"Don't you remember? Yesterday, BeachBoy, the prescriptions? It's the hospital bed you wanted."

My homecoming can't be worse than the ordeal of the past few months. I squeezed my eyelids shut, then opened them, "Yeah, okay, sure, thanks. I know you meant well." I took a step forward with the walker, eyes glued to the floor, to maintain my balance. "Could one of you move the wheelchair out of my way? It's important to me that I walk into my home."

They both stood there like pillars of salt. My husband said, "Let Linda push you, that's her job."

I never felt more unloved and abandoned in my whole life. To escape the tidal wave of waterworks welling up, I had to keep walking. I struggled with the walker, not wanting to admit the carpeting was much more difficult than the tiled floors of the hospital. Ahead of me the last 10-feet of gold carpeting looked like the never-ending miles of the Sahara Desert.

My husband piped up, said, "Come on, Mary! Let Linda push you. It'll be faster that way. This is going to take forever."

Dryly I responded, "I'm not supposed to sit, remember?" An adrenaline surge of indignation moved my body forward. "I promised Dr. BrownEyes I could handle the walking distance to the bathroom. I might as well get used to *that* now." I couldn't hide the anger in my voice.

Almost there. One more step. You can do this. Near the hall bathroom, I stopped to take a break. Through the entry I saw a six-inch tall, white plastic, donut-shaped riser had been placed on the ceramic rim of the toilet. "Where's the portable commode with armrests? Like the one I trained on in the hospital?"

"Insurance won't pay for that style."

With one more excruciating step, I reached the threshold of our bedroom, utterly exhausted, physically, and emotionally, I stood there. There was "my" hospital bed. Our marital bed pushed to the far wall. The two were as far apart as possible. It was a struggle for me not to cry.

Linda roughly grabbed my arm and leg, as I gingerly climbed onto the hospital bed. Aaron sorted through items on his valet on our dresser. Without looking up, he said, "Linda can stay until 5 pm today. I'm going to run some errands, then grocery shopping. I'll pick Cameron up on the way home."

Incredulous, I shouted. "You're leaving?"

"Hey, I need a break. I've been coming to the hospital every day. I'm going to work in the morning."

"Tomorrow? You've been off work for almost a month. You can't spend one day with me?"

"It was your idea that I stay with Cameron."

"Yes, for one week. No one anticipated multiple surgeries. I thought we'd spend my whole first day home together, the three of us, as a family. Please, go pick up our son, bring him home. I really need to see him."

"Later, he's playing."

"Can't you stay a few minutes?"

He looked at his wristwatch. No answer.

My heart sank. "Could you at least bring the roses into the bedroom? Did you forget them in the pharmacy?"

"No. I threw them out. I couldn't carry the suitcase and push you in your wheelchair. I tossed them in the garbage can in your room, on the way out."

"That's what that noise was! Why would you do that? Those kind, wonderful nurses are going to think I threw away their gift. How could you? I offered to hold them on my lap."

"You threw out the flowers I gave you." He shrugged, "What's the difference?" With a quick peck on the cheek, he left. The front door slammed shut.

The next morning, Cameron galloped into my bedroom, as he gleefully announced, "Mommy's home!" He climbed my hospital bed railing. With my arms around his little shoulders, I held on tight.

Linda arrived, "I need to change the sheets."

"I haven't even been home 24-hours."

"That's my job." When she finished, after I climbed back in, my toes were squashed almost *en pointe*, ballerina style under the top sheet. Linda refused to loosen. "They must be tight enough to bounce off a quarter. That's how I was trained." She left the room.

Cameron and I devised a scheme. He scooted underneath the top sheet, stealth mode, and at the corner pushed upwards. It loosened, somewhat. "Good enough. Thanks, Cameron." I was able to wiggle my toes.

When I couldn't bend, due to the brace, to remove my socks, Cameron again burrowed under the sheet, tugged them off. Without any toys in the room, I used my socks to improvise a puppet show for my son. As the day wore on my two-year-old son scampered back-and-forth to his room, brought his books, puzzles, and little cars to my hospital bed for us to play with.

From the living room of our 1,600 square-foot-house, I heard maximum-volume soap operas, hour-after-hour, from that TV. Linda had made it clear: her only job was replacing sheets and food delivery—previously prepared by my husband—three times a day. When I asked if she could bring Cameron his lunch, she refused. "My agency doesn't provide childcare."

At first, I followed her orders, "You can feed him off of your plate." Then I realized if I asked her to bring the Ninja Turtle plated food and juice box my husband had readied for Cameron, she didn't recite company policy. She did agree to bring my son's diapers so I could change him.

On my own for my bathroom trips, without the leverage of a commode armrest to push against, I stumbled, as I tried to stand upright with only a non-locking walker to lean against. The donut seat riser fell to the floor. I lurched against the counter.

My mother arrived late that afternoon for a couple of hours. I pointed to the pile of sheets on the floor. "Mom, can you throw those in the washing machine? Linda doesn't do laundry. Aaron will be tired when he comes home from work."

"I don't know how to use your machine. Show me."

"I'm not allowed out of bed, for a month, remember? The knobs are simple. I can explain."

"No, I came to visit with you."

I closed my eyes tight, and sighed, "Okay."

After my mother left, hours went by, no Linda. When she eventually showed up, I asked, "Where have you been? I've been calling you?"

"I go outside. Your husband said not to smoke in the house, because of his lungs."

Aaron called the agency, furious, "Get someone out here who knows how to do their job, and make sure it's a non-smoker. I have asthma." When he hung up, he said to me, "I bought you a long extension cord, so the phone reaches your hospital bed. I don't have time to make these calls. Call the insurance company yourself tomorrow and tell them this donut thing is worthless. They need to pay for the kind you need. And tell them, there's no one here to help you. You're on your own."

When I called the insurance company, I explained the severity of my surgeries, the spinal cord impingement from the CES, thinking it made a difference. The clerk answered, "You're only 33 years old. The portable commodes with handles are for elderly patients."

I insisted, "That's what I trained on in the hospital. I can't stand without it to lean on. I can't risk a fall."

"You could pay out of pocket."

We hung up. I dialed the medical supply store. The adult-sized version of my toddler's potty-chair was delivered that afternoon. The two sat directly across from each other in the hall bathroom.

Pinch Hitters

Ten days passed. My sister Judy took me to have the staples removed. The resident's replacement positioned my post-surgical x-rays up on the monitor. I almost passed out. It looked like scaffolding at a construction site. The half-dozen screws were large enough that I could count the threads. I was petrified.

The new resident was also surprised. "I didn't know x-rays magnify the size of the screws."

Judy dryly responded, "They're not magnified. Those are two-inch screws." When he turned away, she made a face, while she crossed her eyes.

Dr. BrownEyes arrived and proceeded to remove the staples from my incision. I asked him, "My mother wants to know how many stitches I have."

"If I had to make an estimate, the tissue beneath the staples, I'd say about a 1,000."

Judy interjected, "Tell Mom, it was a 100."

While driving, I asked my sister, "Should I take one of the pain pills once home? I haven't taken any yet since being released, I don't want to get impacted, again."

"No. You'll end up a drug addict. You're out of the hospital, you don't need narcotics anymore."

That night I cried, unable to cope with the pain from the physical exertion of the day. Aaron slammed the bathroom cabinet shut, carried the pills in his open palm along with a glass of water. He grumbled, "You're taking these. Now! Why do you listen to your sister?"

I reluctantly agreed. Within an hour, I felt deliriously drugged, weird, woozy, like the whole world was fading in and out and spinning at the same time. The morphine and then the lesser narcotics, in the hospital, only took the edge off the pain.

"I feel strange. This isn't the way the drug made me feel in the hospital."

"It's supposed to make you feel weird."

"No, it's not. Where did you have this filled?"

"The hospital pharmacy, we picked it up on the way out the day you were discharged. Don't you remember?"

I forgot. *Let's not talk about that day.*

"Bring the bottle. I want to see the label."

He handed me the bottle from the medicine cabinet, returned to his bed, plopped down, and channeled through sporting events.

The label on the bottle listed 60 mg, as expected. Luckily, one of my guardian-angel nurses had taught me a valuable lesson. "Make it your habit to look at your pills, not only labels. Know what they're supposed to look like."

I dumped a few into my palm. "Aaron, these aren't the same pills!"

"Sure, they are. They're from the hospital. It's your imagination." He returned his attention to his TV.

I called the hospital's pharmacy. After being put on hold, the tech returned with a light, happy, voice. "Sorry about that. Looks like someone picked up the manufacturer's bottle and slapped your label on top. Peel it off, does it say 180 mg?"

"Yes."

"Some of our drugs are pre-packaged. Guess they misread the script. You should contact your doctor. He'll need to call in a new prescription with the correct dosage. We've already recorded this bottle as being dispensed. There are no refills. Throw that bottle out. Plus, start drinking large quantities of water. If your condition worsens from the overdose, go to the Emergency Room, especially if you start vomiting. Even with a new script hold off taking any pain pills for a few days. A narcotic overdose is hard on the liver and kidneys."

We hung up. I shared the distressing news. Aaron jumped up, "I'll get you a glass of water."

It was a rough night. The next day, I remembered Dr. BrownEyes' business card. Late Saturday night, I left him a message, hoping mine would be first in the queue for Monday morning.

When the phone rang at 8:00 a.m. Sunday morning, I snatched the handset before it could wake my husband. With amazement and delight I recognized the male voice on the other end of the line. Dr. BrownEyes said, "I've notified the proper department heads about the overdose error. I'm so sorry that happened.

"This morning, I spoke with a pharmacist friend of mine. We've put our heads together and have come up with a plan. Along with the correct lower dose mild narcotic I'm prescribing an antihistamine. Trials have shown that when taken together the allergy med will boost the narcotic effect, without increasing the actual drug in your body. How do you feel about this approach?"

"Yes. Thank you. I can't believe you called on your day off. Thank you! Thank you!"

That Monday, my mom arrived in a downpour. I didn't tell her about the overdose. She stood looking out the windows of my bedroom while the blustering storm raged, and torrential rains fell. Cameron scrambled up his father's bed to join her. Together they sang, "Rain, rain, go away...come again another day."

"Mom, can you bring a diaper and wipes?"

"We used cloth diapers when you were little."

"This is what we use now-a-days. Can you try to find them?"

As our conversation bounced back and forth, so did Cameron's eyes, like someone watching a tennis match. He was munching his pacifier with increasing speed. He bounded off the bed, returned, dragged the package of diapers, and handed them to me. My toddler son had the weight of the world on his little shoulders. His piercing brown eyes and old-soul face seemed to have taken it all in. Our eyes locked in solidarity. I think he knew the two of us were on our own. Our mutual love enabled my recovery.

After the overdose, my sister helped every Saturday for a full eight hours. It was an enormous relief to know my son was safe and well-cared for. She brought delicious home-cooked meals, too.

After two months of bed baths, and dry-wash products for my hair, my sister said, "Time for a seated shower." I couldn't stand without the walker, so she washed off and bleached a white plastic chair from our backyard. Even with my arm around her neck and shoulders, her arm around my waist, I couldn't shift my weight to bend my knee over the lip of the tub. Judy supported my sagging body while she moved each of my legs. Under the waterfall of warm water, she joined me, fully dressed. She had brought a set of dry clothes for herself.

Once seated, she gently pulled off my bandages, washed my back and then my hair. To be in my own home, my own shower, and to feel the warmth of flowing sheets of warm water cascade off my body was nirvana.

The minute my husband arrived home after work, my sister left. Her weekends were for her chores and time with her husband. Each time, Aaron complained. "Why can't she stay an extra hour or two to give me a break? I need to relax before taking care of you and the baby."

Every week I responded, "I'm sorry."

On each succeeding visit from my mother, she criticized my husband. "The bathroom off your bedroom is filthy. It smells like the men's room at a gas station."

I put down Cameron's book. "My walker doesn't fit through the doorway on the little bathroom. I only use the one in the hallway, plus, it has the elevated commode."

"I'll clean it for you, today. But I shouldn't have to do housework when visiting. Your husband said he hired a lady. The house is dirty, no one has cleaned anything. There are toys all over the living room floor."

"I wouldn't know. I'm not allowed out of the bedroom. Cleaning isn't a priority right now."

"When is your husband going to blow the leaves off the roof? Or clean the fireplace grout?"

With that I closed the book. "Cameron, go play in your bedroom. I need to talk to Grandma." When we were alone, I lost my cool, shouted, "Are you kidding? The grout is a grey color, it's not dirt. And who cares about the roof right now? Don't you realize how serious my surgeries were?"

"I don't appreciate your porky attitude."

Oh, not now. Not the speech.

"You had a place to live, food to eat. I took care of you. I kept a clean house. I didn't drink. I didn't smoke. When I die, I'm going to ask God why he did this to me."

I'd heard her tirade so many times about my scoliosis I'd come to imagine her at the Pearly Gates, waving a fist. I always felt sorry for God.

Then a shadow of fear flickered across her face. My empathy shifted. "What's wrong, Mom?"

"On the phone this morning, you asked for orange juice." With the store 200 feet away, she walked over daily for groceries and gossip. "In the parking lot, two guys grabbed my purse."

"Oh! Mom! Why didn't you tell me when you arrived? Are you okay? What did the police say?"

"Police? What police? I took care of them." Her stony face signaled *no arguing*.

"Meaning ...?"

"I fought them off." She clicked her tongue. "They didn't know what hit 'em. I got in a couple of good knuckle punches." She huffed, "I grew up in a tough neighborhood. I know how to defend myself."

"Mom, you're 73 years old. Weren't you scared?"

In seconds her mood shifted. Her face was crestfallen, eyes teared. "They ripped the strap on my purse." She held it up. Her lower lip quivered. "I have to go to the shoemaker to get it fixed." Before my sympathy could percolate further, "If it weren't for you, none of this would have happened. I wouldn't have been in the store today."

"I'm sorry. I'll never ask you again."

"Well, you had better be sorry. You shouldn't have had any of these surgeries. There was nothing wrong with your back." She waved a fist, picked up her broken purse, and stormed out. Over her shoulder, "It's too dangerous for me to come here, anymore. Tell that woman your husband hired to do your grocery shopping for you and clean up!" She stormed down the hallway.

"Happy Thanksgiving, Mom." I called after her.

The thud of the front door slammed shut.

That first month in bed all day and night, when not playing with Cam, I spent hours listening to the radio. My eyesight was too blurry to read or watch TV. Each week brought a different aide. I soon learned, no one stayed in the house. "No, I didn't hear you. I go outside to smoke." Or "I go outside to pick up twigs." It was infuriating.

Eventually, the month passed, finally I was allowed out of my bedroom. It had been two months since I'd seen the rest of my home.

As I cautiously ventured down the hallway on my maiden voyage, the latest aide watched. My gait was a Frankenstein-type lurching. The extra weight of the newly added spinal stimulator threw off my balance even further. The doorway to the living room was blocked by an ocean of toys scattered across the floor. "Could you clear a trail?"

"No, Ma'am. That's not my job. It was like this when I started working here."

Determined, I held onto my walker tightly, tried to kick a path through the debris. Stopped short. *A fall would be disastrous. I can't let Dr. BrownEyes down.* After retreating to my hospital bed, I picked up the phone and flung it. The handset and base flew apart, dial-tone buzzed.

The aide came running. "Did you fall?"

"No, I'm good. The phone fell." *Not a lie.*

The calendar page turned to December. Judy and her husband Ed came to visit. They brought a Christmas tree they'd cut down from their acreage. The scent of pine was incredible. Cameron and I joined them. I noticed the tornado debris of toy rubble had been pushed along the perimeter of the room, as if snow-plowed to the curb.

The holidays came and the holidays went. I wanted my old life back. New Year's Day, January 1991, I lay in my hospital bed, looking at my face in a hand-held mirror. I screamed. My husband came running from the living room, where he'd been watching the Rose Bowl. He exclaimed, "Did the rods break, again? I'm calling 911."

I erupted with laughter. "No. I found a few grey hairs. That's all." The past months had taken a toll.

Aaron didn't laugh, "At age 33?"

The latest aide, Frida, was a recommendation from one of our neighbors. We had used up our insurance benefits for in-home health care and were paying out-of-pocket. Ironically our cost was less than half of our insurance company's "professionals." Frida was completely different. "I like to stay busy when I'm in a client's home. Anything you need: cleaning, laundry, cooking. Or help with your son."

Those first months were nothing but a perpetual roller coaster of a bad dream. The end of January 1991 approached—the upcoming bladder surgery was next.

Frida washed dishes at the kitchen sink. With my hip brace locked, I leaned against the wall like a telephone pole. She initiated, "Mary, have you thought about putting Cameron in daycare? I know he's all you have, but even a few weeks would be beneficial for both of you. You can build up your strength for your next operation. Cameron can play with other children, fresh air. He won't go outside here without you."

"It's been six months. I'm allowed in the backyard now. Plus, my old friends will be coming by with their sons, soon. The eight of us, four moms and four kids, used to visit weekly for play dates. I know Cameron misses them."

Frida dried her hands, said nothing. Then as if an afterthought, "Well, they haven't showed up yet, have they?"

Within days, one of the moms called, left a message, she'd be by for a visit. I was delighted to prove Frida wrong. When she arrived, I asked, "Where's your son? I thought our boys could play together."

"I can't stay long." I propped my body against the wall, as she transferred her home-cooked meal to one of my casserole dishes. "This way I don't need to return. We'll do a playdate when you recover."

Another six months later, when I was finally able to join them, they no longer met in each other's homes. By then they took hour-long walks in a historic neighborhood with a canal filled with ducks. I didn't have the physical ability for the distance. That was the end of my son's playgroup. My entire family paid the price for Dr. Fixit's surgical error.

As my condition improved, I declined some of Frida's offers. "No thanks. I can take care of myself, now." Cameron, was playing on the floor, listened intently and munched his pacifier like a rabbit on too much caffeine. He scampered off to his bedroom. I slowly ambled with my walker to follow him. Once there, I was puzzled. He sat on the carpeted floor bare bottomed, with a new, clean, unfolded diaper next to him. He had pulled the tape, and taken off his own dirty diaper himself, and precariously hung it over the edge of the opened diaper pail. "What are you doing, Sweetie?"

Brightly, with sincerity, Cam answered, "I help Mommy. I care myself." In his toddler vocabulary, he repeated what I had just said to Frida in the kitchen.

A two-year-old changing his own diaper? Things can't be that bad? With the phone book on my lap, I made a dozen calls to daycares. Someplace where he could play. No one would take a two-year-old in diapers. Not even our respective religions unless we each converted. That Cam had relapsed while I was in the hospital with a spinal cord emergency wasn't an acceptable answer.

In tears, one more call. A gentle-voiced woman at a local Presbyterian church listened. On hold she located her director. The superior's voice was warm and cheerful. "I'm so sorry. You've gone through so much. Technically, per our guidelines, no. That's the best part of my job. I have the authority to make exceptions. Yes, we'll take your son."

The word "yes" was soon followed by the word, "Nooooooooo! Stay home, Mommy!" Cameron shrieked, with his little arms outstretched, over his father's shoulder. The morning goodbyes were gut-wrenching. I stood in the foyer, leaning against my walker as I kissed my son's face.

"Cameron, Mommy's boo-boo will be all gone soon. Then I can take you to the park again."

Before long Cameron was making new friends at school, having fun on their playground, and coming home with his "Helper of the Day," badge on his shirt. He sang the corresponding enthusiastic song: "I'm Helper of the Day. Yes, I'm helping all the way…."

It was a good decision. Frida had been right.

Not long after Cameron started day care my mother-in-law called. It had been two months since we last spoke. Frida was in the garage doing laundry. I was in the kitchen when the wall phone rang.

Surprised, to hear her voice, I asked, "Where have you been? Did you go out of town?"

"I didn't want to bother you. I speak with Aaron almost every day. I heard you have a private nurse. It must be nice to be waited on hand and foot all day long. Does she give manicures and pedicures, too?"

Bewildered, I pulled the receiver away from my ear, stared at the handset. "Um, no." *Doesn't she have any idea of what's been going on around here?*

She continued. "I hear you need a wheelchair. Have placed Cameron in day care. Plus, a blue, disabled parking permit. I was thinking, wouldn't it be better if Aaron and Cameron move in with me? Your mother and sister can take care of you, there. I'll have an attorney draw up papers, you know, make it legal, for school, things like that."

My son! You want to take my son? I felt sucker punched. Again. I couldn't breathe. It was as if all the horrors of the past few months shifted out of view, behind a diminutive two-year-old toddler clutching a teddy bear. Instantly, nothing else mattered. *My son!*

Before I could collect my thoughts, she continued, "You must know you'll never be the same. You do know that don't you? How can you raise Cameron? You can barely walk. And you have another surgery coming up, and who knows how many more after that."

She's five hundred miles away. I can barely make it down the hallway. I'd never see my son again. A fury I had never felt before welled up. Every shred of strength left in my body locked into place, like an internal armor. I felt like a half-dead, fire-breathing dragon that had come to life to defend its young.

My voice roared. "You want me to give up custody of my son?"

"That's not what I meant."

"You are not taking my son from me!"

"I'm only trying to help."

"I'll send you a Helper of the Day badge."

"Pardon?"

"Nothing. Bye."

"Well, think about it. At least until kindergarten."

"He won't know me in three years!" I slammed the receiver so hard that a nearby picture rattled to the floor. I collapsed against the kitchen counter. Shaking, I unclenched my fists, as the overstretched ivory cord swayed across the harvest-gold wallpaper of our outdated kitchen in front of me. *I'm not giving anyone a reason to take my son.*

Without hesitation, I pushed off the counter, dialed the hospital and cancelled my surgery. I lied. "Yeah, everything is healed." I still had difficulty urinating. *No more surgeries. I'm not losing my son.*

After that conversation, it still took me agonizing minutes to walk the 30-foot distance from my bedroom to the kitchen, with one difference. Once in front of the dust-covered wheelchair—still there from the day I came home—I stopped, turned, carefully held onto my walker, then gave it an angry kick. "No one is taking my son away from me."

When Tigers Fly

February 1991 marked a major milestone. It had been six months since I first fell in our circular driveway in August. I was allowed to walk outside my house.

Frida watched, while holding Cameron on her hip. With my cane, I slowly walked to the cluster of rural-style mailboxes 100 feet away. The distance felt like the impossible destination of a lunar landing. Along with a mind-boggling sense of freedom, I was confident those were the first steps to regaining my former life.

As I stood there, looking back at the house, I tried to remember life "before." That faraway memory felt like a lifetime ago. I could see Cameron's little hand waving, from our large living room window.

Leaning on the cane for support, I returned his wave. *Concentrate, put one foot in front of the other. Mommy is coming home.*

It was all trial-and-error in those early years. I didn't discover the limitations of my rebuilt spine until after a new injury occurred. When the grass started to grow again in March, Aaron hired someone to cut our acre-sized plus lot, since I couldn't. Foolishly, when the man asked that I carry his five-gallon gas can a few feet over to him, I obliged without thinking. It took weeks to recover from my mistake; the pain the next day was so severe I couldn't stand.

Eventually, I was on my own. Frida and I hugged our goodbyes. I was allowed to remove the locking leg attachment from my brace, ecstatic to finally be able to sit again after six months. Plus, that meant I was permitted to drive again after half a year.

I did have to give up my Chevy, due to its manual transmission. Dr. BrownEyes said, "The clutching action with your left leg is too much stress for your lumbar spine." That, along with the gas can incident, should have been my clues. I was not the same physically.

Even though I was still wearing the back brace and spinal stimulator, I was excited to finally leave the house, with my son, by myself. I thought a short trip to the mall would be okay. I wasn't worried. Cameron could easily climb into and out of his car seat on his own. I had my cane to lean on when walking.

Cameron was fully potty-trained, again, thanks to the teachers at his daycare. But I didn't consider he would need to be lifted onto a toilet in the mall.

I had to improvise, quickly. On the floor with my right knee bent, thigh pressed up against the toilet for support I extended my straight left leg. Then held Cameron's hands as I instructed him to walk on my leg. He thought it was a game. At my waist, I had him sit side-saddle style on my right thigh while I scooted him onto the toilet.

Once I conquered how to move my son without using my back, my sense of empowerment increased.

Yet, there was still the emotional side to deal with. Cameron asked, "Mommy, don't you love me anymore?"

"Of course, I do! Why would you ask that?"

"You never pick me up anymore."

Not picking up my son or being able to drive a stick-shift seemed to be temporary issues. I didn't know at the time: I was at maximum recovery for physical ability. I would never pick up or carry my son again.

That summer, 1991, Cameron turned 3 years old. I was wearing a bathing suit in the backyard, while he splashed in his kiddie pool. He noticed my scar, for the first time, screamed, with a toddler's red-faced ire while his lower lip jutted out. "Mommy! You said your boo-boo was all gone? It's still here." He pointed an accusing finger. His eyes squeezed shut, as he wailed. I held him tight, tried to explain, "No, Mommy's boo-boo is all gone, on the inside."

I was the one who didn't understand. From the reflection of a full-length mirror, I looked the same. But anytime I bent to pick up throw carpets to mop, stood for more than a few minutes to cook a meal, or lifted even a half-full bucket of water, the pain was insanely intense.

I took frequent breaks to lie down. The pain subsided enough that I could maintain vertical, again, but for a shorter increment as the day wore on.

My pain budget was small. A dollar a day to spend, chores like vacuuming or grocery shopping costly, each easily a fourth of my daily ability.

In July 1991, ten months post-op from my CES surgeries, one month out of my back brace, I had a routine appointment with Dr. BrownEyes, along with new x-rays.

"Mary, we have a new obstacle." He popped my latest film on the screen, but unlike past visits, didn't hit the switch to illuminate them. "There's been substantial growth of fusion bone."

I looked at him blankly. "Isn't that what we wanted?"

"The fusion mass is growing too well. New bone doesn't form unless old bone is being destroyed. You need to quit wearing the spinal stimulator."

"Why?"

"As you know, it's an experimental device. The settings for the electro-magnetic field were too strong. New studies have found—."

"I thought it was safe…What happened?"

"You no longer have separate vertebrae." He hit the light switch.

The screen revealed an s-shaped (due to the scoliosis), solid bone, where the separate vertebrae of a spinal column used to be.

Dr. BrownEyes continued "I've scheduled an exploratory surgery."

Incredulous, with a clenched jaw I mumbled, "Another surgery?" *Doesn't this disaster ever end?*

August 1991, a few days before my scheduled operation, a woman from the business office called. "Your surgery has been cancelled. Your insurance won't cover a glitch from an experimental device."

"Wait. They paid for the unit, but not for complications caused by it?"

"Yes. That's correct."

I was relieved. Dr. BrownEyes never mentioned the overgrowth of fusion bone again, and neither did I. The damage was done.

September 1991 marked the one-year anniversary of my scoliosis re-do, CES spinal cord emergency, and subsequent hardware failure surgeries, along with a few months completely out of my back brace. One day, while 3-year-old Cameron rode his tricycle, I walked beside him to our mailboxes. Life was almost normal. I didn't take my cane. I thought we were safe.

As I opened our mailbox, I heard a galloping sound from behind us. *A horse? Here in suburbia? Nah!* I turned, looked over my shoulder. A large Doberman—easily 80 to 100 pounds—was bounding down the middle of our black asphalt road, straight towards Cameron.

With a scoop, I snatched Cameron under his armpits yanked him upwards off his trike and hoisted him over my head. His shoes dangled at my shoulders while massive, muddy paws pounced on my chest, then my upper back, as I twisted my spine, circled, and I tried to keep my body between my son and the lunging, barking, all-teeth exposed, dog. With each quarter turn, the dog pounced again.

Attempts to elbow the dog meant Cameron's feet lowered to the open, barking, jaw. I couldn't knee the dog without losing my balance. I screamed over and over, "Get down!" I hoped a neighbor would hear, despite our muffled, heavily wooded acre-sized lots.

A man's voice called out. The pet ran off to its owner. I abandoned Cameron's tricycle. Carried my sobbing son in my arms. Then discovered I was unable to run, no matter how much I tried. My only option was to walk as fast as possible.

Inside, our own 80-pound German shepherd was agitated. She paced, panicked, between the two of us— Cameron and I had collapsed onto the carpeting, both sobbing. Later, I found her paw prints, and tufts of fur, halfway up the glass, curtains torn. She must have heard my screams and tried to break through the window.

All movement became anguish for months afterward. At every opportunity I was flat on the living room couch. My surgeon's hospital no longer authorized their doctors to write prescriptions for patients more than a year after surgery. I no longer had a family physician. Without any pain meds there were no options except to tough it out.

How could a minor oversight result in such intense misery? A book on pain management via guided meditation and imagery helped. I learned to still my breathing, the shallower the better. The book said to assign a color for the most severe episodes. I came to think of those as the purple zone. The book also said to pick a color and an image, to represent "no pain." I chose blue and a bird soaring. When I was outside, the broad expanse of the sky prompted my meditation practice. When the worst of the pain abated, I eventually learned to use my imagination to visualize myself ice skating, doing gymnastics, or playing tennis. My body had zero limitations in my thoughts.

The dog jumping event was a major turning point in my life. It took many months to recover. There had been no limitations after my original scoliosis surgery. The minimal functionality of the latest version of my spine was alien.

I thought a lot about my father during those many months. One memory led to another. My father had been a meticulous record keeper. He analyzed everything. He was a young man during The Great Depression of the 1930s. He knew how to be thrifty. Then, when I was in high school in the 1970s, he'd been promoted from postal inspector to some type of time-efficiency manager. He would literally follow postmen around with a stopwatch, recording their every step. Then map an alternate route that took fewer steps. He didn't have any friends at work after that.

Details annoying to his carriers resulted in greatly reduced expenditures for the district. From his days of counting pennies in his youth, to counting minutes in middle-age, my father had found his true vocation. He loved the challenge. It became a game of logic to him.

As an adult with chronic pain, I learned every minute mattered, and every ounce counted. My father's attention to detail and my knowledge of timing led to an idea. What was the tipping point? Walking, how far? Sitting, how long? Would the type of chair make a difference? Reaching, how high? Bending, how low? Lifting, how much weight? I pulled out a notebook, drew the lines for a table and proceeded to map out a plan to resume my life and survive. Granted, I still had to give up many things in my new life, but for the rest I would find a way.

I analyzed each movement, as if under a microscope. If I couldn't eliminate the source, could I reduce the intensity? How could I alter my surroundings? Myself, how I did things? The items I handled. Over the decades, I even perfected sequencing of activities for maximum duration.

It wasn't all boring statistics. Some ideas came about by serendipity, or despair, during purple zone days. As a parent, I had to adapt. One day Cameron and I were playing catch in his room. It had been raining non-stop for days and we had tired of books, puzzles, and board games. I thought of them as "bored" games.

We tossed a palm-sized stuffed animal back and forth. A wild toss from me resulted in a collision with the spinning ceiling fan. The little teddy bear, wearing a cape, zipped across the room "flying." We both laughed, loudly. I almost didn't recognize the sound. It had been so long.

"Mommy, can we do that again?"

"Yes, but let's lie on the carpet." *Heavenly pain relief for me.* In short order, the small bear's larger cohorts joined our play, and they became a squadron. As we flung them into the high-speed fan blades, most failed their mission. Cameron and I were showered with teddy-bears. We laughed, and laughed, and laughed until we both cried.

Then we extended our giddiness to interspecies flight. There were flying tigers and dinosaurs. When a member of the squadron hit at precisely the correct trajectory for its stuffing weight, it would whizz across the room at warp speed, to the distant corners of our one-room universe. Sometimes one would rocket to the far-reaching galaxy of the bedroom across the hall. We howled until our sides were sore. It became silly, non-stop giggling, with complete abandon. It felt good. Each successful hit resulted in a shower of dust, like a convoluted blessing. Cleaning had to wait for low-pain days.

We played, while I rested my back by lying on the floor. My life started to feel normal again. I was still me.

Months later, Aaron questioned, "What happened to the ceiling fan in Cameron's room, it's tilted at a weird angle." At first, I didn't put it together. When I realized what had happened, I didn't confess. For my son and I to share riotous laughter was well worth the cost of a replacement.

Decades later, when I became a grandmother, and Cameron a father, their baby cried while I visited one day. On autopilot, without forethought, I picked up a stuffed teddy bear and eyed the ceiling fan in their apartment, to console my grandchild. Adult Cameron didn't hesitate to interject. "Don't even think about it, Mom. We're renting, I have a security deposit."

"Oh, you remember that?" We both laughed.

In those early years, before Cameron started kindergarten, I took him to my appointments with Dr. BrownEyes. Without a ceiling fan to destroy, I resorted to other games to amuse a preschooler. Cameron's favorite was Paper Towel Baseball. Batter! Batter!

Wet brown paper towels from the cubicle sink were wadded up into a "ball." Cameron pitched from the far side. I pivoted my open palm from the elbow like a mini bat. Bam! Home run! With no place to run, we whisper sang, "Take me out to the Ballgame...."

On return visits I often asked, "Why does my whole body hurt since the CES surgery?"

If I stood for too long, my upper back felt like it was either on fire or as if the muscle was being ripped off the bone. My hips felt like non-stop electrical shocks. Even my rib cage hurt if I did too much.

Dr. BrownEyes always patiently explained. "Those are the areas above and below your long-spine fusion, they absorb all the impact of movement now. Your spine problems are severe. The goal of your CES surgery was to reverse impending paralysis." He reiterated his last sentence frequently over the years. I felt ashamed for asking.

On every additional visit, my first question was always the same: "Is it okay to pick up and carry Cameron now? He doesn't weigh much for his age."

"No. My son is only a few years older than Cameron. I'm keenly aware of parenting challenges during the toddler years and I'm in good health. Yes, you're fortunate Cameron doesn't weigh more. There might be a cosmic plan out there, after all. However, weight is weight. The effect on your spine is the same. The trauma from the surgeries alone is quite extensive. I expect complete recovery to take five years."

Five...Years... My son will be eight years old before life is normal again?

It took decades to fully comprehend, that my spine was like a fragile old teacup that had been shattered and glued together too many times. The teacup looked the same on the outside, but its function was gone. Any sitting, standing, or walking came with a time limit. Eventually, I learned three hours a day was my maximum function for those activities. I came to think of it as my spine time, or vertical time.

To help, Aaron pulled the car to the front door, for drop off and pick-up. So, I saved my limited walking duration for inside of buildings. At the mall he carried my purse over his shoulder because the weight, no matter how much emptied out, worsened my upper back pain substantially. Teenage girls cupped their hands, whispered to each other, laughed, and pointed to us.

Aaron growled, "She has a bad back. What's your problem?"

I was anxious to rejoin the real world, on my own, without anyone's help. Volunteering seemed an option for transition. I called several agencies and explained my spine limitations. Each person said the same thing. "We don't have anything for someone with limitations like that." One young girl offered a solution. "We'll put your name on our list. As soon as a volunteer becomes available, we'll send them out to help you."

"I'm not asking for your help. I'm offering to help."

"You can't do anything."

"You're wrong. Maybe I could …."

"No. You're not healthy enough to volunteer."

In defiance I dialed another number anyway. The Director of a local botanical garden answered. "We need someone in our gift shop. Meet me, tomorrow, 1:00 p.m. It's okay to bring your son."

"Is there a place to sit?"

"Yes, our volunteers are elderly, and need to sit. Sounds like you'll fit right in."

"Perfect. Thank you."

The next day, super excited, we waited. Cameron and I sat on the deeply ridged, rain-weathered, wooden steps of the old farmhouse's front porch. Along both sides of the steps were moss covered terra-cotta pots of plants. It started to rain, and then poured. We retreated under the rusty metal awning. I tried to look through the dirt-encrusted window, wiped away a smudge of grime with a tissue from my pocket. There were glazed ceramic pots, garden books, and wind chimes for sale. *I'm going to love being here.* The rustic old building with wood floors was quaint. I spotted an old-fashioned register, and a barstool. *No chair? I won't last long without a chair back to lean against.*

There was no opportunity to ask. Cameron and I played the Alphabet Game repeatedly. We sang songs. After two hours of waiting and dozens of mosquito bites on each of us, the rain slowed, and we meandered along the muddy path to the parking lot. I kept turning, hoping someone would emerge from the bamboo forest in the opposite direction.

Once home I called the Director. He guffawed. "Oh, I forgot all about you. Afraid that's my norm with volunteers." I didn't reschedule, too embarrassed to admit the stool, "for elderly volunteers," wasn't enough support for my spine.

By spring 1994, when Cameron finished his kindergarten year, I went to my local community college. I had come up with a list of seven physical limitations. Their software only screened for "lifting forty pounds."

1. Can't carry anything over 3 lbs.
2. Can't lift things over 5 lbs.
3. Can't stand in one place for more than 15 minutes.
4. Can't walk continuously for more than one hour.
5. Can't sit in padded chair for more than one hour.
6. Can't sit in unpadded chair (hard back) for more than 30 minutes.
7. Can't sit on bench (no back at all) for more than 30 minutes.

The Career Counselor barely glanced at my paper. "People with bad backs need jobs where they can remain seated all day. You'll need to train for an office job. Due to your issues, we'll enroll you for only two classes: typing and introduction to personal computers."

The combined weight of my two textbooks were too heavy to my spine to carry in my backpack. Determined, in the garage I found an old metal luggage cart, a neon orange plastic crate, and a bungee cord. The assembled unit looked stupid but enabled wheeling my books to class. Other students stared. Years later I saw black foldable versions being sold in stores.

Aaron suggested I take the heaviest textbooks to an office supply store to have them cut in half and rebound. That made them less painful to carry, lightened my rigged-up cart, and, of course, killed their resale value.

I soon learned that, like others with invisible disabilities, we live a chameleon existence. We blend in visually. The internal effort and struggle required to participate in even the most minor activity is hidden from the rest of the world. For us there's not only a glass ceiling, but a glass floor, and glass walls as well.

12-Pound Anvil

The community college campus was built on gentle rolling hills. Single and double-story buildings connected by wide, open, covered breezeways, provided shelter from both the heat and torrential rain of a semi-tropical climate. My typing class had thirty students. No one spoke. Our typewriters were on small, grey, metal desks.

I sat in the second row behind a young man who, like everyone else, was wearing jeans and a T-shirt. At our second session I paused in front of his desk and introduced myself. He responded with a deep voice, "Great to meet you, Mary. My momma called me Anvil because I weighed twelve pounds at birth. Over the years that shortened to Anvy.

"Your nickname has nicknames?"

At the same moment we both answered, "Of course," we laughed. I disclosed that I'd done the same with pet names through the years. Samantha had become Sir Muffin. Sydney Carton—named for the Dicken's character—evolved to Sid the Cat, then City Cat. I felt right at home with this stranger.

Anvy typed by holding the unsharpened lead-end of a pencil in his mouth and used the eraser tip to press each letter on the keyboard. I learned that he had broken his neck four years earlier when he was sixteen. He had become a quadriplegic after diving headfirst into the shallow end of a swimming pool.

Out in the breezeway, waiting for class, one day, Anvy powered his wheelchair over. "Hey, I've been watching you."

With his words I froze and was propelled into a total *déjà vu* moment. *Oh, no, here we go again.* This was the same community college, where twenty years earlier, a different classmate had also initiated a conversation with those exact words.

As I emotionally braced myself, Anvy didn't say anything about my scoliosis being "obvious." He said,

"You're in a tremendous amount of pain, aren't you?" His tone of voice was sympathetic, not accusatory.

"Yes. But, how would you know that?" I felt relieved to be accepted.

"I've got eyes. I can see the look on your face. The longer you stand, the worse your pain. Your back doesn't hold you up at all, does it?"

I looked at the ground, blinked to restrain the tears. "No, it doesn't. I never thought of it that way."

"I can tell when you're hurting. Your legs turn into an A-frame, wider and wider. You're starting to look like the Eiffel Tower, a short Eiffel Tower." Being teased about my height was nothing new. Being compared to the French monument was unexpected. We both laughed, heartily, and became instant friends. He told me things about myself I hadn't been aware of. There was no mirror in public places to reflect what others saw. Or was it that he saw me in a way others didn't notice?

Anvy continued. "You're always leaning against a post. Why don't you sit down? I'm in a lot of pain too. My neck, the part that's not paralyzed, is in constant spasms. I've seen you struggle to walk in from the parking lot. Don't you have a disabled parking permit?"

"Yes, but I only use it on the worst days."

"Oh, Mary, you're going about this all wrong. You need to use your permit everywhere you go. Then, maybe, you won't reach such severe levels."

"I hadn't thought of it that way."

"Sit down. I'll come over there." His deep voice boomed with bemusement. His eyes winkled. His broad smile revealed beautiful, perfect teeth. He chided, "Come on, we've got a half-hour before class."

"Okay, okay." I felt like a lost duckling being gathered up. Scanning the area, I found a ledge with an adjacent column to lean against.

Anvy blew into a gadget on his wheelchair, reversed and repositioned himself. "How did you get hurt?"

I gave him the abbreviated version. When I finished, he asked, "Are you registered with Disability? Do you ever use a wheelchair?"

"I'm not disabled. My husband and his family think I should apply. My doctors are adamantly opposed. They all say the same thing. 'Once you start using a chair, you'll never get out...'" I looked at the cement, embarrassed.

"You mean you're not disabled the way I am? Don't worry. You didn't hurt my feelings. With Disability, I'm talking about a department here at the college."

Briefly I stretched backwards, then forward, for some relief from the hip anguish of a seated position.

Anvy noticed. He whistled. "You have trouble sitting, too? Your family might be right."

"My doctor said five years for a full recovery. I have another year, then my spine will be normal again."

"Well, you know what they say. 'Da' Nile ain't just a river in Egypt.'"

"Egypt?"

"Skip it. The Disability Department here at the college can provide accommodations."

I must have wrinkled my forehead.

"They provide different desks in my classrooms, taller ones, so my wheelchair fits underneath them. They'll do the same for your disability. Does the padded chair in our typing class help?"

"Yes, as long as I don't sit too long."

"They'll reserve padded chairs in all your classrooms."

"I didn't know that."

"Shoot yes! They must have at least 200 thickly padded chairs in their computer lab alone. They don't even need to special order equipment for you. Your accoms are a breeze. My Mama's got a bad back, too. I know all about invisible disabilities. She's had a bunch of surgeries, like you. She only needs a wheelchair when the distance is too far for her to walk."

"I thought people either used a wheelchair or didn't."

"Yeah, lots of folks think that way. You're not the only one. There are people who always need a chair. Then, there are folks like my Mama. She can walk okay in the house, can last thirty, maybe forty minutes on a good day, when out and about. Anything more than that and her back gives out."

"I don't think a wheelchair would work. I can't sustain sitting upright, even in a padded chair. My surgeon said no more than twenty minutes tops. That's accurate, for class I tough out the pain for the last thirty minutes."

He frowned and sighed. "Okay, let me think on this. I know! How's about we get you a stretcher?" His eyes shined with whimsy. We both chuckled. I didn't have to fake being okay with Anvy.

The next time we spoke, before class, Anvy said, "I'm graduating in a semester or two. Then I'm going over to UF, get my bachelor's degree. You should do the same. Then I'm going to organize national disability groups. We could use someone like you, Mary. Working together we can improve housing, job opportunities, and discrimination."

I was inspired by his enthusiasm. Anvy continued, "Hey, Mary, come over to my house, meet my momma. She'll cook you up some of the best grits and collards you ever tasted. Give you lots of pointers about managing a permanent injury."

Over the remainder of the semester, we had many conversations in the breezeway before class. We shared our medical experiences. I didn't take him up on his offer to meet his mother. I should have. He often relayed her helpful ideas.

The season changed to early spring. The Red Bud trees were blooming, bursting into pink blossoms. That morning it rained. While waiting for him before class, I noticed a pair of wrens building a nest in the crevice of a loose rain gutter. When Anvy powered over, he too looked at the birds, then looked down at the puddle of water beneath them. He commented, "That's a lot of effort for a bad location." Then he continued, "Mary, does your doc prescribe meds?"

"No. Nothing. No one will write. Family doctors all said, 'Ortho needs to write.' Ortho said, 'See your family doctor.' They all say the same thing, "Someone should be treating you. Your spine issues are severe." It's like being stuck in a revolving glass door. I can see through the glass, it looks like I'm going somewhere, then when I push to move forward, I'm only going around in circles."

"Mary, are you saying you don't take anything for pain? Not even a muscle relaxer?"

"I rely on over-the-counter pills, those newer drugs that are like aspirin. It's better than nothing. The doc who treated my upper back injury in the 1980s, from pulling a vine, said I could take it indefinitely. He said there was no need for a prescription, to take four pills instead of the directions to take one."

Anvy frowned, asked, "Umm, how many pills a day are you taking?"

"It depends, some days up to sixteen."

"Aren't you worried about your liver?"

"No. Dr. Ribby said to take as many as I need."

"Oh Lordy, girl, what am I going to do with you? You can't take that many pills, not forever!"

"How would I know? It's an over-the-counter medicine. I thought it was safe."

"Well, you better make it your business." Anvy sighed. His eyes were no longer smiling. "Doctors only know about drugs from their latest drug rep. Now, don't get me wrong. Docs know how to rebuild a body. They're good at that. They don't have a clue about the aftermath. Mary, it's fantastic the way you learned to manage. Pretty smart coming up with all sorts of shortcuts. You'll still need a doc to write for breakthrough episodes."

"Breakthrough?"

"What you're calling the 'the purple zone,' like when that dog jumped on you and your son. You're barely treading water to keep up. Add a new injury? You're sunk. Without an established relationship, a new doc or the ER is going to dismiss you as a 'drug-seeking patient.'"

"Huh?"

Anvy hooted a friendly team-player's teasing. "You don't get out much, do you? Where'd you grow up, a convent?" He laughed, not waiting for an answer. "Your doctors don't have a clue what you're dealing with. Pick up some of your spine x-rays. Take them with you when you meet a new doctor. That should help."

"Is that allowed?"

"Yes! Mary, these are your medical records."

"Are you in a lot of pain today?"

"Yep, how you know dat?"

"Your language…is different."

"Told that 'Afore. Yeah, if the pain don't fry your brain, the drugs you take for it will. Hey, Mary, one more thing. You listening? This is really important."

"Yes."

"It's okay not to be the same anymore."

The last time we chatted before the semester ended, Anvy said, "Mary, I finally figured you out. You're too good an actress. People think you're one of them. You're not. Then, when you do ask for help, they think it's a joke. A cane would clue them in. They can't see your pain."

"I try not to use my cane. I don't want people to see my limitations. I want them to see my abilities. Besides, my hand goes numb, and I drop it all the time. Doc says its nerve damage from my upper back. Not worth the pain of bending to pick up."

Anvy grunted, "One lame excuse after another."

Even though he teased, I knew he fully understood my Catch-22 frustrations: walking, sitting, standing, bending, and lifting. It was a lot to juggle. I looked at my wristwatch, "Class is starting."

Inside our classroom, I started to take my seat.

"Hey Mary, wait. I need to talk to you. You've made this semester a lot easier. Thanks for being my friend. Lots of folks are afraid to chat with people in wheelchairs, as if paralysis is contagious."

"Oh! Anvy, thank you for all your help, there were so many things I didn't know." I patted him on his shoulder in solidarity.

"Mary, I can't feel your hand."

"Oh! I'm so sorry. I forgot."

"Touch my face. People forget what they don't live. And people can see my chair. No one sees an x-ray of your spine. They don't know what you're dealing with."

The following semester we didn't have a class together and, like other budding friendships, neither of us rescheduled our cancelled lunch plans. We did talk on the phone now and then. His parents rigged up his handset at his home. As much as I appreciated his friendship, I winced when he said I was disabled, too.

We lost touch with each other. One spring day, I alternated between cooking dinner and watching the local 6 o'clock news in the living room. The opening story covered the torrential rain, flooding, and standing water from the storm. I stepped into the kitchen a minute to stir the chili.

Back in the living room, I'd missed the beginning of the next news report, and only heard the announcer's last words. "… accidental death by drowning…a 22-year-old man."

With my head bent down, I wasn't looking at the TV. I was picking up the family debris of the day from the carpeted floor using the long-handled grabber tool that Anvy's momma recommended. *She was right, blessed relief from bending.* The newscaster continued. "The drowning victim was a recent graduate of our local community college, accepted at UF for fall semester."

With the anchor's next words, I jerked my head upright. The tool, a lost sock, missing puzzle piece, and a toy car dropped to the floor. "The student, a quadriplegic, fell out of his wheelchair when it flipped over on a raised patch of sidewalk. Unable to move, he drowned in a four-inch puddle of water."

I found myself an inch in front of the TV. It was Anvy.

Riptide

Anvy's imparted knowledge was clear, solid, and memorable. His words became treasured wisdom and advice that I used for the rest of my life. However, he had been mistaken about accommodations at our school. My new disability counselor turned down my request for a padded chair. She said, "If I do it for you, I'd have to do it for everyone." *Does everyone have my spine issues?*

When I persisted, she said, "We don't have any." I repeated Anvy's information about their computer lab. "Oh, no, we can't spare any of those." Two weeks before the end of the semester she notified. "We located a chair for you." It was a chrome-frame chair from a 1950s style kitchen set. The forty-year-old red vinyl "padding" was paper thin.

By spring of 1996, we moved to a big city for better employment options. It was a flickering, shining star moment of anticipation and hope for a normal life.

The physical demands of moving—packing, bending, reaching, lifting, standing, and the relentless laps around the house—were an enormous toll on my limitations. It took months for my body to recover. I then applied for ten office-type jobs and received seven job interviews. I made sure to only apply to companies whose disabled parking was within thirty feet of their entrance, to save my limited walking ability for inside. *Counting steps. My dad would be so proud.*

I took a job with a temp agency and was placed with a wholesale nursery located on acres of blooming flowers. As assistant to the owner, I could sit as needed, but wasn't required to sit for more than 20 minutes. On the first eight-hour day, the burning sensation in my upper back and stabbing pain in both hips was intense. Yet, I was ecstatic to be there. By the second day, I crawled into bed the moment I returned home, without cooking dinner for my family. It felt like every cell in my body had been electrocuted. When the alarm rang the next morning, I was still wearing my crumpled work clothes from the day before.

On the third day I dragged myself in, dizzy, nauseated, deep in the purple zone. By the fourth morning, I couldn't stand. There was no choice but to call in sick. Their office manager said, "Let us know when you're better. The owner and I are both very impressed with your work. We'd like to hire you for a permanent position as his personal assistant. We can wait a couple of weeks." I was so happy.

I went to see my new family doctor. His stand-alone, white, stucco building was nestled among crepe myrtle trees in full bloom—Cherokee pink and lavender. The dark yellow hibiscus and magenta oleander blossoms were magnificent.

Dr. GoodVibe's broad shoulders made it easy to imagine him playing football when younger. His sandy brown hair and beard offset his faintly freckled face. He looked like a big fuzzy teddy bear. I took Anvy's advice and brought an old spine x-ray to the appointment. Dr. GoodVibe wrinkled his eyebrows. "You have severe osteoarthritis of the spine." He looked at my intake form. "Why, no anti-inflammatories? Isn't anyone treating you for this?"

"My original surgical report from 1983 listed 'osteophytes along the spine.' Is that arthritis?"

"Rheumatology isn't the specialty of orthopedic surgeons. Let's start by having your hips x-rayed. Issues sitting might not be spine related."

I was relieved. *Not my back this time.*

When the results came in, Dr. GoodVibe said, "You have arthritis in both hips, the left is fairly severe."

I burst out crying. "I'm only 38 years old! How is that possible?"

"The areas above and below your fusion must bear the weight of your movement. In your case, that's your thoracic spine and your hips. It's to be expected. Plus, did your surgeons harvest donor bone marrow from either hip?"

"Both. One in 1983, and the other in 1990."

Dr. GoodVibe, leaned back in his chair, sighed, and frowned. "That's old school. These days surgeons use cadaver banks."

"Why?"

"The latest studies show harvesting causes permanent damage. I'm concerned about your sacroiliac joints, too. They look abnormal."

"What's a sacroiliac joint?"

"It's part of the hip."

"Should I see my surgeon, Dr. BrownEyes?"

"No, that's not necessary. There are tons of orthopods here. Plus, we need a hip specialist. In the meantime, I'm writing you a script for arthritis medication." He scribbled on his pad. "You'll need to return every few weeks for a blood test, to check for liver damage. That's a potential side effect."

The world ceased to exist. My thoughts careened around the unfamiliar word "orthopods." A grasshopper? *No, they're arthropods. Pod, a cluster of fish or whales? Are Orthopods whales with bad backs? Snap out of it. What?*

Dr. GoodVibe hadn't noticed I wasn't listening. He kept talking. "...meanwhile the arthritis meds will become a diagnostic tool."

Is this like the day Dr. Mayberry slid in the word "plastic" to reference the catheter? The muscles in my body tightened, my anxiety climbed. When I recovered from my dazed state, I interrupted. "Doctor, wait, I phased out. Slow down. What's an orthopod?"

He chuckled, "Sorry about that. It's slang for a physician who specializes in orthopedic medicine. He picked up his phone handset. "Let's start the referral." He cradled the receiver with his neck, as his finger zig-zagged across the faded-blue ink of a piece of paper taped on the phone's base. After he punched out the number, he covered the receiver with his right hand while he waited for the call to connect. "Mary, records from your 1990 surgeries would be helpful." To the person on the phone, "Is that the soonest available?" He hung up.

"Mary, have your records mailed to this specialist." He scribbled the doctor's name on a note pad. "The soonest available is a month away. In the interim anti-inflammatories and bed rest are all we have."

I took a positive attitude. *A new orthopod might have fresh ideas.*

When my appointment date arrived, I was confident there would be an answer. I looked up at their ten-story modern building. By then Cameron was in third grade. *There won't be any paper-towel baseball or laughter here. I'm on my own.* I had not realized how much my son's presence anchored my emotions.

The elevator arrived on the fifth floor. Once checked in, the receptionist instructed, "Wait here. His nurse needs to speak to you." She turned, continued typing at her computer. There were no chairs, so I leaned against the counter. Upside down, on their side, I recognized the hospital logo and city from the 1990 surgeries, plus my name. *Oh, good, they arrived in time.* A nurse briskly walked in my direction. From the hallway, still a dozen feet away. "You need an MRI. You shouldn't have come in without one."

"My records ...."

"Yes, the doctor's seen them." She arrived at the counter, reached over the ledge, and turned the thick stack upside down. Gruffly, "Those aren't your concern." The receptionist turned from her computer screen, slid her glasses down to the tip of her nose, and frowned at her.

"I recognized my name."

With a harsh tone of voice, she grumbled, "Why are you leaning against our counter?"

"I have trouble standing. Doesn't the doctor need to write orders for an MRI?"

"No."

"I'm pretty sure my insurance company requires a doctor's authorization."

"Use your own money."

"That doesn't make sense. I have insurance. Wait, I can't have an MRI. They can loosen my hardware." *What's going on? What did I do wrong?*

"Well, CAT scan then. Whatever you want."

"I thought I was going to see the doctor today. I've waited a month. My pain is severe. I might have a job, if ...."

She snapped, "No. He's booked up. A month. No, make that two months. Europe. Vacation."

Europe? Vacation? Haven't I heard this before? The receptionist called over her shoulder. "I don't have that information. He has an opening next week." She picked up her pen as if to write. "We can put her in then."

I must be dealing with a misinformed, crabby, employee. Maybe they do things different in big cities. I collected my thoughts, shook off my fears. "I recently moved here. Where would I find a CAT scan facility?"

"How should I know? Look it up yourself." She reached over the countertop, whipped the phone book off the shelf, and shoved it with such force it almost careened off the ledge. I barely caught it in time. The receptionist wheeled completely around to face the nurse. Her jaw dropped open. She seemed to mouth the words, "What's going on?"

I left. Driving home, shaking and crying, without intent realized I'd driven to Dr. GoodVibe's office. His receptionist consoled. "I'm sure he'll talk to you. Please, take a seat. It'll only be a few minutes. He's finishing up with a patient. "I'm so sorry they treated you like that."

Dr. GoodVibe, visibly upset, clicked his tongue. "Of course, they write their own orders for tests. No, you're not a candidate for an MRI. She must be a new employee. I'll write for an x-ray, and personally call them for your appointment to be rescheduled."

"Thank you, Doctor."

A week later I returned, latest film in hand. The same receptionist instructed, "Take the elevator. He wants to see you in his private office on the top floor."

The elevator opened at a carpeted hallway. I saw my new surgeon's name emblazoned on a gold placard next to an open door. Cautiously, I walked in. With each step my body sank into the generously padded carpeting. In the corner was a fake rubber plant covered with a thick coat of dust.

The doctor entered. I turned, reached out my hand to shake his. "Nice to meet you...Doctor?" He stiffly shouldered past without a word. My hand fell to my side. He carried a thick stack of papers. Even sideways I recognized the logo from the hospital of my 1990 surgeries. I followed him. At his desk, he roughly flung my records across his blotter pad. He turned, with an angry voice, said, "I'm surprised you returned. I thought my nurse already spoke with you on your prior visit."

I felt my panic rising. My breathing became shallow as the room seemed to distort into carnival warped mirrors.

Despite a dry mouth, "My family doctor ordered x-rays." I held out the envelope to him. *What have I done wrong? Is this like that neurosurgeon with my spinal cord emergency?* "When seated I have terrible pain in my hip. My family doctor...said...you.... Do you have a diagnosis?"

"Is that all you require?"

"Well, yeah. Isn't that... what doctors do?" I teased, trying to make a joke. He didn't laugh. I shifted my gaze. On his enormous, shiny, mahogany desk was an empty pewter bud vase. In his wastebasket, a few long-stemmed half-dead roses, on the floor, one, solitary, blackened oval of a rose petal.

His eyes followed my gaze, as he whipped the envelope out of my hand, and flung my x-ray onto a wall monitor. He flicked the switch on with annoyance. "Fine, I'll give you a diagnosis. See this black oval area?" He used a gold-plated pen as a pointer.

"Yes, Doctor."

"It's likely a tumor, I suspect cancer."

"Cancer! Are you sure?"

"It's not my field."

"Are you saying the tumor is causing my hip issues? Are you referring me to a cancer specialist?"

"I don't know any." He scooped up my medical records, whipped my film off the monitor, and shoved everything into my hands. "There's no need to return, or to see any other doctor in this building. Do you understand?"

I was trembling with fear as I entered the elevator. *Why is he acting like this?* I did my best to juggle the inch-thick stack of jagged papers and the film. When the elevator opened, his nurse and receptionist were huddled in deep conversation at the counter. As I approached to pay, I heard the nurse whisper. "Yeah, that's her. She's the one...." The receptionist elbowed her into silence. The nurse said, "We'll mail you a bill. No need to stop. Leave. Now."

Once inside the car, without plan, I again found myself at Dr. GoodVibe's office. I didn't wait long. He graciously fit me in between his other patients. He looked at my x-ray, shook his head. "I'm not an orthopedic surgeon, but I'd be willing to wager my medical degree that you do not have cancer." With anger in his voice, "As a matter of fact, I have no earthly idea what he's looking at. I don't see anything that even vaguely resembles a tumor. And that black oval area isn't your spine. It's located inside the sacroiliac joint of your hip. A first-year medical student would know that."

A decade passed before I cleaned out the papers shoved into my hands that day. Under the cover sheet were the medical records from the day I met Dr. BrownEyes in 1990 with the spinal cord emergency. Halfway down the page, "Patient has a retained central line catheter from a 1983 spine surgery." Someone had circled that sentence with such force it was evident where the pencil tip broke off, trailing a ragged lightning bolt of lead across the page. From other records I recognized the name of the hostile surgeon who gave me the fake, cancerous tumor diagnosis. He had been Dr. Fixit's partner from 15 years earlier in other city hundreds of miles away. It was lost on me at the time, but not only was he throwing me out of his office, he basically told me not to even attempt to see another surgeon in that city of one million people.

It was the first of several false cancer diagnoses over the years.

In 1997, once the cancer diagnosis was ultimately proven false, Dr. GoodVibe asked, "Can you return to your former surgeon in your old hometown?"

"Yes. Why? I thought you said there were plenty of Orthopods here. Returning to my former surgeon means hours of driving. Sitting really escalates my pain."

Dr. GoodVibe rushed out a hearty sigh, "I know. But there are too many bad vibes here. I don't know what's going on. You need to be seen by someone. Plus, your spine anatomy is quite complicated. Along with advanced aging components. Your former surgeon likely has a better take on things, anyway."

"Okay."

"Do you have any other questions, before we wrap up for today?"

"Two. A referral from you would move things along with Dr. BrownEyes."

"Of course, I'll call now." He buzzed his receptionist for the number for the out-of-town facility. "While we wait, what's your second question?"

"You seem to be a straight shooter, Doctor. If you only saw my film, how old would you guess my age to be?"

He fidgeted in his office chair and cleared his voice. "I'm afraid anything I say would be unsettling."

"Doctor, all due respect, you brought this up. 'Advanced aging components?' I need emotional healing. You're only going to assign a number to what I already feel and live with every day."

Dr. GoodVibe stood, removed his stethoscope, and hung his white crumpled lab coat on his coffee-stained, royal-blue, office chair. He was wearing a red plaid shirt, unbuttoned at the neck, along with beige corduroy pants. He rolled his chair from behind his desk. When seated in front of me he crossed an ankle over his knee. His suspended boot bounced until a chunk of dried mud fell off. His office was located on the city's fringe, almost a rural area. I decided the pick-up truck always parked in the parking lot must belong to him, as those mud flaps were often covered with local dirt.

His arms and hands were firmly planted on his armrests. "Even if three of your spine anomalies were restored to health there would still be six more."

"That's not my question."

He sighed. "Okay, Mary, I'll put it to you this way. The radiologist who reviewed your spine film called. He thought there was a typo, that your birth year was forty years older than your actual age."

"Meaning what?"

"Biologically, even though 39, you have the spine of an 80-year-old woman."

"Oh!"

He continued. "Your spine would be classified as 'over-operated.' I know there was no choice with the emergency surgeries. However, as each operation averted one disaster, it too, created new problems." He rushed out the rest of his words. "Quite frankly, I'm amazed you can walk at all. Everyone who sees your x-rays agrees."

My left thumb unceasingly rotated my gold wedding band. He continued. "You must have tremendous determination. Moving your body is like driving a car with four flat tires. You'll get where you're going, eventually, but not without a tremendous struggle."

Like all wise doctors, he knew the importance of a pause. He waited for his words to settle. My swirling thoughts coalesced. Finally, I spoke. "That would explain a lot, wouldn't it?" Emotionally flattened, yet oddly relieved. "Thank you, Doctor." It was like being on the Titanic, told to stop bailing with a bucket and then given the reason why.

"I'll return in a moment. You need pain relief. I'll look up your surgeon's phone number myself, my receptionist must be busy."

He left. I found myself staring at a quintessential beach painting on the wall behind his desk, a numbered print signed by the artist. There were all the shades of blue I so loved, gentle, rolling, cresting waves. Golden stands of sea oats. A tinge of teal-colored water was visible at the horizon. I could almost smell the salt air. Feel the sand between my toes. Then my thoughts shifted. *Where are the riptides?*

Before I moved to Florida, I had never heard the word, "riptide." I didn't know anything about hidden dangers. I had only seen artistic renderings of cascading ocean waves, of gently kissed shorelines. I didn't know a fast-moving undercurrent perpendicular to those waves could form like a fast-moving river, swiftly dragging a swimmer out to sea.

I was caught in a medical riptide, drowning. I learned three valuable lessons that day: My medical riptide existed. I was caught in one and fighting against the system wasn't working. Returning to Dr. BrownEyes, swimming parallel to shore, was the only answer.

At home, the house was empty except for our aging dog. I flung my car keys onto the bar stool side of the kitchen counter. They jangled off the edge, clattering onto the floor. I left them there. As I patted the dog's head, I absent-mindedly emptied the entire box, a pyramid of milk bones in front of her. She tilted her head sideways, with a questioning look. Gingerly, she politely picked one off the top of pile, slowly walked down the hallway, circled too many times before she slowly collapsed her arthritic limbs into her basket. She tucked the unwanted bone under her greying muzzle. *I know how you feel, old girl.*

Numbly, I sank onto the couch and waited for the "Your appointment's been scheduled on…" call from my surgeon's office. I heard a squeaking wheel, spinning, as my son's gerbils ran in endless circles. *I know how you feel, too.*

Boomerang

The latest arthritis meds from Dr. GoodVibe didn't work. Plus, I developed skin tags on my neck and armpits. I asked him, "Are these from the prescription?"

"No, that's impossible." He scheduled a biopsy.

During a purple zone day, while lying on the couch, I spotted the latest drug's manufacturer information sheet within easy reach on the coffee table. For the first time in my life, I read all the tiny print, both sides. The very last sentence, on the second page: "In less than two-percent of the population, skin tags have been reported."

I closed my eyes. *Oh! No!*

Dr. GoodVibe was not offended. He thanked me. We cancelled the biopsy and other scheduled tests. I quit taking the drug. The skin tags disappeared. Valuable lesson learned: two-percent patients existed.

Before I knew it, like a boomerang, I was in my former hometown to see Dr. BrownEyes. I stood on the sidewalk in awe of the mountain range of adjoining buildings in the enormous medical complex. *Here we go again.*

The clerk at the information desk commented, "We're the second largest building under one roof on the East Coast of the United States."

"Who's number one?"

"The Pentagon."

Dr. BrownEyes' small, windowless examination room was identical to the one where I had first met him in 1990. My latest tests resulted in another new diagnosis, Bertolotti's Syndrome. The birth-defect-level vertebra was no longer biologically fused to the base of the spine. There was an area of movement, bone sliding across bone.

Additionally, the radiologist report listed, "a halo" around the top of the screws holding my hardware in place. There was no concern. It was decided to be an unimportant artifact. No one knew. As a patient with a bizarre hardware complication, I had entered the less than one-percent zone.

Months went by. My first injection for pain relief failed, as did the second, and third. Since they were a teaching hospital, each visit meant a different doctor, along with a new cluster of students. Each time, I filled out the same questionnaires. Employees inquired with happy voices. "What brings you to clinic today?" "Did you trip?" "Is this a tennis injury?" Each new team was unaware of the prior injections or the reason for them. Overly confident, inexperienced newbies promised, "We can fix you." I said nothing and rolled my eyes when they weren't looking.

Aaron came along for injection number four. In the small cubicle, I was lying on my stomach, while he held my hand. When he squeezed too hard, I looked up to see him wipe a tear from the corner of his eye. "What's wrong?"

"That is one damn big needle."

The student nurse, standing next to him, enthusiastically gushed, "Oh, I know this must be unbearable for you to watch." She patted his hand.

The discomfort from the needle, reinserted several times due to the anomalies of my spine, was zilch compared to the purple zone I'd already endured for months. When finished, the doctor left. Aaron let go of my hand. "I'll get the car from the parking garage, meet me out front."

"Okay."

Alone with the student, she steadied my elbow, while I cautiously climbed off the exam table. She chattered endlessly. The curls of her red hair bounced with excitement. "Isn't it wonderful? All better."

"No, actually, it's worse."

"That's not possible. You know, it's bad for morale, when patients don't appreciate our efforts."

"Maybe there's a delay."

"Oh! No! It works right away." The bouncing springiness of her hair looked like a young Shirley Temple. I anticipated a stamping foot. She said, "You're not thinking about this the right way."

"That makes no sense. How could you possibly know what I'm feeling inside my body?"

She leaned in, squeezed my hand, and whispered, "You don't have my training."

"I appreciate your education, but that doesn't alter my experience—."

"Oh, you're welcome!" She enthused. Curls bobbed. She left. The heavy metal door slow-motion closed, as I imagined she tap-danced out of the room, to sail away on the Good Ship Lollipop.

I finished dressing. *This hurts like the devil.* Slowly, I dragged myself through countless corridors until I arrived at the main entrance. I stood there, hypnotized. *Another failed injection? Where is this pain coming from? How many more times can I go through this? Isn't there an answer?* The automatic glass doors opened...closed, opened...closed, through several cycles.

Scores of other patients, as well as medical providers in uniform, kept walking. I finally broke free from my stupor.

Aaron honked the car horn to get my attention. Once inside, he said, "Hurry up. The game's going to start. There won't be any reception until we're on the interstate." When I relayed the student nurse's comment, he responded, "She's probably right. You're thinking about it the wrong way."

"I know what I feel."

He turned up the radio volume. I reclined the seat as much as possible to ease my pain, clenched my jaw, and shut my eyes. *Don't argue. Keep peace at all costs.*

Exactly two weeks later stretched out on the couch beneath the living room windows and poof, the purple zone disappeared. Gently, I turned my body left, then right. Gingerly, I stood up, took a few steps. *Thank you, God!*

My joy was short-lived. Within days the searing sensation returned, ten times worse. It felt like someone was using a jackhammer to pound steel pylons into my spine. I again ruminated about the latest events. Aaron pointed the TV remote in my direction. "They should have a mute button for wives."

"The game is twelve months a year for you."

"And you never stop talking about your back." He pointed the remote towards me and clicked.

I gave him a wordless thumbs-up and slowly made my way down the hallway to our bedroom. Looking up from our bed, my gaze singled out a solitary blade of the ceiling fan, following its unending circles. Our dog jumped up, I mindlessly stroked her fur, while she licked my face. Then she pawed my chest until I made eye contact with her. "Don't worry, I'll be okay." I kissed the top of her head. "Cameron will be home soon, old girl. Let's pull it together. We need to pretend everything is okay."

Dr. BrownEyes was encouraged. "I'm confident we're closer to an answer. The spinal nerves are like a leaking roof. The source of the leak and where the damage shows up aren't always the same place. When injections into specific areas don't work, we've eliminated those areas as a potential source."

When I asked him to confirm or deny the student's point of view, he frowned. "No, she's mistaken. It is expected that you'll have additional pain for several days. The musculature is greatly aggravated, especially if they pull the needle out to reset." He skimmed my reports. "Apparently that's quite common in your case. Doctors aren't trained on atypical spine anatomy. The hospital should require warning labels for their less experienced staff: 'Student in Training' like teenagers with 'Student Driver' signs on their cars."

I laughed. He had a dry sense of humor, and I appreciated any levity to lighten the intensity of our conversations. He acknowledged my frustrations and validated my feelings. With the release of a pent-up sigh, I asked, "Okay, next? Where do we go from here?"

"We're done with your spine. Next, we'll try a series of injections into your sacroiliac joint. If those don't work, our last resort is exploratory surgery."

"My family doctor mentioned the sacroiliac joints, too. I don't understand. How is there a joint inside the hip bone?"

He slid over his desk-sized spine skeleton. "See this heart-shaped bone at the base of your spine? That's the sacrum. Attached to the sacrum on both sides are the hips, almost like a bird's wings. At their juncture is the sacroiliac joint. The word 'joint' is misleading. It's firm yet flexible. Like the tip of your nose. Not the range of motion like an elbow or knee."

I frowned.

"The tip of the nose can't move by itself—."

"Sure, it can. Didn't you ever watch the TV show *Bewitched* as a kid?" *If I don't laugh, I'll cry.*

He chuckled, adjusted his glasses. "As I was saying, with mild pressure, there is slight movement. This happens inside our hips, too." He pressed his index finger against the tip of his own nose.

"How is this related to my spine?"

"We fused to the sacrum in 1990—."

"So, the stress of all my movements moved to the next unfused level, my sacroiliac joints?"

"Yes. Our goal in 1990 was to prevent impending paralysis."

"Am I returning to the same lab, the same staff?" *Please, no more Shirley encounters.*

"No, SI injections are done in the CAT Scan lab. Extreme precision is required. Likely an hour procedure, they slightly advance the needle, scan, repeat to verify placement. The needle must be as deep as possible before releasing the cortisone."

As the weeks rolled by, the first injection into my SI joint failed, as did the second. *Surely the third would work.* Rather than a dual-person team, there were six doctors inside the glass-windowed booth. They spoke amongst themselves.

On my stomach, I remained motionless. Each doctor in turn stood by my side injecting the needle. Voices from the booth instructed. "Angle left, now, right." "Pull back." "Push harder." They would stop, start again. Lying on my stomach, each time a doctor walked up I observed a different pair of shoes. With their last attempt, something went wrong. As an experienced patient, I spoke up. "It feels like you're pushing the needle through clay. This doesn't feel like the other injections. Are you sure the needle is inside my sacroiliac joint?"

At that moment the needle broke off.

I heard the doctor shout, "Oh shit!" A second voice, from the booth, "Call the OR. The broken needle will need to be surgically removed." A third voice barked. "Wait. Look at the film. It's not too far below the skin surface. We can retrieve it without too much digging. Don't forget your liability and malpractice insurance premiums boys." The sound of light laughter erupted from the booth.

A fourth voice interjected. "You're all on mic, she can hear you."

They did retrieve the broken needle. Afterwards, I questioned one of the doctors. He said, "I too felt an enormous resistance going in. It was my instinct to push harder."

"How could there be something inside my joint?"

"It must be scar tissue. Both of your SI joints are pulled apart due to your extensive fusion. You'll have to ask the referring doctor. We don't do diagnostics."

At my follow-up appointment, x-ray lit up in the background, Dr. BrownEyes confirmed, and further speculated, "That's accurate. It's called a vacuum phenomenon. Once separated, scar tissue fills in. I believe that was there all along. Even with a CAT scan it's difficult to visualize the area. I imagine the first two attempts took the route of least resistance, and assumed they were inside the true SI joint."

Dr. BrownEyes pointed at a dime-sized, black oval area inside my SI joint. "This is another anomaly."

I laughed out loud. "I was told that was a cancerous lesion."

"A medical doctor told you that?"

"Yes, an orthopedic hip specialist."

He placed his palms together in a tented position, closed his eyes for a split second, as he rested his chin on his fingertips. He dropped his hands, and then said, "When your sacroiliac joints pulled apart, that oval was the worst area for damage."

By March of 1997 we had lived in our new home for nine months, six of which I had spent searching for a diagnosis. The purple zone continued to worsen. My husband, son, and I went to a restaurant for dinner. Within minutes of being seated I was nauseated and sweating profusely, purple zone deluxe. It felt like metal scaffolding crashed inside my back. We had to leave immediately without ordering.

The next morning, I called Dr. BrownEyes' office, sobbing. I begged his nurse, "I can't take this pain anymore. Please help."

Within minutes of hanging up, the phone rang. I picked up the handset in the bedroom. It was Dr. BrownEyes himself. He said, "I'm confident this is a nerve impingement. We've eliminated everything else. Our only option is an exploratory surgery. I've been looking at your old films. I'm also concerned about an area near your CES spinal cord compression injury from 1990. You might need another laminectomy at an adjacent level."

I geared up for battle, shifted gears to cold, clear, logic. "Can you repair both of those surgically?"

"Yes." He paused. "Mary, this is another major surgery. I might have to replace your hardware, and that would mean drilling rods into your hips for stability. There are no more unused landmarks along your spine."

With a dry mouth I whispered, "Schedule the surgery."

"I'll call the OR now. If you don't receive a return call within two hours, call my personal nurse. Here's her direct private number. Hang on, Mary. We'll have you in surgery in less than 48 hours."

When we hung up my whole body shook. As I walked down the hall, my legs buckled. After I collapsed against the wall, I dropped to my knees, sat on my heels, and covered my face with both hands, sobbing uncontrollably. *I'm 39 years old. Will this ever end?*

A heavy paw landed onto my shoulder. Opening my eyes, our dog gave a tail-tip wag, and then licked my face.

I sank completely onto the floor, lying on my side, in a fetal position. My dear old girl eased her own arthritic body down next to my stomach. With my right arm around her, my other hand fingered a frayed carpet fiber, unable to function, move, or imagine a future without surgical events.

Eventually, I rolled upright, sat on my heels, and tried to stand. There was a strange sensation from deep inside my body. An intense agony sucked the air out of my lungs. I crashed against the wall and fell to the floor.

Internally, there was a sensation in the middle of my back of a cluster of harpoon-like metal arrows exploding, outward, and stabbing me in all directions. An intense wave of queasiness hit. I broke out into a cold sweat, dripping wet, even worse than the prior day's restaurant episode.

To minimize the searing pain, I curled up, squeezed my eyes shut. Then, almost like a split-second video clip, the anatomy of my internal spine flashed into my mind. I couldn't decipher the image.

Then, slowly, one-by-one, corresponding words dropped into my brain to describe the image.

I knew what was wrong.

"Suicide Blonde"

At our pre-op appointment I decided to trust Dr. BrownEyes. "I think I know what's wrong."

"Okay, I'm listening."

"The hardware is loose."

He snapped his neck, looked at the lit monitor. "The x-rays don't show displacement, not like 1990."

"I'll bet you a dollar. Make the incision, turn me upside down. The whole structure will fall out."

He frowned. "That's highly unlikely. However, I'll take your opinion under advisement." He wasn't dismissive, angry, or even amused that I'd expressed my point of view. It was an honest conversation: his formal education versus my first-hand experience, from living inside my body.

On that day in March 1997, wheeled into the operating room for my fourth major spine surgery, the lights were bright like a sunny day, not glaring interrogation-room blinding like my first surgery.

The young anesthesiologist said, "Dr. BrownEyes has been delayed, an urgent situation with another patient. Do you mind if I play a song? Background music mellows everyone out."

"Sure." *Any distraction from this moment and the reason I'm here.*

I'd assumed it would be the soothing, soft strums of classical instruments like violins and cellos. I anticipated Bach or Mozart. I closed my eyes, ready to drift away. A high-pitched harmonica rang out while maximum-volume vocals shrieked about hoping for death, followed by the screaming reverb and echo of harmonica riffs. Startled and confused I jumped up, one leg slid off the operating table towards the floor. *Was this a celestial warning?* Within that split-second the lyrics revealed the song's title, *Suicide Blonde.*

Once I recognized the tune, my fears morphed into uncontrollable laughter at the irony of the lyrics. I practically rolled off the table. The anesthesiologist took my arm. "You, okay? Guess that was too loud?"

"A tad," I tried to keep a straight face.

The group was INXS, and the song had become a big hit not long after I was released from the hospital in 1990. I had heard it many times on the radio while in bed at home those first post-op months. Memory of that song was permanently entwined with three words: recovery, home, safety.

My entire body relaxed. *I'll be okay. I'm in good hands. My son is eight now, not a toddler. This will be an easier recovery.* I felt a deep sense of confidence. *And laughing? What a fabulous way to start an operation.*

A latex-gloved and green masked Dr. BrownEyes entered the operating theatre, bent elbows, sterile hands held upright.

"Mary, are you ready? Is this music okay for you?"

"Yes, and yes, thank you for asking."

He turned to the anesthesiologist, "Could you turn it down a wee bit? It's background music, not a rock concert, okay?"

I laughed out loud, again: *another operating room, another surgery, and we're talking about the volume of a rock song?*

A memory of schoolchildren on a playground throwing a ball surfaced: A child's voice implored, *"I want a do-over."* *Was this my do-over, a happier memory, to replace my first surgical experience?* I drifted off, "100, 99, 98...."

Surgery lasted six hours. Once on the regular floor I commented to my nurse, "Wow, this is a fancy room." It was an enormous private room with lush drapery, sheer curtains, and quality photography: waterfalls, clear mountain lakes, soft moss of an ancient forest floor. There were two large glass panes with an enormous perpendicular view. Outside were the green leaves of treetops, fluffy soft-looking clouds drifting across the bluest sky I'd ever seen. When I questioned the unusual windows, the nurse answered, "You're in a corner suite."

I continued to gush. "This is twice the size of any hospital room I've ever been in as a patient or as a visitor. I didn't know they had corner rooms. This is like a hotel."

"You've been designated a VIP by your surgeon. I'm your personal nurse, here to ensure the quality of your hospital experience."

Is this a dream? Oh crap! I died. I hate when that happens.

The nurse continued. "Are you a doctor?"

"No."

"A politician?"

"No."

"Foreign dignitary?"

"No. Why would you think that?"

"We're the number one trauma hospital for the entire state of Florida. The helipad is near this room." She pointed to the ceiling. "The VIP suite is designated for the highest-ranking elected officials, including the President."

"The president? Of what? Oh! I must be… in… the wrong room… the wrong floor." My eyes circled. There was state-of-the-art full emergency room equipment behind zig-zagged metal-framed curtained panels. "I don't think I'm supposed to be here." I moved my IV line, started to sit up, to leave.

She chuckled, "You're in the right place. Don't worry. You're apparently a very important patient or you wouldn't be here. Can I bring you a drink? I have a direct line to food service. Would you like some freshly squeezed orange juice? Are you from overseas?"

"No. Here, the United States, where else?" Underneath my sheet, I pinched my thigh.

The nurse continued with smiling eyes. "So, you're not one of Dr. BrownEyes' patients who flew in on their private jet from Saudi Arabia?"

"No. I'm a regular person. What are you saying?"

"Your surgeon is a highly sought-after specialist, internationally."

"I didn't know that."

"You hit the jackpot with Dr. BrownEyes."

"Yes, that part I know."

Later that day, Dr. BrownEyes came in on rounds. His broad smile meant everything went well. I knew there was a possibility they'd installed a fourth set of hardware. I tried to steady myself.

"Mary, I have good news, and more good news. There was significant nerve impingement. As far as the hardware, you were correct. I've never seen anything like this. It was as if someone unscrewed all the bolts by hand. Your body really doesn't like foreign objects. And correct again, if we turned your body upside down, the entire five-rod, six-screw construct would have fallen out. With every step you took, the rods and screws moved, too. The severity of your pain was no doubt substantial."

I took a sip of my freshly squeezed orange juice.

He continued, "The fusion mass is solid and bridged. Your body rejected the hardware in a unique way. I've learned a great deal from your insight. Thank you. When impossible symptoms present, test for the impossible. It turns out on your x-rays from six months ago—the mystery 'halo effect' around the screw heads— is where bone had eroded."

I gulped. *Eroded?*

He continued. "It's an inconceivably rare situation. I've been reading up on the topic. It appears your personal physiology rejected the hardware in a unique way by releasing a chemical defense."

"To break down the metal?"

"No. The bone. Erode the bone around the screws when they loosen the rods fall away. I have more good news. We didn't have to install new hardware."

"Really? It's been fourteen years. Oh! Wow!" A solitary tear rolled down my cheek.

"That's a double-edged sword. We've used up all the landmarks along your spine that can be used for hardware."

"Can't you re-use a former site? Doesn't the bone grow back to fill in those holes?"

"No, I'm afraid not. Imagine a picture hanging on the wall in your house, once the hole in the plaster is too large, it won't have enough purchase, grip so to speak, to secure another nail. The spine is like that too. You'll never have spine hardware, again. However, if you ever need another spine surgery...."

Let's not go there. Then I remembered. "Were you able to retrieve my souvenirs?"

"Yes, here they are...." From his clipboard he produced a small clear plastic bag with a printed label. It contained all the screws and bolts from 1990.

"Where are the rods?"

"We couldn't preserve those. They were encased in bone and had to be disposed of according to law. Why did you want them?"

"Two reasons. When I look in a mirror, I don't see my spine. These validate what I live with every day."

"The second?"

"I'm thinking of hanging them on my rearview mirror along with my disabled parking placard. Once, at a grocery store, little boys yelled, 'You're not disabled. You're not using a wheelchair.' Their parents stood there, didn't say a word."

Dr. BrownEyes said, "I'm sorry. As surgeons we too often forget that when our trauma care ends, your new life begins."

Despite the VIP treatment, I was eager to leave the hospital. Judy, my sister, offered that I stay with her and husband Ed, until I recuperated enough for the long drive home to join my husband and son.

Dr. BrownEyes asked, "How far does she live from the hospital? I seem to recall we had complications following the 1990 surgeries."

"Thirty minutes, tops."

"Okay. Three days, here, non-negotiable, then you can be discharged. Here's my card with my pager number. Call immediately, if any concerns."

Thankfully, recovery from the 1997 surgery was completely uneventful. I had zero complications. Judy and Ed lived on rural acreage out in the country. On the day I was released, Judy drove me from the hospital to their home. She opened and closed the heavy rural gate for vehicles.

There hadn't been any rain recently. Dirt sprayed both sides of the car's windows as she accelerated down the long driveway to her home. Chickens in their coop cackled and guinea hens squawked loudly as they scattered in all directions. The Dobermans circled, barking, from the back field. The goats, in their enclosure, lazily looked up, and then lowered their heads.

As we drove towards her house, we passed under the mammoth Live Oak tree in her front yard, dubbed The Wedding Tree, after my husband and I had stood beneath it twelve years prior when we married. My thoughts spiraled, *three major spine surgeries, plus the cardiac cath. It was all too much for any young marriage.*

After work my sister inspected the wound—another 18-inch incision due to full hardware removal—and replaced the bandages. She snapped a picture of my scar.

One day, while she was at work, my brother-in-law, Ed, a former combat Veteran, sat at the kitchen table drinking coffee and reading the paper. He stood six-foot-four, had broad shoulders and bulging 'Semper fi' tattooed bicep. I'd barely taken any of the narcotics since my discharge. I cautiously navigated my walker the ten feet from my room to the nearest bathroom.

Ed looked up, saw my grimace, dropped his paper, and swiped off his eyeglasses. "What the hell was your surgeon thinking?" Weren't you released from the hospital too soon? Any fool can see you're in a lot of pain."

"I asked to be discharged. I can tough it out."

His reaction came as a complete surprise. He jumped up, straightened his shoulders, dropped his glasses, stood at attention, and raised military straight fingers to his forehead with a full salute. As he lowered his hand, with an outward jut of his jaw, he declared, "Mary, you could have been a Marine. We could've used someone like you in Ko-re-a." He always enunciated each syllable.

I was bewildered. It was an incredibly high compliment coming from him. I looked down, and then looked up at him. I too, straightened my shoulders, as best I could, and stood a little taller at his high praise. I would never have put myself in the same category as him for courage. Ed wasn't only a Marine. He was among "The Chosin Few."

At 19 years old he'd survived the Chosin Reservoir Battle of the Korean War. With temperatures of 48 degrees-below-zero, soldiers' blood froze solid when exposed to the air after being shot. History books recorded 4,000 fatalities. Soldiers, frozen solid with outstretched arms and legs, had their appendages broken off, to fit as many bodies as possible into the few trucks available to return base.

Ed had no amputations. Not even fingers or toes. He too, looked fit to the outside world. Internally he endured horrific pain due to the permanent injury from those sub-zero temperatures.

In 1997 his words empowered my recovery. That memory became a gift carried far into the future. I remember his face, the aroma from that long-gone coffee, more than anything, the tone of his voice, his absolute sincerity. On days I'm overwhelmed with pain I imagine him standing in front of me and I return his salute.

Embers to Ash

1998 was marked by major epiphanies in my life. In the pro column it was the first time I accepted that the damage to my spine was permanent, the old me didn't exist anymore. I started to make peace with that knowledge and looked for any positives in negative situations. In the con column, I became keenly aware that someone else's life was impacted by my spine problems.

My husband, son, and I took our first true vacation that year—not visiting family—since my 1990 CES surgeries. I was still inexperienced about my limitations.

We drove towards the Carolinas, Aaron stopping every two hours so I could take a stretch and walk a little bit, to relieve the pain of sitting. We stayed in a lovely cabin on a gentle slope overlooking a rambling stream. The view, framed by emerald-green pine trees, was striking. A nearby Native American exhibit was educational for Cameron and a small enough area for my minimal walking ability.

Aaron wanted to visit the Great Smoky Mountains and for the three of us to trek to a peak, at 6,000 plus feet, to see the view. I thought I could tough it out. I wore my best thickly padded sneakers, took my cane, and prided myself on pre-medicating with Dr. Ribby's sanctioned quadruple dosing of an over-the-counter anti-inflammatory, despite Anvy's warning. It was the only medication I had available.

The hike was a terrible mistake. I stopped often. Leaning forward released a tension deep inside my spine. Barely a third of the way up the mountain I wobbled and folded to the ground. The front of my thighs felt like cement. The boys were ahead. I called out, "Hey, guys! Wait up...."

We were in the middle of the charred remains of a pine tree forest. The smell of embers from a controlled burn, permeated the air. Those long-extinguished fires enabled new growth. It was a crystalizing moment of comprehension: *My fires are raging.* As I looked around at the metaphorical version of my spine, I noticed another difference. Those leafless, blackened, skeleton trees were all perfectly straight.

Weren't there any bent or crooked ones? Groups of hikers silently split, walked around me, regrouped, two or three looked over their shoulders frowned at me for their inconvenience. As I sat on the ground, I gazed upwards, along the curve of the trail. A wall of greenery blocked my view. I realized the peak was beyond my walking ability.

Aaron returned, bent down, and took my elbow, "What are you doing? People are staring. Get up."

"I can't walk. My legs gave out." Distracted, I watched our ten-year-old son zigzag off the trail ahead of us. "Cameron! Come here!" With my husband on one side, my son on the other, they helped me stand, then walked with me back down the mountain. Once there, a weathered, wooden park bench provided a place to sit. "You two climb to the peak. I'll wait here." They took off.

Surrounded by the barren, leafless trees of autumn's undressing, without decision my body crumpled into horizontal. The raging misery from every cell in my body was unbearable.

I had grown up in a large city where a person lying on a park bench would have been considered a bum. I didn't care who saw me or what they thought.

Brutal shock waves of purple zone felt like I was hit by a truck. My upper back, ribcage, hips, every joint of my body screamed. I flexed the knuckles of my fingers open and closed. Even they felt swollen. I began to cry. *Were all my surgeries for nothing? I can't even walk with my family. I won't be able to climb any mountain, ever.* My tears of defeat became the howling anguished sounds of a wounded animal. The dam, suppressed for years, finally opened.

When the boys returned. Aaron said, "Let's take her back to the cabin. Then we'll go out."

Once in bed, alone, I remained as motionless as possible. I tried not to breathe, to ease the pain. I focused on my surroundings: the faded, lumpy, pastel quilt of pinks and lavenders, the scent of lemon furniture polish from the maple headboard. Motionless as a cadaver, I couldn't find one body part to move without anguish. I did discover I could roll my eyes clockwise and then counterclockwise without pain.

The following day the boys went white-water rafting. I stayed behind. When heavy rains came early that evening, we grilled steaks on a red-brick grill adjacent to the cabin-length porch with a view of a mountain stream. Cameron and I played jumbo checkers while I sat on the cushioned seat of an ivory-white, wicker rocking chair.

"Aaron, come play checkers with us?"

"No. That's a kid's game."

When it wasn't my turn, through the misty haze I watched the swirling waters ebb around small boulders. Raindrops dripped off the edge of the tin roof. All was right in my world. I thought we were a happy family.

The next day with more than 24 hours bed rest, I had recuperated enough to join my family for a brief excursion. We drove down the spiraled roads of the Smokey Mountains. I spotted a little park, "Wait, let's explore here a while." We parked. Cameron and I wandered a short distance beneath the canopied coolness of shady trees. We carefully maneuvered over massive boulders. My husband called out in consternation. "What are you doing? You'll fall, get hurt."

"I'm being careful. I love this place."

Cameron reached out, took my hand, while I steadied myself with my cane. "Mom, let's sit down."

I carefully lowered myself onto the largest boulder. Cameron sat across from me, knees bent, ankles crossed. "Isn't this place beautiful? Look at—." I was pointing to a waterfall hidden in the foliage.

Aaron called out to our son, "Cameron, come with me. She can't walk anymore. We'll go do something fun."

"Aaron, come join us." I patted the rock.

"It's too hot. Come on Cameron, let's go."

Cameron questioned me with his eyes. Then he whispered, "Mom? Want me to stay with you?"

I wanted to say yes. But I wanted the three of us to be together as a family. Dejected, I said, "No. It's okay. It's your dad's vacation." They left.

I straightened my leg, repositioning my cane underneath it as a mini stretcher to ease the hip strain. I swallowed my tears when I heard a forlorn bird's call. My feathered friend also searched for its mate. *Why couldn't the three of us sit together for a few minutes?* I consoled myself: *We'll have family time later. A ten-year-old should be out exploring.* But how I wished they both would have stayed with me, even if only for a few minutes.

My surroundings soon distracted my thoughts. I felt the smooth, refreshing coolness of the boulder serving as my support. With fingertips I explored the crevices of imperfections rippled across the rock's seemingly smooth surface. The forest provided countless mesmerizing kaleidoscope shades of green. I would have stayed there all afternoon. That place was a thousand times more beautiful than the burnt-out mountain top.

At my epiphany moment I realized: *I wouldn't be here if I had stayed there.* I beamed to myself in happiness. I couldn't climb a mountain, but I could sit on an enormous boulder and enjoy all the magnificence.

When the boys returned, we continued driving on the meandering road. After passing a stable, Aaron suddenly u-turned the station wagon and enthusiastically said, "Let's go horseback riding. The mountain trail should be fantastic. You can do that Mary, you'll be sitting."

Once at the stables, I walked, with my cane, over to the attendant. "I need your gentlest horse, please. I have a bad back."

The wrangler was thin and suntanned, wore dirt-encrusted jeans and a sweat-stained, T-shirt. He removed both thumbs from their holstered belt loops. "No, Ma'am, you're not riding any of my horses." He eyed me up and down, chewed, turned, spat out chewing tobacco. "Horses aren't for cripples, Lady."

I'd felt as if I had been slapped, stared at the ground, blinking back my tears, and mumbled, "I'm not a cripple."

"That cane says otherwise, Ma'am."

Why didn't I leave the cane in the car? He never would have known. The three of us riding together would have been wonderful, despite the pain.

When I looked up, on my right were the eager faces of my family, on my left, the firm jaw of the wrangler. I looked around and discovered a make-shift place to sit—a couple of cedar boards across cinder blocks. I offered a compromise. "I'll sit there and wait."

"That's a good three hours, Ma'am."

"That's okay. I don't mind."

Aaron snarled, "You can't sit that long! Forget it. It's only my vacation. Why should we do anything I want to do?" He stormed off towards the car. Cameron and I followed in silence.

Once inside, neither of us said a word. Finally, I found my voice. "Do you want to see that nearby museum? We're not too far? There will be benches, for when I need to sit."

"Sure. Whatever."

We arrived at the bustling metropolis of city buildings and one-way streets. Traffic was intense. Prior to that trip, my husband had always dropped me off before parking, to conserve my walking duration. He passed the entrance, circled continuously. We found ourselves in the middle of a massive intersection. Aaron jammed on the brakes, shoved the gearshift into park, jumped out of the car, and waved his fist at me. "I'm sick and tired of taking care of you, Mary!" It was the first, but not the last time I would hear this over the years. Later, he added, "How did I get stuck with you?"

But on that day, the first time, I could feel the color drain from my face as cars from all four directions honked. Aaron stood there, circled, and in turn shook his fist at each of them. "Fuck you! And you, and fuck you, too!" With that he hopped into the car, rammed the gear shift into drive, held the blaring full-volume horn down, and spun out in a cloud of dust as cars parted to make way for him. We drove to the cabin in silence. Bowled over at the revelation of his feelings, I nervously folded and unfolded the hem of my floral-printed cotton blouse. Until that moment I thought we were happy.

After that trip I quit using my cane. The wrangler's declaration, "cripple" wasn't how I saw myself. I looked for ways to enjoy life, finally accepting that I would never be the same as I was prior to my CES spinal cord injury. Yet, I was desperate to find anything to lesson my pain, to please my husband, so I could more fully participate in family vacations and save the debris of our marriage.

The next years brought a series of futile attempts.

My first rheumatologist diagnosed "Legionnaire's Disease. There is an infection in all your joints." She prescribed antibiotics for six months, along with a muscle relaxer. On the latter drug she said, "You'll need to take this every night, for the rest of your life." I was 41 years old.

Within months my vision dramatically worsened. I bought a pair of cheater eyeglasses. When even the food on my dinner plate looked blurry, I went to an ophthalmologist. He suspected, from my intake form alone, that it was drug related. That was the quickest correct diagnosis I'd ever received in my life. He explained, "Muscle relaxers affect all the muscles in your body. Your eyeball is a muscle too. I'm surprised your rheumatologist didn't alert you to this side effect. You absolutely cannot take a muscle relaxer every day for the rest of your life." He leaned in, whispered, "And if I were you, I'd find another doctor. I'm highly skeptical of that Legionnaire's diagnosis."

The second opinion rheumatologist's blood test confirmed: not Legionnaires. That doctor diagnosed the "felt like I was hit by a truck" pain from the Smokey Mountains trip as fibromyalgia: a chronic pain condition, totally separate from my orthopedic history. "You'll have to learn to live with it. There's no treatment available."

Someone told me about pain management clinics. I had never heard of these before. Once again, my hopes were high. That specialist took one look at my x-ray. "There's nothing we can do for you. Our clinics are for patients who can benefit from pain management. Nothing can be done for a spine like that." He stood up and left.

Meanwhile, a new family doctor, on my first visit, gave an unexpected diagnosis for a sore throat. "Looks like cancer. You'll need to see an oncologist." Emotionally, I fell apart, again.

A month later, at the first available appointment, the specialist was furious, within seconds of pushing down the wooden tongue depressor. "What type of family doctor doesn't know what post-nasal drip looks like?" He hurled the wooden stick sideways across the room, with such force it hit the wall, bounced to the floor near the intended garbage can. He roared, "You're wasting my time. I have cancer patients to see." He started to storm out, paused, with a gentler voice, said, "You should be seen by an allergist. I can't imagine what you're allergic to in the dead of winter." He snapped off his latex gloves and tossed them into the garbage can. I started to cough.

At long last, I finally found an internist who agreed to write a prescription for pain medication. When none of the new arthritis meds on the market offered relief, she insisted I try an anti-anxiety drug. I took one "do not drive, this will make you drowsy" pill and stayed awake for 48 hours. It was as if I drank twenty pots of coffee. "Wired" would be an understatement. I couldn't sit still. I buzzed through chores like a chainsaw until I collapsed in exhaustion. The good news: the house was cleaner than it had been in years. The bad news: when the drug wore off, my purple zone was worsened ten-fold due to all the physical activity.

My pharmacist said to not take a second pill, but to report my reaction to my physician. Her response, "That's impossible. Keep taking them." I didn't. I started to have doubts. One by one, with each new prescription she wrote, entire bottles of prescriptions went into the garbage after taking only one pill. There would always be a bizarre reaction, not one of the typical side effects listed. With one med I cried non-stop for five hours. With another I fell repeatedly, too dizzy to stand. A third meant sleeping for 20 hours straight. With each weird reaction, my pharmacist warned, "Don't take another pill, throw out the bottle, and let your doctor know."

My internist upgraded me to narcotics. I only took them for acute episodes of break-through, purple zone days, like Anvy had instructed, typically ten to twenty pills a year, not the hundreds of pills, dozens of refills as written. When my doctor found out I was throwing them out, she said, "Bring them in. I'll safely dispose of them for you." I obeyed, determined to prove how few I used for acute episodes.

She tossed the vial of narcotics I handed her in the air, dashed to catch them, and noisily knocked a row of instruments off a metal tray onto the floor. She shoved the bottle into her lab coat pocket, lurched. "Thanks, I can't tell you how much I truly appreciate your gifts. They take the edge off my day."

Mortified, I quit seeing her. I felt like a fool.

The replacement doctor, a newly graduated physician, had a different take on my bizarre drug reactions. "It's rare, but a known dysfunction of metabolism. Some patients experience a paradoxical reaction, opposite to the drug's expected benefits."

It was refreshing to be believed.

I had to throw in the towel for joining my husband and son at theme parks, or any place that required sustained walking, sitting, or standing. Instead, I was always on the lookout for anything the three of us could do together, within my physical limitations. *Maybe a merry-go-round at an amusement park? Or a kiddie horse ride at a pizza parlor?* The denied horseback ride in the Smokey Mountains was always on my mind.

In spring a scaled down opportunity presented itself in a quaint little town at their annual Zucchini Festival. By then I realized I had to make the best of my abilities, learning that less was more, physically, and emotionally.

Inside an old barn were splintered wood tables loaded with every possible recipe for zucchini, from breads to cakes. A nearby poster announced a cake walk. Outside the barn, BBQ chicken roasted on the grill as the ashes fell. In addition to the yard bird—what the locals called BBQ chicken—resident cooks served up fresh corn-on-the-cob dripping with melted butter, black-eyed peas, turnip greens, and cornbread along with freshly brewed iced tea. Children and families milled everywhere. In a clearing, the clang of horseshoes sounded when pitched by old men.

A sign read: "Horse Trail Rides." The handlers wore cowboy hats and boots, as they led beautiful glistening mounts through a woodland path around the perimeter. *Okay for my back!* Excited, I hobbled, ahead of my family. "I have a bad back, is that okay? I've wanted to ride a horse my entire life. We'll need three. I turned to my husband, who had caught up, "This will make up for North Carolina." I was ecstatic.

Aaron said, "That's not horseback riding. They're being led on a rope. I'm not a child, and these scrappy woods are nothing like the Smoky Mountains." A leaf fell onto the shoulder of his lemon-yellow polo shirt with the red insignia. He flicked it off. "You two go. I'll see you later." He wandered off after taking our picture.

Listening to our conversation, the wrangler, a woman my age, had been holding the reins of one of the horses. She frowned, looked down, dug her boot heel into the dirt, and then looked up, with a leathery, sunburnt, face. She thumbed her cowboy hat off her brow, and said, "Since you want to ride a horse that bad, we'll work it out. Even if I ride with you, you can hold on to me."

Before I could object, she jammed the reins into my hands. "Here, take these, stroke his mane." My focus shifted to the magnificent chestnut creature. Over my shoulder, she yelled, "Bill, grab 'ole Sara, Seraphim, from the barn, she's gentle enough...and a handful of carrots. Then help the kid."

While I held the reins, she moved to the horse's side and stroked his coat. She turned to Cameron and said, "Now, son, after you're seated, wait 'til your mom's settled. Okay? I want you to follow behind us on the trail. Keep an eye on her, if she looks wobbly, holler out real loud. Got it?"

Cameron answered with a deeper tone than I had heard before, a man's voice. "I can take care of my mother." I did a slow-motion double take.

When Sara arrived, the woman said, "Okay, Bill, let's switch." She patted the mare's neck, handed over the carrots. "Stroke her mane, while feeding her. Take a few minutes, get to know each other. Then, I want you to try to sit on her, on your own."

I was happily distracted. As a city gal I'd always known that the sensation of touching a horse would be incredible. I wasn't disappointed. I almost didn't catch her last comment. "Wait, by myself? I thought I was riding with you?"

"I got me a funny feeling about you. You only need a leg up. We'll help ya'. Besides, it looks like your son has your back." She pointed in his direction.

Cameron nodded. My son was still wearing his white polyester baseball uniform pants and royal-blue team-emblazoned shirt from his softball game earlier in the day. He adjusted his baseball cap and pulled on his solitary batting glove from his pocket. Bill wove the fingers of both his hands as a make-shift lower stirrup, below the leather one. He helped my son mount his horse.

Bill and the woman helped me up. I held the reins firmly, but not too tight. I knew to drop my heels, from my favorite childhood books, while I squeezed gently with my knees. I adjusted my baseball cap, like I'd seen Cameron do with his.

We sat there a few moments while she caressed the dear sweet animal. "Yep, that's what I thought. Horse people are born that way. You're seated like you've ridden your whole life." She chuckled and turned to Bill. "Okay, let's ride."

It didn't matter that we weren't in North Carolina. Or that it was only the two of us. I looked ahead. My—this is the best I can do—experience was life affirming.

I never sat taller than that day in the saddle. I had made it to the top of an equestrian mountain. The view was fine.

Tidal Wave

With each tiny success my confidence grew. I was changing. Soon I tackled another: learning to swim.

When in my twenties, I went with friends to nearby springs. They had reassured me, "You'll be floating. You don't need to know how to swim." While lying on a plastic raft, like I had done as a child in the placid lakes of Ohio, I closed my eyes, oblivious to any danger.

My raft escaped the packed swimming area. When I opened my eyes, I was in the swift-moving current of the canal heading straight towards the Suwannee River. My friends were nowhere in sight. There were a dozen people on the dock. I reached my out my hand. "I can't swim!"

A teenager wearing cut-off jeans crouched down, with both his hands extended, and firmly held my outstretched hand and elbow. Then he flung me off the raft into the water, laughing. "Everyone knows how to swim."

I had gone under. In the murky water I kicked. Disoriented, I couldn't find the sky. Half a dozen people jumped in and pulled me out. The young man collapsed to his knees, crying. "I thought you were joking."

My son and his friends were old enough to swim. *What if they needed me?* When my worries were revealed in the backyard pool with out-of-state relatives, my life transformed in minutes. In the shallow end, an in-law handed over a pair of goggles. "Put these on. I'll tow you to the deep end. I won't let go. I promise. Once there, put your face in the water. Open your eyes. Look at what you're afraid of."

I saw the bottom of the pool. My point of view shifted. That summer I took lessons. It was pure euphoria. Since then, swimming, water walking, and aquacise have become my greatest joys, and eased my daily challenges. For a while, I was able to volunteer with the Arthritis Foundation as an aquatics exercise instructor. In the pool, my students, some in their 80s and 90s, taught me the importance of accepting my limitations, to pace myself, take breaks before my body hit inevitable zero function shutdowns. When instructor requirements changed, they had to teach from the deck, I had to quit. I couldn't stand that long.

I learned I could join my husband and son on some trips if I sat down frequently. The year we went to the Bahamas, I spotted a shiny black, intricately scrolled, wrought-iron park bench. I told the boys, "Explore. I'll wait here." They took off.

The view was breathtaking—crystal clear turquoise waters, dazzling pinks and yellows of tropical hibiscus. Even the foliage was colorful, some ranging from lime, to jade, and emerald greens. Bees and butterflies flew nearby.

A slender, balding, elderly man approached, easily in his nineties. When he spoke, his words came out with a strong British accent. "Might I join you? I can't keep up with my son's family. I miss being in my eighties when I didn't have to be left behind."

I know the feeling. "Please, have a seat."

In short order our conversation turned to politics, and we engaged in philosophical debate to solve the woes of the world. "Your President has led my Prime Minister down the garden path." He leaned forward and pounded his mahogany, gold-tipped cane on the pavement.

When he saw my eyes widen, his voice softened. "Do you follow my meaning when I say garden path?"

With upturned palms I motioned around us, "Like this?" We both laughed. He gazed around. "I suppose despite the commonality of language, there are simply some phrases which do not translate for you Americans."

"If it cheers you up, I didn't vote for this president."

"Nor do I care for my current prime minister."

The wait passed quickly. For the first time I didn't feel left out. I felt privileged for the experience.

At the Grand Canyon, I met an Asian tourist. Neither of us spoke the other's language. We pantomimed our thoughts about the plants growing around the rim. A wrinkled-up nose meant the fragrance wasn't up to snuff.

After that I talked to strangers everywhere, people I never would have met if not for waiting on park benches.

Around my home I planted more flowering plants. In turn the dragonflies, bees, birds, and frogs arrived. My garden became my sanctuary away from my medical world. A hammock and chaise lounge eased my pain. My plants, like me, were rooted in one place, yet we could bloom where we stood.

Cameron, now in fifth grade, helped with my new hobby. He carried my purchases of potted plants. On a visit to a local botanical garden, I bought a four-foot-tall plant. Turk's Cap was a leafy shrub with bright red flowers. I walked ahead of my son as we exited single file through the crowded festival. He improvised because the plant was too tall for him to see over. Incoming shoppers stared. Some giggled or covered their mouth with a palm. Others whispered as they pointed to us. When one person laughed out loud, I turned around. My eyes round saucers when I saw how my son carried my new purchase. Cameron held the potted plant, sideways, parallel to the ground. Almost all the soil had emptied out. The plant was broken in half. The defoliated ragged twig of the top half dragged in the dirt.

"What are you doing?" I shouted.

Cameron's reaction was always like my father: unruffled and pragmatic. He took everything in stride. Calmly, "That's how the other men carry them."

I looked around. Indeed, husbands carried heavy pots by their rims for their wives. Of course, the full-grown versions knew the difference a slight angle could make to preserve the soil. It was hard not to agree with his logic.

At home, I cut away the damaged parts and planted the remaining two-foot, shredded, solitary stem anyway. The plant recovered despite its rough handling. The roots were intact. Within years that shrub reached well over ten feet tall by ten feet wide. Every fall it was covered in dozens of cherry-red blossoms.

Four years passed. In 2002, a newspaper article announced a chronic pain support group was holding their inaugural meeting. As fate would have it, Cameron's freshman year of high school's mandatory orientation-for-parents was the same night. I had been the liaison parent since kindergarten, but asked my husband to sub.

Downtown, through a courtyard of weathered hand-cut stone walls, I walked past flowering rose bushes, cement angel statues blackened from mildew, entered the century-old, gothic-style church building, and through musty hallways into my new life. As a gesture of benevolence to the community, multiple churches over the years opened their meeting rooms for groups like ours. They asked nothing in return.

Members fully understood the chronic pain lifestyle. One woman with severe arthritis ultimately had eight major joint replacements prior to age fifty. Both of her shoulders, elbows, hips, and knees. She said, "The first day I used a disabled permit, kids threw stones at me, yelled out, 'You're not disabled, you're not using a wheelchair.' Their parents stood there. Didn't say a word. I never left the house again." Many of us nodded our heads. We too, had experienced similar confrontations by strangers.

Another person, despite every known medical cure, experienced migraines for over thirty years. As a self-employed business owner, he had an out. "On the days mine are the worst I lie down on the couch in my office with an ice pack over my eyes for several hours."

A twenty-year-old had a shunt implanted in her brain to prevent the backup of leaking spinal cord fluid.

Most people had failed back surgeries. We compared notes. Many of us had similar experiences with the same providers. The journey of our various medical events brought us together. One man said, "Once I realized it's a salvage operation, I had to figure out which body parts still worked, and how to use them to make a new life."

With each meeting, my memories churned. I realized that besides all the horrible events there were the people who had helped. Some were in my life only a few months, like my friend Anvy, others a few days, like all my wonderful nurses over the years. Even minutes of kindness had changed everything: the cousin who helped with my fear of water, enabling me to swim, Ed's salute, riding the horse at the festival.

I was no longer the solitary inhabitant on a deserted island. These people understood the chronic pain lifestyle.

Dr. BrownEyes had once said, "The injury to your spine was like surviving a tidal wave." His analogy indicated the storm was over. It wasn't. The lifelong aftershocks of two surgical errors from 1983—failure to remove the central line and fusion to the wrong level—felt as if I was trapped between a tornado and a hurricane. Either way, the wind was always blowing.

In 2003, the retained catheter fragments had been inside my body for twenty years. Dr. FalseHope had said in 1987, "At some point in the future the last piece will dislodge, loop through the chambers of your heart, and deposit into your lungs." Ever since the 1987 cardiac catheterization I'd experienced constriction-type events, inside my heart. It was always in the same nickel-sized area near the breast-bone side. Using my fingertips or thumb while massaging clockwise and counterclockwise, the tightness would release. The episodes were intermittent, unpredictable, and unrelated to activity.

One day, 14-year-old Cameron and I were sitting on our living room couch, laughing, while we watched a comedy on TV together. One dog lay at my feet, while I stroked her silky soft fur with my bare foot. The other dog was sprawled across the couch, his muzzle resting on Cameron's lap, while my son massaged his floppy ears one-handed.

In a split second, I experienced incredibly strong chest pain. In the past, typically those episodes had lasted a minute or less. This was different. The pressure inside my heart was intense and not letting up. I jammed my thumb against the chest cavity more firmly than past instances.

Those moments froze. I looked across the couch at Cameron. He was laughing at the TV show. Like a vertigo spin, I felt as if I was moving far away from him. Sweat droplets beaded up on my forehead. The dog at my feet jerked her head upright, rested her chin on the couch cushion, as she emitted a low warning growl. Cameron asked her, "What's the matter girl? Come on up." He patted the empty space between us, without turning his attention away from the TV.

I rammed my fist, reinforced with the other hand, against my chest, and used a full-force, all-knuckle massage. I knew the internal battle was fierce. The tiny pattern of turquoise and lime green threads in the fabric of the couch came into focus.

Is this the big one? Had the fragments in my heart broken loose, looking for the exit ramp? A 911 call was worthless. How would I explain a twenty-year-old medical error?

My thoughts shifted to my son. *Am I going to die right here, in front of him? Does he know about the catheters?*

I had to protect my son. It was too late to stop the event. I continued to push against the disturbance with the knuckled fist of my right hand, while I reached for the phone with my left. I made the call. *Dear God, please let her be home.*

Judy, my sister, answered on the first ring. In a hushed voice, I brought her up to speed, ordered, "Stay on the phone with Cameron until ... either way ...." She fully understood the implication. I handed the phone to my son, "Your aunt wants to talk to you."

He had been distracted by the TV. My sister pulled it off with supreme professionalism, asked him one question after another. He politely answered, while he continued to watch the program. "Yeah, school is okay." "Yes, I'm taking Spanish." Every few minutes Cameron looked in my direction, as he answered her with a quizzical tone of voice, "Yeah, Mom's okay. Why do you keep asking about her? She's sitting right here on the couch. Wanna' talk to her?"

I waved off his offer of the handset. The entire episode might have lasted five minutes but seemed like all of eternity. My heart felt like it was choking on a piece of food too large to swallow. Then poof, all the pressure was gone. The sweating stopped. I motioned for the phone and shared my relief with my sister. "I'm okay. It passed."

Dr. FalseHope had said in 1987, "It will feel like a massive heart attack when the last piece moves through your heart."

There was only one doctor who could fully understand my history: Dr. Ritz, the cardiologist who attempted removal of the six-inch—whipping with each heartbeat—piece inside my heart in 1987. I made the appointment, but by 2003, countless patients later, he didn't remember me.

Dr. Ritz scheduled a stress test. My spine couldn't handle the treadmill. We switched to the drug-induced version. The test confirmed: no heart attack. I was 45 years old. The next test was an echocardiogram. I informed the tech about the catheter fragment embedded in my heart near the tricuspid valve. "Are you a doctor? Most patients don't know that level of detail." After the exam, she said, "There's nothing there."

In the decade plus since 2003, I've never had that odd chest pressure again. An x-ray to confirm a fifth piece in my lungs was deemed unnecessary by the cardiologist. For my own peace of mind, I had to believe the last catheter fragment had moved through my heart. I was somewhat relieved, *finally, after all these years, no more catheter issues.* Wrong again.

Rubber Band Man

The jasmine was blooming in May of that year. On the chain link fence the flowering vine was twenty feet long and eight feet tall of heavily scented, pinwheel, white flowers. Over the years, not only had I never trimmed the vine, but had encouraged its growth by using fruit-tree mesh and poles to double the height of the fence. Eventually, the massive wall of flowers encroached on the walking path.

It must have been a Sunday. Aaron had the day off. That afternoon I trimmed the vine. Soon my clothing, baseball cap, and hair were covered with whip-like marks from the sticky sap of countless cut stems. My neck, bare shoulders, and arms above my elbow-length garden gloves broke out in red, leathery hives. There was no sneezing. I had a dry hacking cough, then wheezing. My throat felt strange, almost as if swollen.

I took an over-the-counter allergy medication and showered to remove the sticky residue from my hair. Within minutes of leaving the house for errands, my wheezing became a high-pitched choking, almost crowing, like a whistling sound.

Aaron asked, "Are you okay?" He didn't wait for a response. He turned the car and headed home.

Ultimately, a friend recommended her allergist. "Doctors aren't trained to deal with the unknown. If they don't know the answer, they assume the patient isn't reliable. He's the best diagnostician I've ever met."

My initial appointment with Dr. Achoo didn't start off well. The doctor, a thin, tall man, came into the exam room. He carried my intake form and was immediately dismissive. Without looking at me he diagnosed, "Asthma."

I knew he was wrong.

At the receptionist's counter, I paid my bill, headed towards the door. As I turned the knob to exit, a man's voice shouted, "Wait! Wait!" I looked over my shoulder, Dr. Achoo bounded across the room like Superman on a mission, his necktie and coattails flying. At my side in seconds, his fingertips barely touched my arm. He held my intake form on a clipboard. "Please forgive my ignorance. You wrote 'retained catheter lungs?' We need to talk. Please, come to my office." He motioned. "I insist."

I shook his hand off my elbow. "That's old news."

"You're right. It's not asthma, it's an allergic reaction."

An allergic reaction to what? My curiosity got the better of me. We walked past his receptionist, she asked, "Doctor, what about the other patients, their appointments?" She motioned towards the packed waiting room.

He lifted his chin, declared, "They wait."

We went to his private office. Across from his enormous grey metal desk I sat on a worn, cracked, leather, wingback chair. My chair and his were identical. Overflowing stacks of research journals covered his desk, edge to edge. Around us, we were surrounded by floor-to-ceiling bookcases with unevenly crammed books, journals, loose articles jutting out.

I eyed him with caution. *What's his angle?*

Dr. Achoo asked, "Would you like a cup of coffee?"

"No." I frowned, eyes narrowed, lips flat-lined.

He buzzed his receptionist, "Hold all my calls." To me, "Why are there catheter pieces in your lungs? Why wasn't the central line removed when it broke during surgery?"

I hesitated. Other providers, who thought they'd "made discovery," were typically defensive and angry if I told them the truth. So, I gave him the "Oh, no big deal" version.

"We must schedule emergency surgery. These catheters must be removed from your lungs today. I know a surgeon ...." He picked up the receiver on his desk phone.

Now someone cares? I found my voice. "No. We've already tried that many years ago. They can't be removed." I stood up to leave.

Dr. Achoo hung up the receiver. "Please, sit." He motioned with an open palm.

I exhaled. *He doesn't doubt my experience.*

He reached down and opened a drawer, withdrew a side-bound spiral notebook, clicked his pen, and wrote my name in large letters on the cover. As he turned to the first page, he looked up. "You need my help. Let's talk."

I snapped, "Doctor, there's nothing to talk about." My memories churned: *The minor mistakes, the major errors, and being abandoned as a patient.*

He didn't flinch, maintained a clinical stance. He knew my anger was justified. We looked at each other. He put his pen down, straightened his shoulders, and folded his hands. With complete sincerity, he said, "I'm so sorry my colleagues did this to you." He blinked his eyelids quickly. "No one ever apologized to you, did they?"

"No." My body released decades of pent-up anger. "Thank you, it has been twenty years." *You shouldn't be the one apologizing.* I held back the tears.

"Good. Now we continue." He slapped his palms onto his desk. "Now, you'll take coffee? Yes?"

I nodded. He buzzed the receptionist again. "Please, to bring two cups of coffee. Tell the other patients, my apologies, reschedule for another day." There was a pause as he listened. He answered her. "Yes, all of them," and hung up the phone.

Dr. Achoo stood up, took off his lab coat, hung it on his chair and rolled up his sleeves on his crisply starched, pin-striped, shirt. As he sat down, he slid down the knot of his coarsely woven maroon tie. "You said you've had trouble breathing inside of hospitals?"

"Yes."

He wrote in his notebook, looked up. "Continue."

"When I visit friends or family in hospitals, I break out in hives, coughing, almost choking. My sister teases about it, "You're allergic to hospitals.""

Dr. Achoo leaned back, covered his mouth with the curved index finger of his hand, and noisily tapped his pen on this desktop with the other hand. He seemed displeased. "Please, continue."

"The worst episode happened in a first-floor surgical waiting room—I didn't go further into the hospital that day, so it makes no sense—it started with a choking cough, non-stop sneezing for at least twenty minutes. I left, went to a nearby drug store and bought an antihistamine. A few hours later, the surgeon came in to brief me. 'Everything went well. Go home. Your relative's sleeping.' When I tried to speak, my voice came out in a rasping croak. Shrill, like a whistle. My throat felt funny, almost as if swollen. The surgeon didn't say a word. Everyone in the waiting room stared at me.

"Once home I was surprised to see my reflection in the bathroom mirror. Half of my face was puffy like a pillow. My right eye almost swollen shut, as if hit by a baseball bat."

Dr. Achoo held up a stop-sign palm. "One moment please." He cleared his throat. His lips puckered as he slowly enunciated each word. "Half...of your face...was swollen...and the surgeon... said nothing? Did I hear you correctly?" He sounded angry.

"Well, yeah, but I wasn't his patient."

"That makes no difference. He should have personally escorted you to their emergency room. The sound of your voice, as described, is called *stridor*. That, along with swelling of the face, is an emergency medical situation. If you didn't take that medication when you did, your throat would have swollen shut, you would have died."

Dr. Achoo searched and noisily slammed each metal drawer shut. He reached around and patted down the pockets of his jacket hanging on his chair and pulled out a small recording device. Which hospital? "What's the surgeon's name? I'll call him personally to advise him of his ignorance."

"I don't want to get anyone in trouble."

Impatiently, "It could save someone's life." Little did I know at the time it would be mine.

Dr. Achoo pushed a button on the device and recorded. "I must cross train all physicians at Mercy Hospital to recognize anaphylaxis. Start with the ER staff."

I was so relieved. He wasn't angry. One thing was clear: Dr. Achoo was a team player, like Dr. BrownEyes, and Dr. GoodVibe. I felt authenticated as a human being. I wouldn't be abandoned. He was the type of doctor who always put his patients first.

Dr. Achoo said, "You're fortunate to be here. This is much worse than I'd anticipated. In my country we have a saying. 'First God taps you on the shoulder with a feather, and then if you ignore the warning, he throws a brick at your head.' Your hives were the feather. The swelling of your face puts you at the brick level. Your body is in a chronic state of allergic reaction. Any additional allergen will push your immune system over the threshold."

Threshold? *Where had I heard that before?*

Dr. Achoo continued, "Like filling a cup with water, at some point only one more drop, we call the threshold, causes the water to spill over. With the immune system, it's a medical word that relates to allergens."

A memorized answer from a physics exam, decades earlier, came to my lips: "Due to the adhesive properties of the hydrogen atom, the surface tension of a full cup of water curves in a convex manner. Upon maximum volume, an additional solitary droplet breaks the tension."

Dr. Achoo responded, "Excellent! Yes! Correct."

He then questioned topics that seemed bizarrely unrelated: my clothing, balloons, food, even what plants I was growing in my garden. He assembled clues like a lawyer preparing for a closing argument. Hours later, when we finished, he summed up all my odd experiences through the filter of his knowledge. He stood up, scanned pages of handwritten notes. He paced between precariously towering stacks of books on the floor. An index finger shot towards the ceiling. "My first clue was the burn, from the adhesive on the sticky-strips used to close your surgical incision from your first 1990 surgery."

With each proclamation, another finger popped upwards. "Number two, your burn-like hives when trying on bathing suits in 2001." The welts had been so severe that the supervisor at the mall department store filed an incident report, took a picture, and then gathered all the suits to ship to their corporate office.

Dr. Achoo continued, "My suspicion was confirmed, with clue number three, when visiting hospitals, hives, difficulty breathing, and swelling of the face." He held up four fingers, "Plus, your allergic reaction while trimming a plant in May of this year. The white sticky residue you described from your jasmine vine is called latex."

Dr. Achoo closed the notebook. "You have an extremely severe latex allergy. At upcoming appointments we'll discuss your food allergies."

"I don't have food allergies. What's latex?"

"Any product made from rubber. There are many in today's world: balloons, car tires, rubber bands and many more, especially in hospitals. As far as food allergies, yes you do have them. I used to be a chemist before I was a doctor. On a molecular level some foods are so like latex that the body's immune system doesn't differentiate. I suspect your skin is saturated with histamine." He reached for his ring of keys on his desk, and then ran a solitary key point along my forearm. A bright red line appeared.

Dryly, I pointed out the obvious. "Maybe, I'm allergic to the metal in your key."

He bobbed his head side-to-side as if saying, "Maybe." With pursed his lips and his index-finger tapping his chin, he said. "It's unlikely, but a valid point." He walked around his desk, opened a drawer, and pulled out a plastic spoon. He repeated the exam using the bowl part of the spoon. A twin line appeared.

Not convinced, I responded, "Allergic to plastic?"

He shook his head in the negative. "Highly improbable. However, go ahead and run your own fingertip, not the nail, down your arm."

Trifecta! Three parallel inflamed lines. "But I didn't sneeze while cutting the jasmine. Now that I think about it, I haven't sneezed in years. How can this be an allergy?"

"That's very bad news. The immune system has three ways to remove an allergen: sneezing, coughing, runny nose." He patted his stack of journals. "Scientific studies indicate that sneezing expels at the rate of 40 to 100 mph.

"Our bodies are marvelous machines. When the body is unable to expel the allergen using one of those three methods, the more complex immune system takes over. Anaphylaxis is a severe allergic reaction. The body's misguided quirk to stop the allergen can result in swelling of the throat so quickly that all oxygen supply is cut off, causing death in a matter of minutes.

"There's no cure for latex allergies. I can teach you what to avoid."

At subsequent visits Dr. Achoo said, "You have the worst latex allergy I've ever encountered. You're reactive to not only natural, but artificial latex, too, as well as airborne latex particles. The relative who teased you was ignorantly correct. You are allergic to hospitals, the air in hospitals. Those hundreds of latex gloves being snapped on and off send latex particulates into their ventilation systems."

I couldn't believe what I was hearing. This was a whole new medical disaster. The future ramifications were daunting. Yet, it didn't add up. When I left his office that day, I turned and asked, "What about...."

Dr. Achoo was busily writing notes at his desk. He glanced at me. "We will meet many more times. Not to worry." He looked down and waved me on. "Weekly appointments until we sort everything out."

"Doctor, that's not my question. On our first appointment why did you run after me in the waiting room? What about the catheters changed your mind?"

"The catheters are made of latex. Didn't your other doctors ever tell you that?"

Muddy Boots 1987

I felt like a zombie driving home that day, the same thought circling repeatedly: *The catheters are latex, and they're trapped inside my heart and lungs. Wasn't there an allergic reaction like this a long time ago?* Once home, my memories catapulted all the way back to 1987, the emergency room, nurses, those muddy rubber boots.

December of 1987 had been memorable. It had marked my first Christmas without my father, our third wedding anniversary, and ten weeks since the attempt to remove the catheter from my heart. And I was ecstatic to be two months pregnant with Cameron.

My latest adopted stray dog was being treated for mange. In the car on the way home, I had the worst allergy attack of my life. I sneezed and coughed non-stop. The hour-long drive was through desolate country roads, not a phone booth in sight. I had only seen my new obstetrician once and didn't think to ask about the safety of an over-the-counter allergy pill I'd used for seasonal allergies.

When finally, home, the front of my black sweatshirt was saturated with snot, I'd used up every tissue and take-out napkin in my purse and car. A call to my OB's office sanctioned the use of the over-the-counter allergy med. It was too late. My symptoms escalated to choking and high-pitched wheezing.

When Aaron had arrived home after work, he took one look at me and rushed me to the hospital emergency room. Once I was settled, he went in search of a pay phone to make the necessary calls to our bosses and family. The ER staff called Dr. Mayberry, my family doctor, to supervise the treatment. That's how it was done in those days.

Dr. Mayberry had arrived wearing hunting camouflage, his pants tucked into muddy, half-opened, rubber boots. He stood with his arm crooked as if still holding his rifle. Then he marched over to my bed, pulled his stethoscope from a, well-worn, leather, medical bag, and listened to my lungs.

I cried, between muffled sobs, "The baby! The baby! Please, no drugs. They'll harm the baby."

Dr. Mayberry's typical crusty approach and loud booming voice evaporated when his patients were in emotional distress. He stepped away, leaned against the wall. A plop of wet mud fell off his hunting boots onto the highly polished floor.

At that moment two nurses entered: a male nurse, "Mike" per his name tag, and a mature, decades older than typical, female nurse wearing a student's uniform. The woman took a step backwards in virginal-white, new shoes. She cringed, nostrils twitched, and her lips drooped in a frown. She eyed my doctor as if he were a hobo off the last train out of town.

Despite the female nurse's recoil, she advanced with a cheery voice. "Doctor, can I get you a—," as she started to drag a chair across the room in his direction.

Dr. Mayberry roared, "Well yes, I would love a hot cup of coffee."

"I was going to say chair."

He barked, "Cream? Yes. Make that cream and sugar. Make sure it's nice and hot." He stepped over to me. To the nurse he said, "Now get along. I'm busy taking care of my patient."

"Doctor, shouldn't we send this patient for diagnostics?"

Mike silently mouthed, "No."

Dr. Mayberry sighed, squeezed my hand for a moment. "Everything is going to be all right. Your baby is perfectly safe. I'll be right back." He walked across the room and stepped out without answering.

The two nurses engaged in a whispered conversation.

"I'm not a waitress.... This is 1987. Because I'm a woman, he thinks—."

"You offered him a chair.... The Doc treats everyone the same, medical students, too. He wanted you to watch, observe, and learn. No one respects the nursing staff more than he does."

"How dare he show up at a hospital with muddy boots? That's not sanitary. I'm a nurse—my husband is a doctor."

"You're still a student. You haven't graduated yet. I'll take over. Go on to the next patient."

She left with a puzzled expression on her face.

During their conversation I had seen Dr. Mayberry in the hall, standing off to the side of the door, eavesdropping on the nurses' conversation. When our eyes met, he held up a silencing index finger over the pursed lips of his mouth.

After the student exited, Dr. Mayberry blustered into my room, "Mike, I need a few minutes with my patient." He placed a weary palm on Mike's shoulder, leaned in and whispered.

When Mike left and we were alone, Dr. Mayberry started with, "Is that woman done huffing and puffing?" He let out a deep sign. "I'm glad I'm closer to retirement than starting out in medicine. Now-a-days we've got all these new-fangled tests. They're so busy running their diagnostics, they plum forget we're all human beings. You and I jawing is part of the healing." He pulled up a chair and sat down.

Hiccupping through my sniffles, I repeated, "Jawing?"

"Talking to each other," he stretched his neck, towards the hallway. "She thinks I'm too old to be a doctor. Offering a chair! Humph, I should have sent her out for donuts." His laughter was contagious. Dr. Mayberry's eyes squinted. "Good. Laughing requires more oxygen than talking. I run my own diagnostics. Now, wipe your eyes. This baby is gonna be fine. The medication you need will not injure your child. I don't know what you got into, but, if this continues and your lungs shut down completely, this baby will be in trouble."

"Yes." I clenched the blanket with my hands.

Mike re-appeared pushing an IV pole and holding a glass vial with a rubber stopper. Dr. Mayberry stood up, gestured for Mike to enter, and instructed, "Set up the asthma medication. I'll spend the night in the hospital. I'll be catching forty winks on the couch in the employee lounge. I want to check on her personally every couple of hours. If she has any issues in the meantime, I'm here. Come wake me."

As the doctor and Mike switched places, Dr. Mayberry patted Mike on the shoulder, "Glad to have you on-board with this case. You're our best nurse."

In the open doorway I could see Dr. Mayberry with his hands akimbo on his hips. He bellowed, a brief pause between each word, "Where's...my... coffee? Where's...that... student? Can't she see I've been out hunting all day in the rain?"

Mike chuckled. "He keeps all of us on our toes. He's our best doctor." He rolled the IV pole over to my bed, hung the clear plastic bag, opened the vial, and injected the needle into my arm.

As I sniffed, I asked, "Does this mean I have asthma?"

"No. A medical problem that mimics asthma doesn't mean genuine asthma. I saw you listed fragmented pieces of catheter in your lungs on your intake form." He stretched his neck sideways towards the empty hall. Then leaned in, with a set jaw and a hard stare into my eyes, tersely whispered, "They shouldn't be there."

The Deep End

After I remembered the emergency room nurse from 1987, I realized the correlation with the 2003 crushing chest pain event: those were the two years the catheter had been actively moving through my heart. Once I arrived at that conclusion, I fully believed Dr. Achoo. "When the full immune system is involved, it's not a one-day reaction. It can take weeks to months for everything to settle down."

Dr. Achoo training ER staff on anaphylaxis at that small private hospital saved my life. One day, another choking cough and face swelling episode occurred after walking across a neighbor's fresh cut "grass" which was a huge swath of freshly cut poison ivy. Within five minutes I drove myself to the hospital, two miles away. As I pulled into their parking lot, I knew I had made a terrible mistake. I was out of time. At the ER drop-off bay, I shoved the gear shift into park, jumped out, and left the car running, driver's door wide open. As I sprinted through the opened automatic glass doors, the security guard ran behind, yelling, "Hey Lady, you can't park there! This is an emergency room."

At the ER triage window, I cut in front of the woman standing there. I had both my hands around my neck, completely unable to speak by then, due to my throat swelling. The triage nurse took one look at me, jumped up, ran out, and grabbed my waist as I sank to the floor. The other nurse, over the microphone, announced, "Code Red. ER," then ran out to help.

Inside the triage cubicle, the nurse had me sit, a doctor ran in with an IV bag. A third nurse, taking my blood pressure, whipped off the cuff, "BP is bottoming out." The doctor injected the needle into my arm as the triage nurse held the bag over my head until a fourth nurse ran in with an IV pole.

They didn't even have my name.

When Cameron arrived, I burst into tears, "They towed my car."

"Mom, the security guard followed you inside. He parked it for you. He figured out what was going on."

When I had my follow-up appointment with Dr. Achoo, he was pleased. "Excellent. Their ER staff followed my training protocol completely."

I saw Dr. Achoo for several years before we truly resolved the "threshold" items that kicked my immune system into overdrive. Since I couldn't do anything about the catheters in my lungs, all other allergens had to be eliminated. Foods I had eaten my whole life, like bananas, pineapple, and cream cheese, set off massive hives. Dr. Achoo also correctly identified food additives like guar gum and xanthan gum. Thickeners found in almost all processed food, like ice cream, bottled salad dressings, even green olives. I had to read labels religiously.

A decade or more after Dr. Achoo left town, the terms "allergy asthma" and "latex anaphylaxis" became distinct diagnoses. Like all brilliant physicians, Dr. Achoo was lightyears ahead of his colleagues.

In the interim my duration for walking had dropped off even further. With increased frequency, I had to stop, take a deep forward bend from the hips. Shopping was restricted to stores with shopping carts to lean on for support. Yet, I noticed I didn't have any of the heaviness in my legs when bicycle riding within the ten-block radius of our subdivision.

When a new fourteen-acre dog park opened near us, and our dogs ran off leash, I had to sit every ten minutes. The front of my thighs felt heavy like cement pillars. Fortunately, the park had plenty of benches and hammocks throughout.

The newspaper listed a free seminar, by an orthopedic surgeon, about problems walking. As I sat in the audience of elderly attendees, everything the surgeon said described my symptoms. She even mentioned riding a bicycle, "It opens up the base of the spine when leaning forward." Afterwards, at the podium I was given her business card, "You have spinal stenosis. It's my specialty. Make an appointment. I can fix this. I'm sure it's the cause of all your back limitations."

I was in high spirits, even though I knew the last sentence wasn't true. A month later, when my appointment came up, I brought all my prior surgical records, as instructed. Upon arrival I was sent for a scoliosis panel. It had been twenty years since my last film. All my other x-rays over the years had zoomed in on specific areas. No one ever saw my whole spine.

When the orthopedic surgeon arrived, along with another doctor, she repeated her promise. "I'm going to fix your spine." She took the x-ray from the large manila envelope and flipped on the switch of the light box.

I was sitting on the exam table three feet away. As the "other me," was revealed, they both gasped, the surgeon shouted, "What did they do to her?"

The two doctors shot comments back and forth.

"What a total monstrosity!"

"Who was her surgeon?"

"This is the most botched-up spine I've ever seen!"

Embarrassed, angry, and emotionally wounded, I spoke up, "You know I'm sitting here. I can hear both of you."

They turned to me with scathing looks. The surgeon flicked off the switch, hurriedly shoved the film into the envelope. "No one can help you." They stood up to leave.

"Wait. You said—."

"Spinal stenosis is a condition of 80-year-olds."

"I'm 48. Did you think I was in my 80s when we met at your lecture? What about my trouble walking?"

"Buy a treadmill."

"What difference does the walking surface make?"

They left without a word. Another door closed.

Once again, I retreated to Dr. BrownEyes. His latest office was an elevator ride up a few floors. As always, I went for new x-rays first, and hand-carried them to him.

While I waited for my ally in his office, black crows gathered in the treetops outside. I slipped the radiologist's report out of the envelope and read it. When an inexperienced patient, I'd thought those reports were the final words. With decades of experience, I knew it was a split-second decision by someone unfamiliar with my history. I was relieved: no red flags.

Dr. BrownEyes never read those reports. He made his own diagnosis based on the actual film. As always, my surgeon had a pleasant demeanor, shook my hand, and made brief chit-chat about non-medical topics. He always asked about my son, by name.

He adjusted his glasses, positioned his face an inch from my latest film. I wasn't ready for his diagnosis. "You do have spinal stenosis, but not for the same reason as everyone else. I suspect the outer dura of your spinal cord is herniated."

"That's not mentioned on the report."

Dr. BrownEyes was refreshingly honest. "She missed it. I could walk downstairs and show her. However, that wouldn't advance your medical care. I want you to be seen by a highly specialized neurosurgeon who deals with this type of problem. I'll call in orders for an MRI, so you have that done before you see him."

My appointment with the latest neurosurgeon came to pass. I was immediately at ease. His professionalism, intelligence, and sincere concern put him in the upper echelon of providers with Dr. BrownEyes. Neither of those superior surgeons ever overlooked the importance of empathy. The first thing Dr. Neuro said, "I'm sorry to hear you're having trouble walking. I can see why your surgeon suspected a cord herniation." He made eye contact.

"Surgically, I'm experienced. Most of my patients are football players who come here from all over the country due to blunt force trauma injuries. However, in your case I'm not convinced that's a completely accurate diagnosis. Let's reconvene after a second MRI zooms in on a particular area in question."

At our second appointment, Dr. Neuro said, "Your case is quite puzzling and extremely rare. I've consulted with other top surgeons across several spine specialties including your Dr. BrownEyes. We are not reaching a consensus on a diagnosis. At best we have three theories. To be clear, we're all guessing."

My entire body relaxed. I appreciated his honesty. He continued. "Our first theory concurs with Dr. BrownEyes: herniation of the outer dura of your spinal cord. We are talking about an encroachment as thin as a piece of paper. That's why it's so difficult to visualize, even on MRI. However, that's all it would take to elicit your symptoms.

"Theory two, your spinal cord is tethered to your spinal column by scar tissue from your multiple surgeries."

I swallowed. "And number three?"

"Our third supposition is lumbar claudication due to the severity of your scoliosis. It's possible your spinal cord kinks like a garden hose. Fold a hose in half and the running water stops. Your scoliosis is quite severe. The cement-like heaviness in your thighs, and the relief you feel when leaning forward—opens the base of the spine—indicates you're not receiving enough spinal cord fluid to your legs."

"Is that the same as leaning forward, riding a bike?"

"Yes. The movement provides enough fluid to your legs to enable you to walk again, briefly."

"Can anything be done?" My fingernails dug deeply into my palms. *Are we really having this conversation?*

"We could surgically remove the side of your vertebral column, at four or five levels. Hopefully, but unlikely, your entrapped spinal cord would release on its own."

Tersely, I asked, "And then it dangles there free floating in the middle of my body?"

"No." He took a sheet of paper out of a drawer and drew a picture. "After the spinal cord is freed, we build a cage-like device, an artificial spine, so to speak, and attach it to the vertebral column, above and below the worst curvature of your spine."

My brain felt as if it was on overloaded circuits ready to explode from the latest impossible conversation. *Does this twenty-five-year-old medical disaster ever end?* Thanks Doc. I looked at the paper. "Is this drawing accurate? Shouldn't the spinal cord be equidistant in the middle of the vertebral column?"

"Yes, it's correct. Due to the severity of your scoliosis your spinal cord is slammed up against the side walls of your spine. Like a crooked tree in the forest trying to grow towards the sun, the spinal cord also tries to straighten itself. Here's a cross-section."

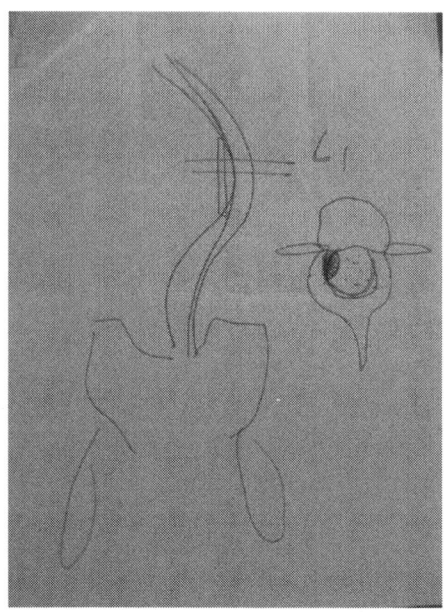

"So, that dark oval is where my spinal cord is located in the spinal canal?"

"Yes."

It was, yet again, a surreal conversation with another surgeon. I kicked my emotions into clinical mode. "What's the anticipated success rate?"

"There's a 50% chance of permanent paralysis. I highly suspect your cord is tethered by scar tissue. Anytime we must manually manipulate the cord it's dangerous. I don't recommend the surgery. However, that decision is up to you."

I stayed focused despite the shell-shocked diagnosis. The luxury of emotion, tears, and anger, had to wait for later in the day. "Do you have a long-term prognosis?"

"I don't know. None of us knows. It would be best if you put up with the symptoms as best you can. Surgery must be the absolute last possible option. If the situation escalates to the point where you can't stand upright at all, we'll proceed. Dr. BrownEyes will continue to oversee your primary spine care. I'm a phone call away."

Once home I petted both the dogs, tossed them treats, and tugged on my bathing suit. Nearby, I had a community pool membership. By then I'd discovered I could wear a bathing suit, despite the latex, if I stayed in the water. If I let the suit dry on my skin, I broke out in massive hives.

Alone at the pool I stood in the shallow end, swirled, with a straight arm, circled, left, then right, stiffly splashing the water with increasing anger. Not only due to the medical events of my life. The waves rippled with resentment over having to tell my spouse about one more medical issue. Indifference had become the norm.

I swam to the deep end, started to climb the ladder, turned, swam a few more laps, kicking for all I was worth. *Can I force the spinal cord fluid into my legs?*

When I climbed out onto the pool deck, squeezed most of the water out of my hair, slipped on my cover-up. *Should I attempt this dangerous surgery?* I forced back the tears. *Would my homecoming be like 1990? The roses? He threw out my gift from the nurses.*

I made up my mind. *No. I'm done.*

Driving home, I abruptly turned into a grocery store parking lot. A first for me, to shop so casually dressed.

"Well, someone is loved." The cashier commented on my solitary purchase.

"Yes, I am." I declared with a sense of purpose. Droplets of water fell onto my shoulders from my wet hair.

I bought myself a dozen dark red roses in their most expensive crystal-looking vase.

Adams' Own Rib

The spinal cord diagnosis with Dr. Neuro was the last straw. I went from conquering minor fears to fearlessness. There was nothing left to lose.

My husband and I took our first couple's only vacation since becoming parents. I still had high hopes we could reconnect. On a cruise to the Bahamas, I was confident I had learned to juggle all my spine issues and wouldn't disappoint him.

On a private island, the sand was warm between my toes, countless palm trees swayed in the breeze. I was more than content to sit on the beach and read a book. Peach-tinged clouds striated, while sea birds called to each other.

Aaron wanted us to go snorkeling. I thought we would stay close to the shore, like the one I had to skip when we were first married because I didn't know how to swim. A seventy-foot boat took us out into the open ocean waters. Peeling paint, fuel tanks, and thick, greasy ropes covered the deck. Everything smelled of gas, oil, and dirty rags. It was the type of private enterprise the cruise line warned us to avoid. Another passenger slipped on the steps while boarding and fell, bleeding substantially. It was clear the crew had no first aid training.

When the snorkel gear was handed out, I could smell the rubber as soon as I put the mask over my mouth and nose. Diving off the height of a large boat into the open ocean, fear of anaphylaxis from the mask, and an untrained crew, caused me to freeze in my tracks.

Aaron didn't see it that way. He barked, "You never want to do anything with me." He dove into the ocean with the other passengers. Once again, I stayed behind.

The next day, Aaron decided we would go parasailing, "Your back can handle that."

"No, I can't risk a rough landing. You know that."

While I watched him from a beach chaise, I noticed other couples. They laughed, chatted with each other, while they sipped their fruit-laden Caribbean drinks. I was the only person sitting alone.

When Aaron returned, I suggested, "How about a swim? We can do that together."

"No. I don't feel like it."

"Well, let's sit together, have a drink, enjoy the view."

"It's too hot."

"Okay, let's take a walk together on the beach? It's so beautiful here."

"Why bother? You can only walk for twenty minutes."

"But it would be twenty minutes together."

"Nah, that's not fun."

Behind him, I spotted a floating dock, off the shoreline. "Look! Let's swim out there! We can do that."

"You can't swim that far. You can't do anything." He walked away, "I'm going to the ship to watch TV."

"We're in the Bahamas! Watch TV at home."

He kept walking, didn't answer. I didn't follow.

When he was 100 feet ahead of me, a rage welled up inside of me. *I'm tired of being left behind. Why won't you join me for the things I can do?* Through cupped hands, yelled at the back of his head. "Yes, I can. Watch me!"

I kicked and splashed my way into the ocean, dove when I reached water deep enough, and swam for all I was worth. Half-way, breathless, my ribcage was in agony from the pain. *I can't stop. I must prove to him that I can do this. And to myself.* I kept swimming. Once at the bobbing wooden structure, shaking with effort, I dragged my body up the ladder. Once on top I crumbled onto my hands and knees, gasping. Cautiously I stood up, maintained my balance with A-frame legs, while I straightened my shoulders as much as possible. There was a sense of impossible triumph. The dock dipped and bobbed in the gentle tide. The sun glistened off the undulating turquoise Bahamian waters. I waved goodbye to the man standing on the shore. It was over between us. We separated.

When divorce was inevitable, Aaron called, "Let's grab some lunch, talk."

"I'm going swimming."

"Okay, I'll meet you there."

"No, I'd rather go alone."

"You've asked me a million times to go with you."

"And a million times, you said, 'no.'"

He insisted, I gave in.

We swam a lap or two, I was out of breath, had to stop. At the deep end of the pool, within minutes a heated argument erupted.

Angry, abruptly I twisted my spine in an awkward position as I hyperextended my arm to swim away. I heard a loud "pop" in my upper back.

We left the pool and went our separate ways.

Once home, with a new area of pain escalating, I called Michael, my acupuncturist, for an appointment. Luckily, he was available the following day. Throughout the evening, the purple zone pain dramatically worsened. It was as if someone had shot me with an arrow in the upper back, where I'd heard the popping noise, that penetrated my torso, and exited out my heart. The "entry and exit" points, both the size of a nickel, were on opposite sides of my body.

I sobbed as the night wore on. Someone in my support group had once said, "We only have two levels: tolerable and intolerable."

Now at the intolerable level, my only option was a hospital emergency room visit. I debated: *ER Staff won't understand my complicated spine history and its many ramifications. I can't take this any longer.* At midnight, I called Cameron. He had moved out months earlier. While waiting for him, I discovered that circular movement of my shoulder worsened the pain sensations. A memory struggled to surface. *Haven't I experienced this before?*

When 19-year-old Cameron pulled up in front of the house, he ran up the sidewalk. He put one arm around my waist, gently held my hand, as we walked to his still-running car. Twenty feet looked like twenty miles.

Once admitted at the ER, I explained the "exit" point of the straight-as-an-arrow skeletal path. Without intention I pointed to my heart.

The ER, of course, had to rule out a cardiac event. They drew blood, ordered a CAT scan. It was torment to move onto the machine. Then I was given a drug cocktail: morphine, muscle relaxer, and an anti-anxiety drug. Morphine had been one of a few drugs my body tolerated. The brand of muscle relaxer was the one I'd quit using years ago. Typically, it would put me into a dead sleep for twenty hours. The three drugs barely provided any relief, and I was awake all night.

I tried to explain. "I'm a chronic-pain patient. This isn't my normal. My upper back popped. The pain is like an arrow through my body."

Each occasion the doctor nodded and left.

After a long, restless night, at eight a.m. the ER doctor came in with a cheery diagnosis. "Good news. No heart attack. You're clear to leave."

"I'm still in as much pain as when admitted. Don't we have a diagnosis?"

"You'll have to follow-up with your own doctor."

At home, I called Michael to cancel our afternoon appointment. "I haven't slept all night." He intently listened to the events of the night before. "Why not come in anyway? I'm sure my treatment can help."

"No thanks. This is way beyond acupuncture. Morphine barely helped. There is a serious injury."

"Of course, as you wish. However, why not both? Call your surgeon's office for an appointment, likely they won't see you for a few weeks, right? I'll fit you in this morning."

"Okay."

Michael's office locations through the years nurtured all the senses. The waiting areas were always impeccably clean, the walls painted in relaxing and aesthetically pleasing colors. The air fresh, clean, with a faint hint of some essential oil.

Buddhist prayer flags were strung across the ceiling in the receptionist office. An eighty-gallon tropical fish tank was filled with brightly colored fish. I pressed my face against the cool glass, and for a moment pretended I was snorkeling in the Bahamas with someone who didn't think I was a burden.

Michael greeted me promptly. We walked into his examination room. Under a window were shelves of Chinese herbs. Another wall showcased his many diplomas.

While lying on the examination table, I felt a mild sensation of warmth from the table-length heating pad. The floor-to-ceiling window overlooked a small, enclosed area, with a koi pond, and surrounded by colorful tropical plants.

I felt loved and cared for. More than anything, I felt safe, even if he couldn't help.

Michael took my pulses—there are multiple pulses in Chinese medicine—checked my tongue, face, and eyes, then started treatment. His style of acupuncture had evolved over the years. Rather than leaving the needles in for an hour, he quickly inserted them at key *chi* locations. When he finished fifteen minutes later, he re-checked my pulses and frowned. "That's odd, there's no change."

I knew this wouldn't work.

"Did you say it's immediately to the side of your spinal column? Do you mind if I palpate?"

In the two decades I'd seen Michael, off and on, first for pain management and then for other medical issues, he had never examined by touch. I trusted him yet had reservations.

"I don't think that's a good idea. My spine is really messed up."

"I have a license. I've kept it up to date. Massage therapy prior to acupuncture school. Only light pressure. I'll advance slowly, half an inch increment. If you experience discomfort, advise. I'll stop anytime you direct."

"Okay, go ahead." *After the previous night this can't be any worse.*

Without changing my position, Michael very gently squeezed his fingertips under my left shoulder. Lightly, he touched the base of my neck, rotated his fingertips in a gentle, circular motion, downward, along my spine. Within two minutes, he stopped. "I believe I've discovered the source. Your rib is pulled out of the vertebral column. Not completely, only partially. That would explain the intense pain. I can easily pop it into place. May I continue?"

"Are you kidding? Are you sure, Michael?"

"Yes."

"The ER ran tests, even a CAT scan. Surely, this would show up?" I continued to ramble, both out of nervousness, and anticipation. "I'm afraid. You're not a doctor. Well, not a Doctor of Medicine. Sorry, I didn't mean to say that out loud."

"No offense taken. May I try?"

"Yes, but please be careful."

For a split-second he barely pressed on my rib, and poof, all the pain was gone. 100%. Completely. Gone.

I sprang upright in astonishment. Gently I rotated each shoulder blade, in circles. Forward, then backwards. I expected the feeling to return. It didn't. "Oh, come on. How did they miss this?" I felt a combination of disbelief, anger, and confusion.

Michael, deeply engrained in his Buddhist teachings, gently guided. "Your spine has been dramatically altered, first by nature and then surgically. Many provide medical care based on ideas memorized from a book, not by what they see or feel. It's better to forgive their ignorance."

I exhaled a long, pent-up sigh. I worried about the return of symptoms. My body resumed its normal diminished levels of function, with tolerable pain when juggling activities.

I kept having the nagging feeling that I'd experienced this before. Weeks later I remembered: the pulling vine incident on Father's Day in 1987. Ironically, it was the year I'd first met Michael, desperate for relief, and willing to try anything—even acupuncture. At the time the pain worsened dramatically when a physical therapist had me use an over-the-head weighted pulley for exercise. When I told her she said, "That's impossible." It was almost a year before I could partially raise my arm over my head, again. It was the worst possible treatment for a pulled rib.

I scrambled through my old medical records. There it was. Dr. Ribby's report from 1987. At our initial appointment he'd written, "Pulled rib." Later he denied it, and said I misheard the word "arthritis." His records indicated he knew about the fragmented catheter pieces in my lungs.

Even worse, twenty years later the 2007 version confirmed that the original diagnosis had been correct. It was a sobering moment.

Slaying the Dragon

In my fifties, single, I reflected on my life. *What could I have altered?* My thoughts scanned decades, forks in the road, where I'd made the wrong turn. *I was young, naïve, trusting. The first scoliosis surgery was a mistake, at least with that surgeon.* The errors from that operation opened a Pandora's Box of complications for the rest of my life.

My memories swirled with regrets. Dragons of bad decisions had devoured my soul. *Would I have graduated from UF if I had never met Dr. Unknown?* Probably not. Despite having a high GPA, I was ignorant about survival in a large university setting, first-generation, an introvert, no mentors.

After my first lecture at the University of Florida's campus in 2007, I was asked to return a dozen times to share my story. Each visit to campus, my heart ached with remorse about dropping out decades earlier.

An epiphany occurred. *Why not? I'm not a kid anymore.* Scaly skin, jagged teeth, and claws came into mind, not only mine. *Could I confront, and slay, a particular dragon from my past?* It, too, was reptilian: Go Gators! University of Florida, here I come.

The movie, "Apollo 13," had come out in 1995, five years after my CES surgery. I took great inspiration from the scene where character Ken Mattingly painstakingly searched for a way to "power up" with "only enough amps to power a toaster." That scene became an allegory for my own physical abilities and further reinforced my father's teachings about "efficiency management." Over the decades I had finessed every nuance of my standing, sitting, and walking limitations to "power up" with the least "amps" possible. However, a large university campus would be an enormous challenge.

I still volunteered with UF health-care students. In 2010 that trio of students, for their class project, produced a booklet for me. "UF, where to start?" Listed on the first page: "Contact the Disability Department." I made a folder in my email account: "UF Bound." But did nothing.

The following fall semester I mentioned my regret to a friend, an alum from the College of Veterinary Medicine. She encouraged my application for readmission. Then she provided the skills necessary to navigate the bureaucracy of a major university. The studying part was like riding a bike, granted a rusty one.

Thirty-four years after I dropped out, I sat in an entomology classroom on the UF campus as an incoming junior. It was May of 2012. I was lucky; every single chair was thickly padded. The best quality possible.

I flew through the first two semesters on my son's words, "Mom, I'm so proud of you." In other semesters, on-line classes accommodated my physical limitations. The course work was tougher than I ever could have imagined. I hadn't had a basic science or math class since 1977. Many times, I was ready to quit. Between friends and staff from their Disability Department, I had plenty of mentors.

It became the most incredible three years of my life. As expected, there were many obstacles to overcome, especially with my physical limitations. However, I never could have anticipated a freak accident. I swam a lap in a campus pool one day, no goggles, rolled onto my back to float in the 12-foot end directly in front of their lifeguard, before my return lap. From the water underneath there was an odd sound, almost like helicopter propellers, louder and louder, as if coming closer. I couldn't respond fast enough. Nor could I have anticipated the danger.

Within seconds I was thrown several feet airborne by a football-player-sized, hefty young man, whom I had seen earlier holding his breath on the bottom of the pool, at the shallow end. I didn't know he'd switched to the deep end. He slammed into my body so hard, once airborne I rotated, came down face first. In that split-second, I gathered my wits: *hold your breath, you're going under.* When I bobbed up the student said, "Sorry" and hurriedly left the pool.

I felt disorientated, swam to the shallow end, and stood there dazed until I realized what happened. Then I returned to the lifeguard, questioned her.

She said, "Yes, that was a hard hit. I thought you were okay. You've been in the shallow end for fifteen minutes." I thought it was only a few seconds. That should have been my clue. She brought me an ice pack for my throbbing jaw and shoulder.

Within hours the pain started. The 300-plus-pounds collision of the young student's body against mine was a major whiplash for my overly fused spine.

The ensuing weeks were purple zone distress, and a wicked concussion. My head felt like it was full of cotton. My family doctor advised, "No reading, no computer use." My dentist, "Soft food for the next month, until your jaw heals." I had no choice but to drop a class. Then another.

The pain became unbearable, I was devastated that not only had I likely lost the semester, but my bachelor's degree as well. Then things got worse. As fate would have it, despite having dozens of well-executed cortisone injections over the years, this time things went wrong.

Ultimately, after multiple tests, the doctor said, "The drug is trapped between the bone and the sheath covering the bone. None of the drug went into the intended area. Not only can we not reinject the space, but the pressure of it being trapped there will create significant additional pain for the next month until the drug reabsorbs into your body."

"Isn't there anything you or your team can write for, for pain?"

"No. My partners and I decided not to get involved."

I nodded my head. *I've heard that one before.*

Dr. BrownEyes, in semi-retirement, was my last hope. "It appears there is new damage. With surgery we'll have to drill rods into your hips this time."

My knees buckled. I collapsed against the wall in his office. Without turning my head, I weakly said, "I can't do this anymore." Still flattened against the wall, I looked at him, "In 1997 you said I'd never have any more hardware."

He sighed. "Not in your spine, Mary. We've used up all those landmarks. Now it's your hips we must stabilize."

Months went by, more testing, and it was confirmed that the "I feel like I'm in hard labor," searing hip pain was still the trapped cortisone drug. We cancelled the surgery.

Dr. BrownEyes referred me to an out-of-town doctor who used a botanical drug, rather than cortisone. It offered some relief without side effects. Which was a first and wonderful for me as a patient. When I questioned why other doctors didn't use it, she said, "No patent. No profit."

Somehow, that year I finished the semester. Before I knew it, the third year passed. I was graduating.

Graduation day was on May 1st, 2015. Due to a remodel project, graduation ceremonies were switched to their 80,000-seat football stadium. I knew the five to six-hour ceremony—grads had to be there two hours before the procession—far exceeded my combined duration abilities for walking, standing, and sitting at a solitary event. Behind the scenes, thousands of graduates stood in lines assembled with their respective colleges. I waved to my department classmates, as I walked past. They asked me to join them. But I was led to meet up with another graduate who was also disabled. She wore a hot-pink Hawaiian lei around her neck. I introduced myself, we chatted. Her walking limitations were worse than mine. A portable elevator would move her wheelchair onto the stage. She said, "I can walk thirty feet as long as I can sit again right away."

Prior to the opening ceremonies the two of us were escorted onto the empty field. Arranged in long rows on temporary plastic flooring were 8,500 empty white folding chairs for the graduates. They looked like an army of white, sea birds, with folded wings. My new friend and I were seated in the absolute last row, far corner. I stood up, circled, and searched the massive audience of 30,000 visitors in the end zone. *How would I find my son?* He had waited by himself in the stands, when I joined the other grads, two hours earlier.

My small flip-phone buzzed under my gown. My son sent a text, "10 o'clock." Before I puzzled too long over his message, the phone rang. "Mom! Turn around! I'm behind you." There on the lowest level of the stadium seats, not fifty feet away, stood my 26-year-old son enthusiastically waving. We both laughed. There was not one other graduate and guest as physically close as we were to each other. We each had a camera, took tons of smiling pictures of each other while waiting for the ceremony to start. Afterwards, when I asked how he found me, he said, "I saw the one padded chair covered with the white sheet. I hoped it was for you."

Once the proceedings kicked off, I looked over to see my adult son wipe away a tear, then another. He bent his head, shoulders shook, face covered with both hands.

The sunlight shifted from late afternoon to early evening. So did my thoughts. 1990, the picnic table in the backyard, my son, our conversation the night before my CES, spinal cord emergency surgery. It had been almost 25 years. I could still hear his toddler's two-year-old voice as he screamed, *"Mommy! No! Don't go."* It was the worst conversation of my life.

Without forethought, as if hypnotized, I walked across the twenty-foot barrier of grass between us. At the cement wall I stood on tippy-toe and reached up with both arms. My son bent down. Tightly we held onto each other's shoulders. A deep man's voice whispered in my ear. "Mom, I know how hard this was for you. I'm so proud of you. I know what you went through to be here today."

As expected, hours into the ceremony my spine was maxed out for ability. I couldn't hold myself upright any longer. Not even with accommodations. The printed program wasn't being followed despite my dean's assurances a few days earlier. "I've worked here for decades. The College of Agriculture always goes first." Not that day. The assembly was being called forward by rows. Half-way through the program there were still another 4,000 graduates ahead of the two disabled students in the last row. There was no choice. I gestured to my son that we had to leave.

That had been our game plan. Like a trip to the ice cream parlor when you couldn't afford to buy a cone. I had learned to be satisfied with a sample spoon...of time.

I thanked my disability advisor, who sat nearby. She had asked me to let her know when my body couldn't hold up any longer. She surprised me. "I can have you on stage in three minutes. You're walking if you want to."
"Yes! Of course!"

She pulled out her cell phone.

Beaming, I turned to my son in the stands and motioned towards the stage, with a two-finger, walking motion. His wide smile confirmed his comprehension. A young usher in cap and gown appeared. He took me to a black curtained area adjacent to the stage. Groups of graduates then walked single file in front of the photographer. I snaked through the serpentine pattern and turned. There at the end of the line, beyond a sea of strangers, stood my twenty classmates from Environmental Horticulture. We laughed, called out, and waved to each other.

Once I was on stage the Dean of the College of Agriculture recognized me. She leaned in, whispered, "First the official photo, then a quick hug." My son snapped the picture of us embracing.

As I moved past the Dean I paused for a moment, marveled at the massive audience in the bleachers, as well as the 8,500 graduates seated on the field. One empty chair in the front row held a cap on top of a folded gown.

Despite everything I'm still alive. At that moment the stadium lights came on, beyond them a full moon beamed brightly from a cloudless sky, ebbing blues turning to night.

I walked across the stage.

Major Diagnoses:

Adjacent Segment Deterioration (ASD)
Arachnoiditis
Antalgic gait
Bertolotti's Syndrome
Crankshaft Phenomenon

Cauda equina syndrome (CES)
Claudication lumbar spine
Degenerative disc disease (DDD)
Failed back surgery syndrome (FBSS)
Flat back syndrome/Loss of lumbar lordosis

Halo Phenomenon/Pedicle Screws
Hypertrophic bone formation
Fibromyalgia
Foreign objects/heart and lungs (FOB)
Hemi-sacralization of L6 vertebra

Kyphosis
Neurogenic bladder
Osteoarthritic spine
Pseudoarthrosis T6-T7, T10-T11
Pseudo articulation: lumbosacral and SI joint

Rotoscoliosis
Spinal fusion T7 to Sacrum
Spinal Stenosis
Spondylolisthesis
Tethered spinal cord

Thoracic Outlet Syndrome
Trochanteric Bursitis
Vacuum phenomenon SI joints

ACKNOWLEDGEMENTS

Thank you, with deep gratitude to all the members of various writing groups over the years, especially Gainesville Poets and Writers. In appreciation to all the dedicated librarians, near and far, who helped research my medical issues, especially in the days before the Internet. I also thank Westminster Presbyterian Church daycare for taking my son in 1990.

A special thanks to the many friends for their support every step of the way while at UF. I'm also deeply indebted to the many counselors in the Disability Department, professors, and classmates at the University of Florida who facilitated my goal of graduation. Obtaining my degree made writing this book possible.

Facebook support groups: from scoliosis to latex allergy, cauda equina syndrome CES, and everything in between. Thanks to you, I've read of other experiences. I'm humbled. I've chatted with CES survivors globally. I'm saddened to learn, to this day, the diagnosis is still being missed. We've united and reassured each other about our life-changing experiences and challenges. Thank you.

The x-ray on the cover is from my 1990 surgeries. For additional pictures, commentary, and information visit: www.facebook.com/BB2020MT

BOOK CLUB DISCUSSION TOPICS

1. There are several themes throughout the book: water, nature, abandonment. Discuss one. For example, when do scenes with water empower versus harm?

2. Several unnamed characters offer Mary advice to overcome her battles. Name two. How do their few words, or actions, empower the main character?

3. In the first chapter, "I saw a patch of blue sky, the only light in the enclosure of ... sheer ... cliffs." Does this scene echo for the reader later with the dream about being trapped in the grotto? Plus, a third time?

4. The heroic, Drs. Mayberry, BrownEyes, BeachBoy, GoodVibe, Acho, and Ritz, all had similar characteristics. What traits make for a good doctor?

5. How do the psychologist and acupuncturist directly change the course of events? What would have been the outcome without them?

6. Name some of the main character's triumphs. In what way can small victories change a life?

7. There are many people with invisible disabilities. Name some disabilities that, although not obvious, limit a person's function.

The author MT Adams is available for book club Zoom meetings. Contact her at bb2020mt@yahoo.com.

Reviews on Amazon, Goodreads or Barnes and Noble websites are greatly appreciated.
Thank you for your support. MTA

---

[i] Alexander, A. L. compilation, *Poems That Touch the Heart*. Garden City Publishing, 1948.

Printed in Great Britain
by Amazon

28800381R00141